MW00784504

FrameWorks

Other books by Matis Weinberg

Patterns in Time
Rosh haShana

Patterns in Time
Chanukah

FrameWorks

BEREISHIT ~ GENESIS
parashot ii-xii

Matis Weinberg

AN FJP BOOK
The foundation for jewish publications
BOSTON - JERUSALEM

The Foundation for Jewish Publications, Inc.,
15 School Street, Boston, Massachusetts 02108
www.fjp.net

Essays originally published
in the weekly *FrameWorks* journal by FJP, Jerusalem.

ISBN 1-892984-00-8
LIBRARY OF CONGRESS CATALOG CARD NUMBER 98-74417

Printed in Israel

3 5 7 9 10 8 6 4 2

BOOK DESIGN BY DAVID WILLNER

To SR
with love

CONTENTS

CONTENTS

CONTENTS

"*Parasha? forget about it!*"

"Anything else you have, we'd be interested," he said. "Parasha? forget about it! An old policy. If we publish on the parasha, first thing you know every rabbi in the country would be sending us his Shabbat sermons. No way we would even look at it."

He was right, of course. No work is so inconsequential as one with infinite malleability, and nothing is so oppressively irrelevant as blanket relevance. The Torah portion read in the synagogue on the Sabbath usually serves as generic raw material for whatever the pulpit must deliver that weekend: current affairs or Bar Mitzvah fare, fund raising or consciousness raising, political commentary or theater review. It was unfair all the same, I thought as I replaced the handset, because that was precisely why I had resolved to write these essays in the first place.

Torah is my life. That implies the same sort of relationship to Torah* as saying "Science is my life" implies to science, and is entirely different from saying "I am a Talmudist" or "I am a scientist." It projects a concern not just of mind-set or career or interest or skills, but of identity, of passion for an entire vision of reality, of membership in a vast ongoing enterprise of relentless exploration and discovery. As in any affair of love, there is an intense desire to share beauty's vision and power, especially with those who misconstrue her as beast (theology, perhaps, or technology, as the case may be). As in any affair of love, adulteration is an act of war, dilution is demeaning, and charlatanism is beneath contempt. The uses often made of Torah (and sometimes of science) can be all of those. Yes, he was right about many sermons. But personally I feel the same pain and

*Not in the sense of the *Chumash* ("Five Books of Moses") or the *Tanach* (the "Old Testament"). Here I refer to the ongoing and boundless enterprise itself, not to any particular work.

mortification about much of the "pop-Torah" genre that does manage to get published.

Is there an alternative? I once thought that any "popular" presentation just couldn't escape the unctuous patronizing, couldn't rise above the moralizing pap and oversimplified pablum that are the just desserts of reducing a grand, rich, and integrated whole into glorified sound bites that insult the intelligence of the serious reader (and speak volumes of the writer). Then, on the cover of a popular weekly magazine I saw a Harvard professor – a paleontologist, for heaven's sake! A certain Stephen Jay Gould, who *lives* science, who spends his time studying snails and making punctuated waves in the staid halls of evolutionary biology, was communicating meaningfully, intelligibly, and broadly enough to be interesting to millions of readers. And at that moment I knew: if it can be done with paleontology, it can be done with Torah.

The gentle reader is probably chuckling good-naturedly at my naïveté. Science, after all, is as real as nature herself and bound to serve up some universally significant findings that speak to nearly everyone. Religion, doctrine, tradition – they may have a place along with pop psychology in the larger book stores, but universal significance? And the gentle reader would be right, given those suppositions. Yet wrong simply because Torah is not about religion, doctrine, and tradition any more than science is about snails. Science provides a framework for the systematic and fundamental description of nature, and in doing so certainly has much to say about snails. And about nearly everything else in the physical world: quarks and hormones, probability and gases, and the evolution of galaxies and brains. Torah provides a framework for the systematic and fundamental description of reality, and in doing so has much to say about nearly everything that we find altogether relevant: history and identity, law and love, raising children and making choices, and the evolution of existence and consciousness. Both science and Torah provide complex and integrated maps of the universe; both are uncompromisingly rigorous; both forcefully and properly reject loose speculation, system building, and untestable claims about universal harmonies. You would never confuse science with alchemy, and you should never confuse Torah with doctrine. I remain convinced that what is doable with science is doable with Torah.

But *how* is it done? I set out to read everything Gould had written and was writing, and found myself enjoying it immensely. Throughout two decades of monthly articles in *Natural History* magazine (and five volumes of collections), the man does not try to explain the science he was living. Instead, he writes of what the living science was explaining – its implications for baseball games and Hershey bars, coincidence and crackpots, Mickey Mouse and literary bias. Yet, hardly noticing, his readers come gradually to recognize the patterns of evolutionary biology, its postulates and processes, the framework it provides for viewing the universe. No question that his monthly column justifies its title, in Darwin's own words: "This View of Life."

Such an elementary yet wise solution. Avoid dilution and distortion by not even attempting an oxymoronic "simplified account" of the fundamental breadth and wholeness of a vast, interrelated system. Use a pointillistic technique instead. Provide enough illustrations, samples, and models to gradually elaborate the conceptual framework which alone can offer the intuitive and visceral recognition of a complete "view of life." And stick to Gould's own rules: no compromises with conceptual richness; no bypassing of ambiguity or ignorance; removal of jargon, of course, but no dumbing-down of ideas.

There is a natural and venerable focus in Torah for this sort of technique: the parasha.* Through the millennia, the reading of the weekly

* This word is a popular misnomer (though similarly defined in even the finest English dictionaries) for what is properly the *sidrah*. The *Chumash* was divided into 54 portions that would allow for annual (including lunar leap years) completion in a weekly public reading (there was also, in *Eretz Yisrael*, a triennial apportionment of *sidrot*). A *parasha*, on the other hand, is technically a paragraph, marked by an indent or a mid-line blank space in the Torah scroll. *Parashot* can be as short as a single sentence and as long as an entire *sidra*.

portion has provided a Torah rhythm and focus for the "man in the street." It became the universal "popular" text, studied on every level with every method, so ubiquitous that it served to designate time and anchor events.[1] Pointillist in its formulation, each parasha is built around the interplay of themes complex enough to touch upon fundamental reality, yet simple enough to illuminate a single concept. The 54 parashot✱ supply a substantial reservoir of themes that help elaborate this Torah view of life, a conceptual framework for exploring creation.

What approach shall we take to the parasha? Why not continue the parallel with science: Nature speaks to us very simply, in ways so down-to-earth that any child can understand. Only in the past centuries have we learned not to be fooled by that simplicity, to recognize that nothing is as challenging as that which is most simple. We know now that nested within the simple expressions of nature is all the boundless complexity of the natural world and its underpinnings, impervious to our wishful thinking, speaking its own mathematical language. Torah also speaks to us very simply, in a style so down-to-earth that any child can understand. We must never be fooled by that simplicity, recognizing that nested within those simple expressions of Torah are all the boundless complexities of creation, the underpinnings of mind, time, law, life and death, impervious as gravity to wishful thinking. Anyone who would speculate upon nature on his own terms instead of hers, lives the life of a fool, not of science. And anyone who would speculate upon Torah on his own terms lives a "religious life," perhaps,[2] but certainly not one of Torah.

The reader, then, must also play by the rules. But who makes the rules? If what you are looking for is Bible Stories, psychological insights, or self-help homilies, the answer is: nobody does. You can comfortably engage in

✱ Actually, 53 of the 54. *Parashat Bereishit* is not "pointillist" by any stretch of the imagination. It foreshadows and subsumes the content of the other parashot, in such breadth and concentration as to effectively remove it from this treatment. In effect, all the rest of the *Chumash* expands the condensed information of *Parashat Bereishit*, and in these essays we will often have cause to address it extensively. I look forward to the publication (also with FJP) of the entirely different approach of *FrameWorks* to *Parashat Bereishit*.

the popular diversion of do-it-yourself midrash and the like, just remember that it is difficult to come out with more than you put in – like experiencing Japanese culture by taking a package shopping tour and staying in the local Hilton. If, however, you want to authentically experience a different system of thought, if you want to share your own insights and experiences as part of a vigorous, ageless process likely to flourish long after current fads expire, then you need to recognize that the rules are part of the game, set within.

Every system functions along a set of principles and consistent postulates around which it is constructed, every system follows internal rules of logic, and every system communicates in a "language" with clear conventions. The more sophisticated and foolproof (by this I mean only and literally "proof-against-fools," offering ad-hoc conjecture as fact) the system, the more correspondingly subtle, exacting, and complex are the principles, rules of logic, and conventions of language – and the more demanding is the peer review. Again, consider modern science – a system hundreds of years old, developing still through the combined genius of many thousands of humanity's best minds, who not only have made the discoveries of science, but also have explicated the principles of the scientific approach, its logic, and its language of mathematics. Not to mention the millions who have toiled at collecting and interpreting data, at experimentation and application, and at publication and review, adding here and there their pertinent insight to a noble and ceaseless endeavor. You may have personal objections to some postulates or propositions of science because of religious beliefs or psychological needs, but such objections have no significance within the scientific framework – and you would be ill-advised to hold them unless and until you have fully examined them within that framework. Notwithstanding the trendy postmodernistic belief that all paradigms are created equal, most knowledgeable readers will have no difficulty appreciating all this as it applies to science – but not as it applies to Torah, which they take to be a mixed-bag of promiscuous conjectures that can mean anything you wish them to mean. Nothing could be further from the truth.

Torah is a system thousands of years old, explicated through the combined genius of thousands of people, among them individuals universally recognized as possessing some of the finest minds in history. Its principles, logic, and language are formally and exactingly defined in a literature encompassing tens of thousands of volumes. Its propositions and discoveries are the subject of a peer review that has never been equaled, with intense and sometimes brutal debate that reverberates across the years. Millions of enthusiasts have toiled at proposing and testing new theories, at collecting data, at publication and review, and have added from time to time another piece to a magnificent and boundless enterprise. You are certainly entitled to hold personal objections to some postulates or conclusions of Torah, but such objections are irrelevant within the Torah framework. You may even wish to gut the existing system, but it is awfully easy to throw out the baby with the bath water out of sheer illiteracy and egregious ignorance (and rabbinic appellation, unfortunately, offers no guarantees in this respect). Bracket yourself for a few hours, and take this opportunity to survey the system from within.

Am I suggesting that you temporarily subscribe to a single, absolutely "True" way to look at reality, whether in terms of science or in terms of Torah? No, a hundred times no – and I say that neither for fear of political incorrectness nor to still suspicions of transgressing the only cardinal sin left to our multicultural, polyveritous, and pluralistic society: bigotry. (Indeed, I plead unrepentantly guilty of the primally bigoted persuasion that one conclusion may be vastly superior to another.) I say it because the notion of fundamentally dissimilar paradigms of equal truth is deeply embedded in Torah: the Sinaic fragmentation into seventy primal languages[3] later engraved on stelae[4] and elucidated by Moshe;[5] Sumchus' forty-eight alternatives;[6] R. Yehuda haNassi, author of the

Mishna, and his successful incorporation of thirteen alternative models;[7] the requirement for seventy distinct[8] approaches within the Sanhedrin (a unanimous decision is ipso facto rejected[9]); the proclamation that polar views represent concurrently "the words of Living God"[10] – these scratch the surface of a profound and pervasive current. And I say it because "Torah speaks in the language of human beings,"* as must ultimately be true of science, simply because language reflects the working of our minds, the map of reality that defines, for us, the universe – and the language of humans is the only language we can ever know. But what I *am* suggesting is that there are tenable and earnest criteria for avoiding both the intellectual solipsism of finding exactly what you already know or what you set out to find in the first place (consciously or not), and – much worse – the emotional solipsism of profoundly "experiencing" the god that is none but self projection. The rewards for playing by the rules go far beyond the intellectual and the emotional, for informed consciousness makes authentic experience of reality beyond oneself possible, and nourishes an enriched humanity and vital spirituality more free of self involvement and idols of the mind.

I want to share with you in this series a taste of genuine and thematic parasha-style "learning," exploring together texts, questions, patterns and frameworks so that you can get some sense of what it is like from the inside. Though mere vignettes, these essays cover a fair spectrum of appealing issues and I have tried to make them accessible on a wide variety of levels, at times presenting a single and basic idea in a personal voice, at times ranging far and perhaps provocatively afield. Even in the more difficult pieces I will avoid technicalities that would be unappealing to the reader with little background, but I will not avoid complexity or controversy (I expect to have as much fun here as you, and most

* Berachot, 31b. There are literally dozens of occurrences of this principle throughout the Talmud. Though there is disagreement about whether the principle holds even for *redundancies* in the Torah (cf. for example Nedarim, 3a), there is certainly no disagreement regarding the fundamental concept. As Maimonides puts it, "All is presented in the mental constructs of human beings who think in physical terms, and Torah speaks the language of human beings...." *Hilchot Yesodei haTorah*, 1:9.

certainly did not address this book exclusively to beginners). And I will attempt to convey the interwoven congruence and interrelated nesting of the diverse texts and approaches within the various fields of Torah thought: halachic, aggadic, kabbalistic, talmudic, philosophic, and more. Along the way I hope you will discover some of the relevance and excitement of "this view of life."

Some Notes *on* Usage

There are an awful lot of childhood and childlike preconceptions when it comes to the Bible (or *Tanach*, in Hebrew). To help avoid them and in the interest of authenticity, I use Hebrew names for the characters and books of the Bible (say Iyov, not Job), unless the English is close enough to the original (thus Isaiah, not Yishaiah). I use the unfashionable *ch* for the *khaf* and Ḥ for the *Ḥet*, except when a name is so well recognized that it would seem bothersome (so Rachel, not Raḥel). As this is not meant to be an academic work, I generally chose readers' comfort over technical consistency. Translations are my own, unless otherwise indicated.

Concepts that do not accurately translate into English are presented throughout in transliterated Hebrew (*Ḥesed*, then, not "loving-kindness"). Though such words are initially defined in the essays, there is a (sadly oversimplified) glossary for use when memory fails. Authenticity is also served through using now and then the original Hebrew texts in the margins – if you are a Hebrew reader you will appreciate this most on those occasions when you suspect me of shockingly fabricating a translation.

Tractate references are to the Babylonian Talmud unless otherwise indicated; biblical commentators are on location if no further reference is provided; common and familiar sources are not italicized.

One more thing: The Talmud makes a practice of citing popular aphorisms, epigrams, and proverbs[11] (at times from the most unlikely[12] and even repudiated[13] sources) to illustrate its conclusions. You might suppose that this is merely by way of popular illustration, but there is more to it, as it also happens[14] that the Talmud will first quote the adage and then ask: What is the Torah source for this statement? Keep in mind that Torah is viewed as a powerful framework for reality, and you'll find that the point here is the cross-referencing of human experience with theory, much as science books love to address such questions as, 'Why do curve balls curve?' or 'Why do we experience optical illusions?' (not to mention 'Why do apples fall?'), questions that often serve to unearth hidden and serious principles. Conversely, the piquancy, poignancy, and humanity conferred by real-life experience distilled in literary dressing serve to transform the purely cerebral into the sharply experiential: Life into Torah, Torah into Life. I emulate this vintage style by offering throughout the margins popular cross-references to these essays, using everything from Broadway and best-selling songs to science and the classics, and I have had a lot of fun (I think it probably shows) noting the universality of certain concepts, or the subtle differences in the way a maxim would be taken in a Torah context, or, sometimes, the vivid contrast in approaches. Where the quote bears further study, I include detailed sources; otherwise just the author will do. Enjoy!

1 *Ba'er Hatev, Hilchot Ta'anit*, 580:9; *Shela, Vayeshev*, 297a.

2 Though not by Torah standards, where "religious" could only mean "fulfilling the Sinaitic Covenant," which is not satisfied by ethical behavior and the keeping of mitzvot. See Vayikra 22:3,14 and related Sifra.

3 Shabbat, 88b.

4 Sotah, 32a.

5 Rashi, Devarim 1:5.

6 Eiruvin, 13b.

7 Nedarim, 41a.

8 *Mishne Torah, Hilchot Sanhedrin*, 10:5. Cf. Sanhedrin, 34a.

9 *Mishne Torah*, ibid., 9:1.

10 Eiruvin, ibid.; Gittin, 6b.

11 E.g. Berachot, 8a, 32a, 43b; Shabbat, 62b; Pesaḥim, 28a, among many dozens.

12 E.g. Ḥagiga, 13a; Yevamot, 63b; Bava Bathra, 98b.

13 Cf. Sanhedrin, 100b.

14 E.g. Bava Kama, 92b; Bava Metzia, 107b.

II Noaḥ

The New World

Many readers pay scant attention to the heavy dose of "begats" in this parasha. It is easier to focus on the epic dramas that bracket them, beginning and end: the chronicle of the Flood and the story of the Tower of Bavel (Babylon), respectively. But there is much to learn from the prosaic and tedious midsection in which we read of the development of the primal Seventy Nations. These postdiluvian *B'nei Noaḥ* ('Children of Noaḥ') entities developed within an environment strikingly different from the antediluvian world described in *Parashat Bereishit*. It's a whole *New World*, and the standards, expectations, life-styles, and moral vision are new as well. Humanity's place as a species is strategically redefined here to provide the wholesome prerequisites for renewed evolution.

THE NEW WORLD

Columbus Day marks the anniversary of a journey over the deeps to a New World, and falls appropriately in the season of *Parashat Noaḥ*. The year-long "journey" of Noaḥ and his ark, after all, culminated in the same sort of discovery:

> Noaḥ looked upon a new world.
>
> BEREISHIT RABBA, 30:8

The New World was part of a saga ranging far beyond novel geography and agriculture – it changed forever the nature of history, culture and civilization. Noaḥ's "new world" did the same, innovatively defining the nature of Man and civilization.

Parashat Noaḥ traces the transition from a degenerate creation to a regenerating creation; the transition from the Flood to the birth of Avraham. There is a single individual at the focus of that passage: Noaḥ.

> Ten generations from Adam to Noaḥ…
> Ten generations from Noaḥ to Avraham…
>
> PIRKEI AVOT, 5:2

But Noaḥ achieves here not only a transition, he accomplishes something lasting and real in and of itself: he builds the "gentile" world, serving as archetype of nearly all subsequent civilization. Except for that tiny percentage of Earth's population represented by Israel,[1] the Torah views the nations as *B'nei Noaḥ,* "Children of Noaḥ." Their existential significance is defined by the Rainbow Covenant with Noaḥ, and their connection with God is predicated on the "Seven Mitzvot of the Children of Noaḥ."[2] We may build beyond Noaḥ, but his achievement is the bedrock upon which future development is founded. The transition he provided to a new world is part of our everyday lives and the core of our relationship to creation.[3]

And what a transition it was – what a difference between the world before and the world after the Flood. Something fundamental changed on the way to the new world, and the Torah highlights the transformation with contrasting – even contradictory – declarations. Consider the response of God's "heart" to the corruption of man's "heart" which, *before* the Flood, moves God to violent despair:

> *God saw that…all the inclinations of his* [Man's] *heart were only evil, all day long. And God regretted that He had made Man on earth, and was saddened to His heart. God said: I will obliterate….* (6:5-7)

That same corruption of heart becomes, *after* the Flood, the rationale – again in the "heart" of God – for forbearance and acceptance:

> *God said in His heart: I will never again curse the earth because of Man, for the heart of Man is evil from his very youth….* (8:21)

In [Man] all nature is comprehended, in all nature only he is created, and all nature only for him. He is the measure of all things…
THOMAS MANN

This underlying change implies nothing less than a complete inversion of humanity's place in Creation. In the antediluvian milieu, Man encompassed the consciousness of the universe. If he failed, the failure was universal.

> *God said, "I will obliterate humanity that I have created from the face of the earth – from man to livestock to small life-forms to birds of the sky!"* (6:7)

The decision here to obliterate "*humanity*" is taken to include, as a matter of course, "*from man to livestock to wild animal to birds of the sky.*" Man, after all, was the central objective and aspiration of Creation as envisioned before the Flood.

> Everything was created for Man, and if he were destroyed then what would be the point of anything else?
>
> RASHI, 6:7[4]

וימח את כל היקום אשר על פני
האדמה, אם אדם חטא,
בהמה מה חטאה?
תנא משום רבי יהושע בן קרחה,
משל לאדם שעשה חופה לבנו,
והתקין מכל מיני סעודה.
לימים מת בנו, עמד ופזר את חופתו.
אמר, כלום עשיתי אלא בשביל בני,
עכשיו שמת חופה למה לי?
אף הקדוש ברוך הוא אמר,
כלום בראתי בהמה וחיה אלא בשביל
אדם? עכשיו שאדם חוטא
בהמה וחיה למה לי.

סנהדרין קח.

But after the Flood, it seems that suddenly the earth and its life-forms are viewed as significant in themselves, and Man is no more than another twig on an evolutionary bush:

> *God said in His heart: I will never again curse the earth because of Man, for the heart of Man is evil from his very youth. Never again will I hurt all life as I have just done.* (8:21)

Earth's very soil, its mountains and creatures, are reason enough for Creation. Man can have a share – but only as one species among others:

> *Man and beast you save, Lord (Tehillim 36:7)* – You save man in *merit* of the animal, O Lord! . . .
>
> This verse refers to Noaḥ. The Holy One said: All the kindness I did for Noaḥ in the ark was not for him but for the great mountains. . . .
>
> When I remembered him it was not he that I remembered alone, but. . .*God remembered Noaḥ and all the beasts and all the livestock*. . . .*(8:1)*
>
> BEREISHIT RABBA, 33:1

There is a critical difference between viewing Man as just another species and seeing him as the purpose of Creation. His significance as species is in the aggregate, but his significance as purpose may be in the individual.[5] Members of the first ten generations needed to live as individuals, each separately vindicating Creation. The second ten generations, however, lived as investment in the future, through nourishing a world yet-to-be. Their individual lives needed no justification.

This distinction is what lies behind the significant differentiation between the genealogical chronicles from Adam to Noaḥ and the chronicles from Noaḥ to Avraham. The first ten generations report each individual's total lifetime; the second ten report only the time of the generations' overlap, representing the earlier individual's contribution to the future. Note the format of the early records in *Parashat Bereishit*:

> *Seth lived 105 years, and had a son Enosh. Seth lived 807 years after he had Enosh, and he had sons and daughters.*
>
> ***So it was that all the days of Seth were 912 years, and he died.***
>
> *Enosh lived 90 years, and he had a son Kenan. Enosh lived 815 years after he had Kenan, and he had sons and daughters.*
>
> ***So it was that all the days of Enosh were 905 years, and he died.*** *(5:6-11)*

Contrast that with the format of the later records here in *Noaḥ* where no mention is made of total years:

> *Shem lived 100 years, and had a son Arpachshad, two years after the Flood. Shem lived 500 years after he had Arpachshad, and he had sons and daughters.*

Arpachshad lived 35 years, and had a son Shelaḥ. Arpachshad lived 403 years after he had Shelaḥ, and he had sons and daughters. (11:10-13)

The new vision of Man-as-species is different in another way. Before the Flood, Man transcended the animal – he was a steward of life, not wholly part of the food chain. Unlike the animals, he was not a consumer of the "life-within-flesh." His food was limited to the plant kingdom. After the Flood, he became himself a part of animal life, a predator:

All moving life shall be food for you, as with the green grasses, I give you all these. (9:3)

Moreover, as a predator, Man became subject to predation. For the first time, God must extend special protection to Man: animals' instinctive fear-of-man:

The fear and dread of you will be instilled in all the wild beasts of the earth...I will demand an account from the hand of every wild beast.... (9:2,5)

> Because they [men] became open to attack and were easily overpowered by wild animals – as it says, *He is dominated for he has become similar to beast* (*Tehillim* 49:21) – it was necessary to protect them from the animals. (–Rashi, 9:2)
>
> No wild animal will attack a human unless it perceives that human as another beast – as it says, *He is dominated: for he has become similar to beast* (*Tehillim* 49:21).
>
> SHABBAT, 151b

*What a piece of work is man!
How noble in reason!
How infinite in faculties!
In form and moving,
how express and admirable!
In action, how like an angel!
In apprehension,
how like a god!
The beauty of the world!
The paragon of animals!*
HAMLET II,ii

Man as Earth-product, Man-as-animal, the commonality of *flesh* – these are the most striking themes in the new relationship between God and Life. The Rainbow Covenant is achieved here *not* with Man himself, but with *Earth* and with the *flesh* of the earth and with all life therein embodied.

I have placed My rainbow in the clouds, and it shall be a symbol of the covenant **between Me and the earth***....*

The rainbow will be in the clouds and I will see it to be aware of the everlasting covenant **between God and all breathing life within all flesh which is upon the earth***....*

God said to Noaḥ: This is the sign of the covenant that I have made between Me and all flesh on the earth. (9:13,16,17)

God has come to care here for Earth in its entirety. Man's shortcomings as part of Earth are seen by Him as of no great consequence. We are now '*only* human': still children, with hearts corrupted in youthful innocence.[6] There are pretty butterflies and sweet humans with all their human failings, and they justify one another: *Man and beast you save, Lord.* It is man-and-beast together that allows the survival of men-become-beasts.

> *Should I not care for Nineveh, that great city, in which live over one hundred and twenty thousand persons who do not know the difference between their right hand and their left, and many animals!* (*Yonah* 4:11)[7]
>
> – "*Many animals*" refers to evildoers, who act like animals.
>
> TANḤUMA, ZOT HABERACHA, 6

This was the vision of Creation on which the world would be rebuilt, a vision of Earth-as-ark, its life collectively absorbed in a voyage towards completion, from which *God smelled the sweet fragrance* (8:21), and with which a covenant for Life could be made. It was a creation based on sweetness and favor (Hebrew "*ḥen*," חן), without immediate expectations;[8] a creation that would eventually nourish a recreation. There was one human being who was the focus of all this change, the focus of a new way of viewing Creation; one man who made it possible for a very imperfect world to begin its voyage home: Noaḥ.

It was not the *merit* of Noaḥ, not the righteousness of *Noaḥ, the just man* (6:9) that allowed him to survive the Flood. It was the "*wholesome Noaḥ*" (ibid.) who survived – it was his *sweetness*, his *ḥen*, that let him live to begin a new sort of life in a new world:

> The original decree of annihilation included Noaḥ as well, however he found *ḥen* in God's eyes, for we may read the verse as, *God said: I will obliterate Man...I am sorry I ever made them and Noaḥ – [but he nonetheless] found favor in the eyes of God.* (6:7,8)
>
> SANHEDRIN, 108a

זה ינחמנו...
ינח ממנו את עצבון ידינו.

רש"י

Noaḥ was named at birth for an exceptional destiny – named with the two Hebrew letters spelling *ḥen* (ח"נ).

He [Lemech] called his [son's] name Noaḥ (נ״ח), *saying, "This one will succor us from our work and from the anguish of our hands out of the soil that God has cursed."* (5:29)

Adam's years terminate at the birth of Noaḥ, and Lemech felt that what the former had ruined, the latter would now repair.

ḤIZKUNI, 5:29

The initial ten generations had lived in the shadow of Adam, the bearer of mortality and an earth accursed. Their failure was painfully obvious. But Noaḥ was to lead the first generation born after the death of Adam.[9] It was he who would realize the dream of escaping the shadow.

Noaḥ was the first human being to dream of revitalizing the earth,

Noaḥ gave his heart and soul to bring the earth out of its adversity.

ZOHAR ḤADASH, 22b

Noaḥ was the first human being to dedicate himself to being the gardener of the earth,

Noaḥ was a gardener for the pure sake of gardening.

BEREISHIT RABBA, 36:3

Noaḥ was the first human to invent for the sake of the earth,

Noaḥ invented plows, harrows, hoes, and all the farming tools.

TANḤUMA, BEREISHIT, 11

Noaḥ was the first human being to conceive of the earth as ark. He was the first to see the need to tend each piece of an interrelated world and became the one man who would tend the ark as earth. Noaḥ became lover of the earth,[10] knower of the earth,[11] master of the earth,[12] builder of the earth,[13] and even husband of the earth.

Noaḥ, the man of the earth... (9:20)

As in "*Elimelech, the* man *of Naomi...*" *(Ruth, 1:3)*. (—Rashi[14])

Noaḥ, the one who perceived farming as *husbandry,* lived to see Earth rebuilt and settled. He lived to see his new world alive and flourishing.

Noaḥ did not die until he saw the earth settled and growing, until he saw seventy nations ranging from his seed.

TANḤUMA, NOAḤ, 2

We walked in single file through narrow aisles of a greenhouse [located] at...a holding facility for prisoners awaiting transfer to other institutions. Passarella [an inmate convicted of assault and kidnapping] recited the names of the plants as we passed through, and when he came to a bench where there were rose cuttings taking root in containers, he said almost in awe, "Look at that. We're bringing life into the world." ...He stands ready to swear by all the saints that the plants have made a changed man of him.

THE GIFT OF GARDENING[15]

The first ten generations certainly did not ignore God's primary injunction to *serve and keep* (2:15) the earth. However, instead of tangibly tending the earth, they served through the awareness of prayer and their religious connection to God.[16] They declined into perversion and self-gratification, and were lost in the deluge. The second ten generations learned to concretely *serve and keep* through tending Earth with love – through *tend*erness. They succeeded in establishing a covenant with God in everlasting care for life:

> *Never again will I hurt all life as I did now. As long as the earth lasts – seedtime and harvest, cold and heat, summer and winter, and day and night shall never cease.* (8:21,22)
>
> *I hereby found a covenant with you and your offspring after you, and with every living creature that is with you, birds, livestock, and all the beasts of the earth with you, all who left the ark....* (9:9,10)

The wholesomeness of Noaḥ and his descendants is preserved by the Rainbow Covenant and the Seven Mitzvot.[17] Those seven mitzvot are not just a list of important moral principles. They are the specific underpinnings of Noaḥ's entire vision: the "Seven Mitzvot of the Children of Noaḥ." As long as men maintain the commitment to take only what is given them, to maintain respect for all life, for the right to hold property and sustaining relationships, and for Justice – as long as humans live the covenant with God, the earth will flourish and develop. But without the covenantal relationship the decay sets in, and the finest ideas become first theories, then mere conveniences, and at last – burdens.

To create something in the image of nature is to create a machine, and it was by learning the inner working of nature that man became a builder of machines.

ERIC HOFFER

At their finest, the Seventy *B'nei Noaḥ* continue in the tradition of Noaḥ. The commitment to creation, the devotion of whole lives to one tiny corner of the world – a better school, a cleaner road, a finer rose, a single new observation, a beautiful discovery, a mathematical puzzle – the tenderness of gardening in its broadest sense is what allows the world to survive, to grow, to nourish the future still ripening in its womb.

To leave the world a bit better, whether by a healthy child, a garden patch or a redeemed social condition; to know even one life has breathed easier because you have lived.

EMERSON

The Seventy Nations provide the groundwork and footing for the flowering of Yisrael. Seventy of Avraham's progeny would descend to

Egypt to grow into his own identity of *father of many nations (17:5)*. The seventy symbolize the bond between Yisrael and the Children of Noaḥ.

יצב גבולות עמים למספר בני ישראל

When the Most High gave nations their heritage and split up the sons of man, He set the definitions of nations according to the number of the Children of Yisrael. (Devarim 32:8)

Paralleling the seventy individuals of Yisrael who went down to Egypt did *"He set the definitions of nations,"* seventy languages.[18] (—Rashi[19])

יצב גבולות עמים למספר
בני ישראל [דברים לג]
וכמה הם?
כל הנפש לבית יעקב הבאה מצרימה
שבעים שאומות העולם שבעים.

במדבר רבה ט:יד

The rise of the *individual* would begin again – one person as one nation.

Noaḥ lived to nourish the future that would restore the individual as he had restored the species. He lived to nourish the future that would outstrip him, that would restore the service of God as he had restored the service of earth.

Avram stayed in the home of Noaḥ and his son, Shem, and learned from them. . . .

SEFER HAYASHAR, NOAḤ

That new service of God would be forever built on tenderness:

Avraham asked Malkizedek [Shem], "How did you merit to survive the ark?"

"Through charity," he answered.

"But what kind of charity could you perform on an ark – there were certainly no poor people there!?" asked Avraham.

"Charity to animals, beasts and birds!" said he. "We never slept, we tended each species at the proper time, all night. . . ."

It was then that Avraham opened his inn in Be'er Sheva, to provide food and drink and company.

MIDRASH TEHILLIM, 37:1

Whenever man forgets that man is an animal, the result is always to make him less humane.
JOSEPH WOOD KRUTCH

Man will once again be the "height of creation," but only after learning his place upon the land and its life, and only through the many centuries and the countless lives that have prepared and continue to prepare the way with tenderness towards Earth. To forget that is to defeat the future.

1 Cf. Nedarim, 31a.

2 Cf. Bava Kama, 38a.

3 Cf. Ramban, 9:14.

4 S.v. *Me'adam*, ד״ה מאדם, cf. Bereishit Rabba, 28:6.

5 Cf. Sanhedrin, 37a.

6 Cf. Ramban, 8:21.

7 Cf. Ta'anit, 16a: *They covered man and beast with sackcloth* (*Yonah* 3:8). "They separated the animals from their calves and said 'Master of the Universe: If You cannot care for us, we will not care for these!'"

8 Cf. Berachot, 7a.

9 Rashbam, 5:29. The reference, of course, is to the "first" of the listed ten generations born (in 1056 of Torah chronology) after the death of Adam in year 930, not necessarily the first human birth during that period.

10 Cf. Bereishit Rabba, 36:3.

11 Ibn Ezra and Radak, 9:20.

12 Rashi, 9:20.

13 Cf. Ramban (second approach) and *Ḥizkuni*, 9:20.

14 S.v. *Ish ha'adama*, ד״ה איש האדמה.

15 William S. Ellis, *National Geographic*, May, 1992, 58.

16 Cf. Rashi 2:5.

17 For a simplified exposition of these mitzvot, see Aharon Lichtenstein, *Seven Laws of Noah* (New York: Z. Berman Books, 1981).

18 These were the seventy languages into which the Torah itself splintered at Sinai (Shabbat, 88b), the seventy languages in which the Torah was inscribed by Moshe on the stones of the Plains of Mo'av (Sotah, 32a).

19 S.v. *Lemispar*, ד״ה למספר.

II Noaḥ

נֹחַ

The Rainbow and the Tower

Noaḥ spans ten generations defined by two epic events: the Flood, that begins their history, and the Tower of Bavel (Babylon) that concludes it. The primal SeventyNations, the *B'nei Noaḥ* ("Children of Noaḥ"), evolved during the course of these formative centuries that forever define the fundamental nature of humanity. It is here, beneath the Rainbow and its message of hope and beauty, that Man first enters a covenant with God; it is here that we glimpse for the first time the social ugliness that became a model of evil – the works of Nimrod.

There is a theme running through this parasha, defining the historical forces at work throughout the course of this formative epoch; there is a direction to these centuries of seemingly drifting development, a coherent transition between the Rainbow that opens the evolution of this New World and the Tower that closes it. And there are paradigms endlessly instructive, surprising, and undimmed by passing millennia.

THE RAINBOW AND THE TOWER

Noaḥ is a parasha that tells of failure, collapse and reconstruction. The parasha presents suggestive parallels to the forces that have come so dramatically into play during the twentieth century. The stunning failure and collapse of communism comes to mind as an example, a collapse that to me symbolized a vindication. Not necessarily vindication of an *economic* system – clearly the collapse of communism proves nothing about the long term viability of capitalism – but vindication of a *moral* system. Some would agree passionately with such an assessment; others would find it embarrassingly naïve. I suspect that in this parasha the Torah cautions us that both might be missing a significant point.

Kennedy called the cold war "a long twilight struggle," and it was a twilight that continues to baffle and to intrigue. Sophisticates feel a bit sheepish now as they look back at the period. In the *fin de siècle* CNN series, *Cold War*, Robert McNamara explains deterrence but seems amazed himself at its scandalous logic. It does seem out of all proportion that a disagreement over rival economic systems should have been charged with the sort of hatred and fervor that is usually reserved for religious crusades. One would have imagined only *jihad*-driven fanatics capable of blowing up the planet to save the world. Yet nominally intelligent people came dreadfully close to doing just that. Were we all seized by some kind of mass hysteria?

Others see *jihad* as precisely the point. They perceive the conflict in candidly religious terms: atheistic communism warring against the Godly West. They trumpet the triumph of truth marching on – however perilously close we came to nuclear holocaust, that is part of the price one gladly pays for truth's triumph. Yet the injection of religious elements seems facile. Why battle communism – why not just battle atheism? Certainly, providing for the poor and protecting workers from exploitation is not a violation of religious tradition. The antireligious elements of Marxism are not an indispensable part of economic theory – after all, there are religious kibbutzim in Israel practicing Marxist economics (and no one ever suggested nuking them).

But there is a more primal value involved here: humanity. As a teenager I was shaken by Nikita Khrushchev's displays of brutish ferocity. I believed he meant it literally when he made his savage prediction of communist victory: "We will bury you." What would happen to *me* if he really were right about "historical inevitability"? Maybe some people related to the threat of communism in terms of its repressiveness, its poverty, its painful proscriptions – it was profoundly inhumane. To me it had more the nightmarish quality of horror movies: it was *inhuman*.

We got rid of them [communists]. They'd either go against religion or something like that, and that's how you could tell they were communists.
THURGOOD MARSHALL

True, the stuff of a child's nightmare is hardly a rational basis for formulating assessments of good and evil. At the time my reactions were intuitive, a visceral shudder. To an American youth, the Soviet premier appeared more *H. neanderthalensis* than *H. sapiens* as he banged his shoe on a UN desk in an eye-popping display of calculated contempt for the aspirations and simple civility of civilization. Now, however, I have the data I did not have then. I know him now; I recognize where he comes from. His roots and derivation really do lie in pre-civilization, as characterized here in Noaḥ.

Whether you like it or not, history is on our side. We will bury you.
NIKITA KRUSHCHEV

The Talmud teaches that all of *Parashat Noaḥ* is part of an extended Creation narrative. The parasha speaks of a period during which the fundamental construct termed "human" is still primitive. This period terminates only with the development of a template for consummate humanity in the form of the mature Avraham:

> The first two thousand years, until *Avraham and the people he influenced in Ḥaran (Bereishit 12:5)*, were years of *tohu* (chaos).
>
> AVODA ZARA, 9a

Tohu is a primal keyword, the very same word used in the opening of the Torah: And the world was *tohu,* תוהו*, (Bereishit 1:2)*, i.e. still unformed.

This extended narrative describes the intensive program of selection[1] required to inbreed the characteristics[2] we associate with full humanity, a program spanning twenty generations over two millennia:

> Ten generations from Adam to Noaḥ . . .
> Ten generations from Noaḥ to Avraham . . .
>
> PIRKEI AVOT, 5:2

Parashat Noaḥ tells the story of the second set of ten generations, beginning with the children of Noaḥ. But what exactly is the motif of these later ten generations? They do not seem to accomplish very much, appearing only as a cluster of "begats," an outline of a genetic program. But a genetic program – even one that selects for "spiritual genes" – has to reflect a direction of sorts. We ought to be able to say, at least in retrospect, "Ah, yes. So this is where we have been heading all along." That does not seem to be the case in our parasha. In fact, the only noteworthy event besides the Flood and its immediate aftermath is one which appears at the very end of this epoch: the epic of Nimrod and the Tower of Bavel. How, then, can we refer to the epoch of the second ten generations? A hodgepodge of themes hardly qualifies as an epoch – much less as a unified parasha.

Yet, consider again the story of that tower – a thoroughly mysterious story. What was it that these people did that was so wicked? The midrash and the commentators offer various explanations of the depravity of the tower builders: they wanted to battle God;[3] they wanted to worship idols;[4] they wanted to protect themselves from future floods;[5] they wanted to launch a space colony to avoid God's presence on Earth,[6] and so forth. These explanations need to be seen in the context of the unembellished and simple words of the Torah itself.

But the Torah never says that the builders of Bavel violated any Divine commandment or committed some injustice. We are told only that –

> *All the earth was a single language, and a unified expression...And they said let us build ourselves a city and a tower that reaches the sky and make a name for ourselves, lest we be scattered over the face of the whole Earth.* (11:1,4)

Now, that does not sound like such a bad thing, and indeed the Midrash says:

> The wrongdoing of this generation is unclear....
>
> BEREISHIT RABBA, 38:6

They achieved what the West has only been able to dream about – universal understanding, a common language, and harmony. They had a United Nations that actually worked.

Because there was peace between them they were not destroyed....

IBID.

Yet God makes it sound as if this were an unmitigated disaster which spelled the end of everything.

And God said: They are one people and one language and this is what they are doing! Shall they now achieve every evil purpose they devise!? (11:6)

The sort of divergence which has made Pingelapese a distinct dialect of Pohnpeian has occurred many times throughout the scattered islands of Micronesia... "Some Micronesians," he goes on, "have become remarkably versatile linguists." One cannot but be reminded of how animals and plants diverge from the original stock, first into varieties and then into species – a speciation intensely heightened by the unique conditions on islands.... Cultural and linguistic evolution, of course, normally proceeds much faster than Darwinian, for we directly pass whatever we acquire to the next generation.

OLIVER SACKS, THE ISLAND OF THE COLOR-BLIND[12]

In fact, the entire theme of Noaḥ seems to represent a premeditated assault on the very value of harmony we take so for granted. Instead, we hear of 'scattering', 'islands', 'nationalities', 'divergence', and 'separation'.

From these all the Earth was scattered. (9:19)

From these the islands of nations were separated in their lands, each to his own language.... (10:5)

According to their families and languages, in their lands and nationalities. (10:20)

According to their families and their languages.... (10:31)

From these the nations diverged on Earth after the Flood. (10:32)

The essential accomplishment of the Sons of Noaḥ is that they were not only "*fruitful*," they not only "*multiplied*," but they "*scattered across the Earth*." This had been the central charge of God to the new postdiluvian world,[7] and this was the purpose of the Rainbow Covenant He made with its population.[8] Just as Darwin and Wallace found islands and isolated populations to be unique laboratories, hothouses of nature which might show evolutionary processes in an intensified and dramatic form, so did isolates of peoples, *islands of nations* (10:5), develop entirely new societies, languages, and cultures. Through a process of psychological and spiritual speciation,[9] the Sons of Noaḥ formed new modes of relating to the world around them – separated *in their lands, each to his own language*...(10:5). The progression and direction of the *B'nei Noaḥ* period is the clear theme of the parasha. Their legacy can be summed up in a word: Diversity.

The most universal quality is diversity.

MONTAIGNE

It is against this thematic background that we need to see Nimrod and his ideological backlash. Nimrod was diversity's nemesis, the patron saint of Homogeneity.

One language...identical opinions...one nation... (11:1,6)

All the midrashic explanations flow from that central theme: identical *opinions*, דברים אחדים.

Nimrod's mind rebelled even at the individual character of stones and the haphazard variations of mountain terrain – standardization and sameness were the feats of his society.

They came upon a valley in the land of Shin'ar and settled there.
They said to one another, "Come, let us make bricks...and the brick served them as stone." (11:2,3)

Shin'ar was his promised land, the Land of Bavel (בבל), the atavistic Valley of the Flood in which all had been homogenized.

Why was the Flood called *mabul* (מבול)?
For it mixed (*bilbel* – בלבל) all together....

RASHI 6:17[10]

Why was it called Shin'ar (שנער)? That was where all the dead of the Flood were tossed together (*shenin'ar* – שננער).

SHABBAT, 113b

The very scattering that was essential to cultural speciation was Nimrod's terror. Fear of the scattering drove him to the Tower:

Let us build ourselves a city and a tower that reaches the sky and make a name for ourselves, lest we be scattered across the face of the whole Earth!

Yes, Nimrod built a peaceful society – but there are two paths to peace and harmony. One path unites through integration, synthesis, and synergetic achievement. The other unifies through uniformity, homogeneity, and the suppression of distinction. Out of fear and open hatred of everything that the ten generations of Noaḥ might achieve, Nimrod and company chose the latter path. Creativity and diversity were menacing to Nimrod, the original "*strongman*" (10:8). His non-adaptable survivability depended entirely on control and domination. His society was infinitely deprived, for adaptability is the story of life and its development. The new world of Noaḥ was meant to live under

Civilization is a progress from an indefinite, incoherent homogeneity towards a definite, coherent heterogeneity.

HERBERT SPENCER

the multicolored breadth of the rainbow, spanning a scintillatingly multifarious humanity. Nimrod substituted the drab brick and single-mindedness of the straight and narrow tower.

Nimrod's candid enemy was diversity – diversity in all its feverish color, diversity in its expansive endless unpredictability. In its presence, no one could ever own the future, no position could ever be secure, no power guaranteed, no knowledge absolute. As the forerunner of all of the Great Unifiers and Big Brothers in history – as the prototype of the same communists who murdered millions in the passionate name of holy collectivism – Nimrod set out to bury diversity, to inhibit change and innovation by curtailing challenge and variation. There were to be no new environments, no new circumstances, no new testing, no new worlds:

Comrades! We must abolish the cult of the individual decisively, once and for all.
NIKITA KHRUSHCHEV

> *Let us build ourselves a city and a tower. . . lest we be scattered across the face of the whole Earth.*

And that stasis would have indeed been the end of Creation; it was truly the ultimate *evil purpose* (11:6).

If Creation could be satisfied with stasis, it would be nothing more than an eternal arena which offers a never-ending procession of similar souls a chance to win a ticket to an afterlife. But the world is neither static nor eternal, souls are not similar, and there will be all too few offers of moments in the slowly dying sun.[11] Instead, Creation's entire rationale is uniqueness, distinctness, distinctiveness, diversity, and individuality. It presents us a world that must be made whole – and wholeness comes only through the other road to harmony, the path leading to synthesis and concert of variety and heterogeneity. *Shalom* means not merely *peace*, but *wholeness*.

If we cannot end our differences, at least we can help make the world safe for diversity.
JOHN F. KENNEDY

Challenge, responsiveness, fresh vision and growth are not only part of the definition of life – they are the very format of Creation. What God loves most is innovation, *Ḥiddush* – a unique insight never before achieved. The Zohar describes poetically this sensational passion for *Ḥiddush*:

> When new insights in Torah issue from the mouth of a human being,

That *Hiddush* comes and presents itself to the Holy One,
The Holy One takes it, and kisses it,
Crowning it with seventy crowns....

ZOHAR, I:4b

Stasis is the hallmark of death and homogeneity is the final statement of entropy – whether thermodynamic or spiritual. This is why life itself ceased to have meaning to Nimrod and his people. Only ideology made a difference; only the Great Plan was of consequence:

> If a worker fell and died, no one paid any attention. But if a brick would fall they would sit and mourn, crying, "Where can we ever find one to take its place!"
>
> PIRKEI RABI ELIEZER, 24

The evil of Nimrod and the "Generation of the Dispersal"[13] went deeper than mere transgression. They set out to destroy the very *raison d'etre* of Creation. They sought to uproot every possibility of development and advancement. Ultimately, this was the ruinous evil of Nimrod's recent progeny, the communist regimes. It is no coincidence that these purveyors of collectivism were also the merchants of death. It is no coincidence that these lovers of homogeneity were the worst assassins of ecological diversity. It is no coincidence that these masters of standardization supplanted color and beauty with the hopelessly dull and drab. It is no coincidence that these suppressors of creativity destroyed all productivity. It is no coincidence that these enemies of individuality were self declared enemies of God. Their sin was not against beliefs, it was against Life itself.

*Plurality which is not reduced to unity is confusion;
Unity which does not depend on plurality is tyranny.*

PASCAL

The "retribution" visited upon the erstwhile Soviet Union was precisely that which applied to her parent, Bavel: a near instantaneous outburst of ethnicity, nationalism, languages and dialects. All the unfettered individuality so long repressed was explosively released.

> *And God scattered them from there over the face of the entire Earth. (11:8)*

> ...He said to them: You said "*Lest* we be scattered over the face of all the Earth" – now *be* scattered over the face of all the Earth!
>
> TANḤUMA, NOAḤ, 18:1

The final chapter of the formation narrative closes with this last definitive change wrought by God in the *nature* of human life. Diversity became built-in with the dispersion, an insuppressible birthright of humankind. This is the deep vindication that I believe lies in the disintegration of the Soviet Bloc. Not a vindication of a specific code of conduct, but a vindication of Life itself, in all its glorious variety.

The breakdown of this inhuman system provides emphatic reassurance that it was only a passing nightmare after all. It was not suited to survive. It lost no war, suffered no blockade, was defeated by no curious combination of historical accidents – it simply failed the fundamental test of life and evolutionary success: survival. It is reassuring to find hope that the world is a place where the inhuman must ultimately self-destruct.

It is good to know that he who would have buried us is buried. But it is wise to remember that even the finest of us share with Nimrod a dogmatism born of our own fears and insecurities. And wiser still to learn to recognize and to fear those "Great Warriors" who in the name of an Almighty would – and do – joyfully bury everything beloved of the God of Life.

1 Some find it appalling to speak of human selection, as it reminds them of the absurd and repulsive eugenic programs of the not-too-distant past. The fact is that we all obviously engage in reproductive selection, whether we call it that or not. The selection of a mate is presumably made on the basis of our best estimate of someone who has the characteristics and understanding necessary to be a partner in building a fulfilling and significant future, a partner in creating children whose character will represent our personal standard of sheer humanity.

2 There are those who claim that character tendencies are related not to genes, but entirely to environment and (if they are generous) to human choice. The whole point of the continuing selection process in Bereishit, however, is based on the notion of "spiritual" breeding. Every animal lover knows which breed generally exhibits desirable characteristics [at least from the human's point of view!], and I doubt if there is a mother alive who doesn't recognize the general character of her infant within a few weeks of birth. Cf. *Mishne Torah, Hilchot De'ot,* 1:2.

3 Bereishit Rabba, 38:6.

4 Ibn Ezra, 11:1, s.v. *U'migdal*, ד"ה ומגדל.

5 Rashi 11:1, s.v. *U'devarim*, ד"ה ודברים; cf. Bereishit Rabba, ibid.

6 *Ya'arot Devash.*

7 Contrast 8:17 and 9:1,7. Cf. R. Baḥya 11:4; Radak 11:5, and Ibn Ezra 11:7.

8 The Covenant was a response to the unwillingness of Noaḥ to reproduce without guarantees. Bereishit Rabba, 34:6.

9 There are varied approaches to the order of the development. Rashi (10:25; 11:1), Ramban (11:2), Radak (10:32;11:1), and others understand that the development into separate nations and languages described all through chapter ten of Bereishit actually followed the Dispersion. The "*single language*" then was Hebrew, and the other languages developed suddenly.
According to Ibn Ezra (11:7), the description here of the dispersion and the development of language is actually a reference to a long process of differentiation completed after the Dispersion.
According to *Ḥizkuni* (11:7), the development into languages came first, and the Dispersion made people forget foreign languages so that different nationalities could no longer communicate with each other.

10 S.v. *Mabul*, ד"ה מבול.

11 This argument is from Rabbi Moshe Ḥayim Luzzato, *Da'ath Tevunoth*, Section 44.

12 *The Island of the Colour-blind and Cycad Island* (London: Picador, 1996), 239-241, n.15.

13 The midrashic name given those who were *scattered over the Earth (11:8)*, based on verse 10:25. Cf. Ta'anit, 27b; Bava Metzia, 44a; Sanhedrin, 107b.

III Lech-Lecha

לך לך

Avraham and the Superconducting Super Collider

Lech-Lecha is the story of Avram and his transformation into Avraham (Abraham). Renamed because he has grown, he is seen as *Av* ('father') not only of the Jewish people but somehow *"of many nations"* (17:4), mysteriously destined to *"bring blessing to all the families of Earth"* (12:3). This use of '*Av*' without biological connotation is consistent with its primary sense of 'model' or 'archetype', with "-type" implying clear specificity. In fact, this is how the Jewish people can have more than one *Av*, as each is a prototype of a single very specific characteristic—in the case of Avraham, the attribute of *Ḥesed* (compassion, kindness).

There is, then, no room for ambiguity in an *Av*. Yet Avraham seems to act in ways that are inconsistent with his reputation and his historic character, in ways that belie the presumption of universality and tolerance consistent with a *"Father of many nations."*

Avraham and the Superconducting Super Collider seeks an understanding of *Ḥesed* that can provide an underlying unity to the varied faces of Avraham's life-work, and identifies a vision that transformed the search for fundamental knowledge as part of a *"blessing to all the families of Earth."*

AVRAHAM AND THE SUPERCONDUCTING SUPER COLLIDER

Things seem to be getting more complex all the time. I closely followed the debate (renewed annually, both inside the U.S. Congress and out) over spending billions of dollars on a superconducting super collider, the greatest "atom smasher" ever conceived: 83 kilometers long, containing 41,500 tons of magnets and 19,400 kilometers of superconducting cable cooled by 2 million liters of liquid helium. It appears that I was not the only one confused, because the issue was never truly "resolved" – after spending billions, the half-finished project languishes unfunded. So many different issues were raised that it was well-nigh impossible to know what to think. Is science better served by supporting many smaller projects or by massive spending on one issue? Will America lose its technological edge if spending for basic science is decreased? Is research a greater priority than, say, building a national network of shelters for the homeless? Complexity confuses our priorities, blurs our values, bogs us down with disassociation. It must have been sunny when things were unambiguous and clear-cut.

Complexity comes from the Latin *complexus,* "weaving together," implying relationship between many interconnected parts. Multiple issues pulling in contrasting directions, linked in countless ways, fatigue us both intellectually and emotionally. We yearn for a "return to nature," to simple issues. We crave straightforward and clear bearings. Confusion and multiplicity are our undoing.[1]

There *were* individuals once who embodied utter clarity, who personified coherent concepts. They were called "*Avot.*" *Av* does not mean "father" in the biological sense alone,[2] nor is it limited to the other English meaning of father: originator, as in "Founding Fathers."

Observe its use in the famous words of the introductory mishna to Laws of Torts:

> There are four *avot* of damages.
>
> BAVA KAMA, 1:1

An *Av* is a prototype, an archetype. Each of the *Avot* expresses a different fundamental and primary attribute of life and of God.[3] A consummate archetype must unambiguously exemplify one coherent characteristic. "Complicated" as an adjective paired with "*Av*" is oxymoronic.

Avraham (originally Avram) is introduced as an *Av* in this week's parasha, *Lech-Lecha*. He is the most elemental of all: *Av-Ram* translates literally as "preeminent prototype." He is the embodiment of Creation's elemental *Ḥesed* (loosely, "kindness"), and has entered the Jewish psyche and mythos as its synonym:

> God's Attribute of *Ḥesed* said: As long as Avraham lives in the world, there is nothing I need to accomplish, for Avraham stands in my place....
>
> SEFER HABAHIR, 86

If only *we* had such clear-cut priorities. *Then* we would know how to allocate resources. If *Ḥesed* is what life is all about, why siphon off funds that could be used to feed the needy just to build multi-billion dollar scientific projects? It is good to know that somewhere, back at our roots, Kindness came first; philosophy (natural or otherwise) last. It was all refreshingly simple.

And simple truth, miscall'd simplicity.
SHAKESPEARE, SONNET 66

Or was it? The unambiguously Kind Avraham seems to vanish in a fog of complexities when we discover in *Lech-Lecha* that he wages the first recorded world war;[4] that he asks his wife to lie about her status so that the Egyptians would "give me gifts";[5] that his wife accuses him of disregard for her needs when he prayed for children: "You prayed only for yourself – what about me!" she says.[6] He throws out Lot, the nephew who has been with him through all the difficult years.[7] And what of the unkind and intolerant attacks on the belief systems of those whose idols became victims to Avraham's icon smashfests? These are significant inconsistencies, but there is another problem which is far more serious.

Avraham actually possesses an alternative personality – an entirely different facet which gives the lie to the whole idea of coherency and non-complexity. Listen to Rambam's description of the "other" Avraham, a description as traditional as that of the Avraham of Kindness:

> When this giant was still a child he began to explore in his mind; he began to reason day and night, and to wonder.... He had no mentor, no sources of information, and was floundering in Ur – worshiping with them while his heart probed continuously for insight until at last he discovered the course to truth and the just balance using his own cogent cognition. He knew then that there was One God.... At forty he came to full awareness of God, and when he became conscious and knew, he began to debate the people of Ur, and to have discussion forums.... He smashed icons and began to teach the people.... He would travel and gather people from city to city and from nation to nation.... teaching each individual on his own level.... He wrote books...commanded his children to maintain his teachings....
>
> MISHNE TORAH, HILCHOT AVODA ZARA, 1:3

Here we see Avraham as a veritable Jewish Socrates, a monotheist philosopher who relentlessly cut away the cobwebs of superstition and delusions, an uncompromising iconoclast.[8] A genius and prodigy who single–handedly escaped from (and helped to overturn) the intellectual assumptions of an entire civilization, Avraham was the leader of a world movement to stamp out the gods. Electrifying indeed – but hardly a coherent beam of Kindness.

An incisive and probing intellect focused on uncompromising analytic rationality might just possibly manage to *coexist* with sensitive kindness and undiscriminating love. Even so, these attributes make strange bedfellows. Certainly they are far from the single theme that we expect in an archetype. *Avraham was One (Yeḥezkel 33:24)*, the verse teaches – but how? Did Avraham exemplify Compassionate Care as father of *Ḥesed* or did he personify Rigorous Reason as father of monotheism?

So many inconsistencies point to an underlying inadequacy in our definition of *Ḥesed*. Unless we can discover the seamless symmetry in

Avraham's lifework, we miss the point entirely. Moreover, when we do grasp it, I suspect that we are going to find out that *Ḥesed* and superconducting super colliders (SSC) may be close friends. This question of complexity residing where we expect to find simplicity will turn out to be the solution, not the problem. In fact, I make an audacious suggestion: without Avraham there wouldn't *be* any particle accelerators – no one would ever have dreamed of building an SSC!

Chinese scholars abandoned the idea of a supreme being with personal and creative properties. No rational Author of Nature existed in their universe; consequently the objects they meticulously described did not follow universal principles....In the absence of a compelling need for the notion of general laws – thoughts in the mind of God, so to speak – little or no search was made for them.
EDWARD O. WILSON[10]

Did you ever wonder why, of the many civilizations that flowered through history, only one developed fundamental science? The Chinese, for instance, have an exceedingly ancient culture, yet despite technological developments quite early in their history (in rocketry, printing, magnetic compasses, etc.), such inventions provoked no urge to explore natural regularities. Ingenuity and inventiveness failed to foment periods of revolutionary scientific change and enlarged intellectual horizons as they did later in Western society. Even the Greeks failed to produce any significant corpus of scientific and technological knowledge. They advanced in logic, philosophy, geometry, astronomy – but made no discoveries of the great code of nature's laws.[9] Rambam, in the opening words of *Mishne Torah*, tells us why:

> The cardinal foundation and base of knowledge is to comprehend that there is Prime Being which brings all existence into being; and all things extant, from earth to sky and in-between, exist only as an effect of the absoluteness of such Being.
>
> MISHNE TORAH, HILCHOT YESODEI HATORAH, 1:1

Greece and Rome as Babylon and Egypt: so far from being parents of Arts & Sciences as they pretend: were destroyers...
WILLIAM BLAKE

What possible connection is there between this definition of monotheism and a putative "base of all knowledge"? It is precisely the connection that exists between monotheism and *Ḥesed,* the fusion of the two facets of Avraham.

It appears that the idea of a single Supreme Deity was foreign to the early Chinese, and as a consequence the fate of natural science in that culture was a curious stillbirth.
J.D.BARROW[11]

How did Avraham "explore in his mind" to reach Rambam's Prime Being? He had one overwhelming insight: that all the variety and detail in the universe can be traced back, step by step, to ever more fundamental simplicity. Until at last, *after the fact* of Creation, one is left with existence itself as the root, capable of springing forth from the simple energy of "*Let there be Light*" into matter...into protoplasm...into intelligence...into consciousness itself.[12] Existence itself is the root capable of springing forth to all that we associate with the brilliance of Life. Avraham came to recognize the awesome oneness pervasive throughout all expressions of existence. That "One and fundamental Being" which is the source of all the fabulous detail in the universe is precisely the "Prime Being" of monotheism.

Which means that nature is utterly real, and that all existence shares – *From my own flesh I perceive God (Iyov 19:26).* Prime Being is expressed through *Life.* The entire creation is an astonishing exhibition of pure love for life, of a Creative Will expressed in the astounding confluence of critical elements for life. The moment we understand that, we are seized by an awe-filled love and reverence for creation and Life itself. We find ourselves kin to all life. *Ḥesed* and monotheism become one and the same.

It is a wonderful thing to recognize the unity of a complex of phenomena that to direct observation appear to be quite separate things.

EINSTEIN[14]

Ḥesed is not equivalent to "niceness" or "generosity." It is a profound commitment to Life itself, a commitment that may lead to confrontation, conflict, and even war if such are required to assure Life's definitive triumph. *Ḥesed-Kindness*: examine the word. *Kind* means "of one type"; the deepest *kin*ship of all, a shared existence. *Ḥesed* – the universe as *Kind*ergarten, a garden for the children of pure Being, a*kin* in their very source of existence: the *Image of God* (1:27). What clearer statement of monotheism could be made in a word!

By the same token, polytheism implies an existential detachment that undermines nature's unity along with the commitment to *Ḥesed.*

> Why are idols called "other" gods, אלוהים אחרים? Because they are *other* to their worshipers, who beseech them but they never answer. They act as "others," strangers who never saw them before.
>
> MECHILTA, YITHRO, 5[13]

A little more than kin, and less than kind.

HAMLET, I,ii

In the most profound sense, idols are *other* not simply because their "behavior" appears different, but because they *are* different – they share no common existence with their worshipers. As "*kind*-ness" implies care, "in-*difference*" implies just that: apathy, detached separation, unkindness – anti-*ḥesed.*

The very word *kind* expresses in its history the depth of the relationship between Being, Creation, and *Ḥesed*. It began as the Indo-European *gene* meaning 'being', 'beginning': *genesis*. It became *gecynd* (Old English), meaning 'kin' and 'kind', and *gentle*, and the Latin *gnasci*: Nature itself.[15]

'Gene' signified beginning, giving birth, while 'bheu' indicated existence and growth. 'Gene' turned itself successively into 'kundjaz' (Germanic) and 'gecynd' (Old English), meaning kin or kind. 'Kind' was at first a family connection, later an elevated social rank, and finally came to rest meaning kindly or gentle. Meanwhile, a branch of 'gene' became the Latin 'gens', then gentle itself; it also emerged as genus, genital, and generous; then, still holding on to its inner significance, it became 'nature' (out of 'gnasci').
LEWIS THOMAS, LIVES OF A CELL

The greater our kinship to the roots of existence, the more deeply we perceive the reality of nature – and the more we have the right to expect that our minds can actually think the "thoughts of God" expressed in Torah and in nature.[16] Those civilizations who never saw the light of monotheism could not invest in a fruitless pursuit of understanding what appeared to them to be an essentially extraneous and therefore unintelligible universe. You and I would not invest our lives in the mystical numerology of the Pythagoreans. We would not devote our efforts to Platonic Idealism's Ideal Forms, never to be embodied, or the pure classifications of Aristotle, never to be linked together into a single whole.

Curiosity is insufficient to spawn science. There needs to be an assumption that the universe is real, that nature has laws. There must be a sense that those laws have something in common with the laws that govern the functioning of our mind, our rationality, our logic, our mathematics. Such assumptions are based on a world-view uncovered, articulated, and passionately loved by "Avraham the One."

The closer we come to uncovering the deep roots of complexity in simplicity, the closer we come to living the life of Avraham, to knowing God, to revering life. Dr. Steven Weinberg, a physicist who testified before Congress in support of the SSC, wrote:

Whatever one's religion or lack of it, it is an irresistible metaphor to speak of the final laws of nature in terms of the mind of God.
STEVEN WEINBERG[17]

> There are arrows of scientific explanation … we can now look at a pattern that has emerged, and we notice a remarkable thing: perhaps the greatest scientific discovery of all. These arrows seem to converge to a common source! Start anywhere in science and like an unpleasant child, keep asking, "Why?". You will eventually get down to [this] level. …
>
> NATURE, VOLUME 330

Avraham was that child; he first discovered that "greatest discovery." The journey of science is an adventure of rediscovery, of growing awareness of the "common source," of the unchallenged and unsuspected cultural presupposition that was all along the underpinning of the scientific enterprise. It was a foundation built at great personal and intellectual cost by Avraham, bequeathed to all of his descendants.

Ḥesed and the Superconducting Super Collider are kin, indeed. Listen to this remarkable congressional dialogue (quoted directly from the transcript of the Committee on Space, Science, and Technology), between Harris Fawell, a congressman from Illinois, and Don Ritter, congressman of Pennsylvania, who held opposing views on the SSC:

> Mr. Fawell: I wish sometimes that we had some one word that could say it all, and that is kind of impossible. I guess [Dr. Weinberg] came a little close to it...and I jotted down, "Will this make us find God?"
>
> Mr. Ritter: Will the gentleman yield on that? If the gentleman would yield for a moment I would say...
>
> Mr. Fawell: I'm not sure I want to [yield].
>
> Mr. Ritter: If this machine does that I am going to come round and support it.[18]

1 The very first step towards "complete *Avodah*" articulated by R. Moshe Ḥayim Luzzato in *Mesilat Yesharim* is absolute clarity.

See *Mesilat Yesharim,* Chapter One.

2 Just as "*em*" cannot mean mother in the purely biological sense (after all, every member of Yisrael comes from the *Four Emahot* without being the biological offspring of both Rachel and Leah).

3 The *Ba'alei Kabbala* (kabbalists) teach that the archetype is actually a manifestation of the Attributes, or *Sefirot,* of God. Kabbala never teaches anything new, though. It only places the halacha or *aggada* (of the sort quoted here) into a new macrocosmic framework.

4 Avraham worried about this himself, until God appeared to him and said, "*Do not fear, Avram. . . .*" (Bereishit 15:1). Cf. Bereishit Rabba, 44:5.

5 Incredibly, this seems to be his *primary* concern. "*Please say that you are my sister so that they will do good to me.*" (12:13). Rashi comments: "so that they will give me gifts."

6 That she was correct becomes clear when he is later told that Sarah would have a son. He tells God that he is perfectly content with the concubine Hagar's son Yishma'el and actually needs to be persuaded, "But Sarah your *wife* is going to give you a son!"

7 God was upset about this, as well:
"He relates to everyone except his own nephew Lot!?"
BEREISHIT RABBA, 41:5

8 Now, *there* is a word that surely draws from Avraham himself, the first revolutionary, a literal smasher of idols. "Iconoclast" [from the Greek *eikon* (image) and *klaein* (to break)], meaning a person who attacks traditional institutions.

9 Cf. John D. Barrow, *The World within the World* (New York: Oxford University Press, 1988), Chapter 2.

10 *Consilience* (New York: Alfred A. Knoff, 1998), 31.

11 Ibid., p.35.

12 Cf. Rashi, Bereishit 2:4, s.v. *Bayom,* ד״ה ביום; see also *Ohr haḤayim*, Bereishit 1:1; cf. *Shela, Mesechet Shabbat,* Section 77. See also Rashi 1:14 and Bereishit Rabba, 12:4; cf. Ramban, Bereishit 1:1 s.v. *Bereishit.*

13 Cf. Rashi, Shemot 20:3 s.v. *Elohim,* ד״ה אלוהים.

14 In an early letter to his friend, Marcel Grossmann.

15 Cf. Lewis Thomas, *The Lives of a Cell,* (New York: Viking Press, 1974).

16 *Mishne Torah, Hilchot Yesodei haTorah,* 2:2.

17 *Dreams of a Final Theory,* (New York: Pantheon Books, 1993), 242.

18 This rich dialogue was quoted some years after the appearance of this essay by Weinberg himself in *Dreams of a Final Theory,* 243.

III Lech-Lecha

לֵךְ לְךָ

For One Who has Everything

Lech-Lecha is the story of a man named *Avram* who grows here into *Avraham,* the *Av,* or 'father', of the Jewish people. The parasha traces that growth, beginning with Avram's first direct contact with God and his "mission," going on to describe his extensive travels and challenges, his battles and growing fame as a leader, and his 'Covenant of Avraham', founding a new nation linked to a promised land. *Lech-Lecha* ends with God's commitment to a future beyond Avraham: "*My covenant I will establish with Yitzhak, whom Sara will bear to you this time next year.*" (17:21).

For One Who Has Everything looks for a concise and distinct definition of Avraham's mission and the unique people who embrace it. It turns out that no one has ever given a better definition than God Himself, with the simple words that form the title of the parasha and the leitmotif of a nation: *Lech-Lecha.*

FOR ONE WHO HAS EVERYTHING

God presented Avraham with ten specific challenges[1] through which he grew into the *father of many nations* (17:5). Our parasha is named after the opening words of the first of them:

> *Lech-Lecha... Go for you – away from your land, from your birthplace, and from the home of your father, to the land which I will show you.* (12:1)

This was a complex challenge. It was, as the midrash[2] puts it, a "trial within a trial." It entailed not only the building of a completely new life away from all security and early emotional attachments, not only the willingness to take the plunge without knowing where it would lead ("*to the land which I will show you*"), but also a response to something more subtly demanding. The name of our parasha, you see, is more than a convenient handle formed of the opening words. The words "*Lech-Lecha*" – *Go for you* – conceal the definitive formulation of a deeper and more fundamental challenge to Avraham.

To the midrash, the words "*Lech-Lecha*" somehow delineate not only the opening of the process, but its ultimate objective as well:

> The first challenge parallels the final challenge:
> The first challenge: *Lech-Lecha, Go for you – away from your land....*
> The final challenge: *Lech-Lecha, Go for you – to the Land of Moriah....*
>
> TANḤUMA, LECH-LECHA, 3

The first step of leaving the past for an uncertain future seems to bear little in common with the supreme trauma of binding Yitzḥak to an altar in the Land of Moriah. Other than that odd formula of repeated letters: לך לך, "*Lech-Lecha.*" But what implications, what challenges could possibly lie within those simple words that they should symbolize the essential story of Avraham's development?

Consider the deceptively simple explanation of *Lech-Lecha*'s opening Rashi which provides the key to the structure of the entire parasha:

> *Lech-Lecha... Go for you – away from your land, from your birthplace, and from the home of your father, to the land that I will show you. I will make you into a great nation, and I will bless you and make you famous....* (12:1-2)
>
> *Go for you*: Go for your *own* satisfaction and benefit, for there *I will make you into a great nation....* (—Rashi[3])

Avraham not only had to *do* as he was challenged, he had to do it for the right objective: he had to do it *for his own self.*

לך לך מארצך
לך לך אל ארץ המוריה

Suppose Avraham were to have answered God, "I will do everything You ask: I will leave my family and my past. I will follow You without knowing where I am going – but I will do it selflessly, for You alone!" The test would be over – and failed. Everything that Avraham was to learn, implement and teach had to be part of a total dedication to *himself.* He needed to look forward to great progeny,

> *I will make you into a great nation;*

to riches,

> *I will bless you, (with money —Rashi);*

and to fame,

> *I will make you famous....*

These three benefits to Avraham – progeny, riches, and fame – form the entire structure of *Lech-Lecha.* They explain the apparently unrelated stories that follow. After the opening, *Lech-Lecha* is constructed of three graphically divided sections, *parashot,* each one actualizing another of these three blessings:

Money

The first section, 12:10-13:18, details the famine that forced Avraham from Canaan to Egypt, and ends when *Avram was exceedingly loaded – with livestock, with silver, and with gold* (13:2).[4]

Fame

The second section, 14:1-24, describes the war in which Avraham defeats the combined armies of four of the world's greatest powers. It ends with worldwide recognition and Malkizedek's proclamation that *Avraham is blessed to God Most High* (14:19).[5]

Progeny

The final section, 16:1 through the end, tells of Yishma'el's birth and announces the forthcoming birth of Yitzḥak. Here Avram's name is changed to "Avraham" in reference to future progeny: *I have made you father of vast nations – I will increase your numbers very very much, and I will make you into nations. Kings will emerge from you!* (17:5-6).

Lech-Lecha, then, is not only the parasha of Avraham, it is the parasha of Avraham's *blessings.* It is the parasha in which the early Avram grows into his new name and new identity, Avraham. Each section – each benefit to Avram – is a qualitative step towards the consummate "Avraham." Each new step is marked by a new commitment to grant Avraham the Land of Cana'an,[6] the original "*land which I will show you,*" and objective of "*Lech-Lecha.*"

Now, this all seems strangely selfish and egotistical. Did Avraham really make *himself* the focus of his life – or did he turn to selfless service of God and man? Listen to this unique soliloquy, as God explains out loud why He feels so attached to Avraham:

> *"I love him because he enjoins his children and household after him that they cherish the path of God; that they do charity and justice in order that God bring to Avraham what He promised."* (18:19)
>
> Those are the very words Avraham used. He actually enjoined his children: "Cherish the path of God *in order* that God bring to Avraham what He promised!" (—Rashi[7])

One must learn to love oneself...with a wholesome and healthy love, so that one can bear to be with oneself and need not roam.

NIETZSCHE[9]

Not only, then, did Avraham accept the *Lech-Lecha* challenge personally, he saw to it that his children and household would never make the mistake of "Cherishing the path of God" out of selfless altruism. He made it clear to future generations that the purpose of keeping the ways of God – the purpose even of *doing charity* itself – could only be *in order that God bring what He promised.*

But surely "*doing charity*" – the *Ḥesed* which became the hallmark of Avraham for all time[8] – surely *Ḥesed* must by its very *definition* be driven by selflessness and altruism? Not at all.

> *The man of* Ḥesed *cares for his own self....* (*Mishlei* 11:17)
>
> As did Hillel the Elder. He was leaving his students [near the public baths] after walking along with them, and they asked,

"Master! Where are you going?"
Answered Hillel, "I am going to perform a mitzvah."
"What sort of mitzvah might this be?" they asked him.
Answered Hillel, "I am going to shower!"

VAYIKRA RABBA, 34:3

Self-denial is not associated with *Ḥesed*. If anything, it is a hallmark of cruelty:

> *The man of* Ḥesed *cares for his own self, and he who troubles his own flesh is cruel. (Mishlei 11:17)*

I admit to being somewhat subversive up to this point – pretending that this is perfectly intuitive when in fact it seems outrageous. Is the Torah seriously suggesting that *Ḥesed* is meant to be selfish? Is it possible that God would not have loved Avraham had he told his children to keep God's ways "for the sake of Heaven" instead of "so that God can bring Avraham his blessings"? After all, the focus on acquiring "blessings" actually violates a primary element in service of God:

> One should *not* say: I will perform the *mitzvot* of the Torah and study its wisdom so that I can obtain the blessings written therein....

MISHNE TORAH, HILCHOT TESHUVA, 10:1

Is it really possible that Avraham would have failed his test had he insisted on meeting his challenges out of pure love instead of "for himself"? If so there appears to be an awful contradiction here, for Avraham is held up as the model of service "for the sake of Heaven," the paradigm of man motivated by pure love.

> The one who serves out of love, will work at Torah and *mitzvot* and walk the paths of wisdom for no ulterior motive whatever – neither from fear of harm nor to secure benefits – he simply does Truth because it is Truth. The benefits will follow in its wake – eventually....
> This is the level of Avraham *Avinu*, to whom God referred as *"My lover" (Isaiah* 41:8) because he did nothing unless out of love....

IBID., 10:2

העובד מאהבה עוסק בתורה ובמצות והולך בנתיבות החכמה לא מפני דבר בעולם ולא מפני יראת הרעה ולא כדי לירש הטובה אלא עושה האמת מפני שהוא אמת וסוף הטובה לבא בגללה, ומעלה זו היא מעלה גדולה מאד ואין כל חכם זוכה לה, והיא מעלת אברהם אבינו שקראו הקב"ה אוהבו לפי שלא עבד אלא מאהבה והיא המעלה שצונו בה הקב"ה על ידי משה שנאמר ואהבת את השם אלהיך, ובזמן שיאהוב אדם את השם אהבה הראויה מיד יעשה כל המצות מאהבה.

הלכות תשובה י:ב

I believe that we find all this so confusing only because we make many culturally biased – and dangerous – assumptions regarding the nature of *Ḥesed*. The truth is that these two pictures of Avraham are not contradictory but fully complementary, and each is conceivable only and entirely in light of the other. This is the central teaching of the parasha and of the Avraham model, and only in grappling with its subtleties can we begin to understand what God wanted from Avraham – and what Avraham achieved.

Lech-Lecha describes the job that needs to be done; Rambam describes the motivation for doing it. The *motivation* for Avraham's service to both God and man was pure love. Its *objective* needed to be the consummation of Avraham's own self. But such a motivation can exist only in light of such an objective, and such an objective can only be consummated through such a motivation: if you have not both, you can have neither.

Love seeketh not itself to please,
Nor for itself hath any care,
But for another gives its ease,
And builds a Heaven in Hell's despair....
Love seeketh only Self to please,
To bind another to its delight,
Joys in another's loss of ease,
And builds a Hell in Heaven's despite.

WILLIAM BLAKE[12]

"Selflessness," some preach, is a sine qua non of the kind of love expressed in Avraham's *Ḥesed* and in his service for the sake of heaven. But in reality, selflessness precludes love. Love, as Rambam defines above, implies being "without ulterior motivation," having no *external* concern whatsoever.

> The one who serves out of love, will work at Torah and *mitzvot* and walk the paths of wisdom for no ulterior motive whatever. . . .

The motivation must come from *within.* If I want to "*get* something out of it," then clearly I am driven by something that exists outside of myself, something *ulterior.*[10] But the only thing that is not ulterior[11] in any way, the only thing "internal," is my own self. And therein lies the root of the problem of selfish selflessness.

A person who does not experience his own self as significant, who finds personal existence meaningless, cannot possibly be moved by anything but "ulterior" motives. He is *always* trying to "get" something – and all the significance and meaning he manages to wheedle out of life is a lie, because it comes from *outside* his own life. The truly and completely selfish individual is the "selfless" individual – such a one must live on the selves of others in fearful predation. He uses God and other people to find what he cannot himself find within.

How much easier is self sacrifice than self realization!

ERIC HOFFER

History (and, for many, personal experience) makes this observation cruelly clear. Those who seek selfless dedication to others, whose objective is to save the world, who make love a religious goal – those have been more successful at mass-murder, terror and pillage than any Mafia. Only those who are the "servants of God" have succeeded, and continue to succeed, in ruining the lives of countless millions in a sea of blood, tears and, at very least, personal misery. This is no historical coincidence, it is a burning existential incongruity in the concept of selflessness.

The love in the "*loving*-kindness" of *Ḥesed* is not a romantic infatuation with the lives of others; it is an intense identification with and commitment to Life itself. To taste true love, to participate in *Ḥesed*'s love of pure existence, it is absolutely essential to be the "*The man of* Ḥesed," who "*cares for his own self.*" Because the only existence we directly know and experience and love is our own – to imagine a different sort of existence is as impossible as a congenitally blind individual really "imagining" sight. All honest charity, all true care for other and for the universe as a whole, is extrapolation from the immediate experience of Being. Either *Ḥesed* is an expression of love for one's own life or it is based on the worst sort of ulterior motive – a base and sinful attempt to steal significance.

> *Ḥesed of the nations is a sin.* (*Mishlei* 14:34)
>
> All the charity and *Ḥesed* performed by the nations of idolaters is a sin, for they only do it to establish their own significance. . . .
>
> BAVA BATHRA, 10b

As we near the end of the twentieth century, the destructiveness of those whose *motivation* is selflessness has become painfully obvious. What is not as immediately obvious is the other side of the coin: That *Ḥesed* is impossible, that pure love itself is impossible, that acting "for the sake of Heaven" is impossible, unless the *objective* of service is one's own self.

Consider the paradox of "service for the sake of Heaven." If all achievement lies outside of personal existence, then "the sake of Heaven" borders on farce.[13] For no one can possibly do anything without wanting to do it, and in doing something for the sake of Heaven one does precisely what one wants to do, and though presumably one wants to do what one wants to do for the sake of Heaven, that too is only because one wants to do so – in infinite regress. Given that it is an existential impossibility to *exist* as something other than oneself, how can one "want" to serve out of complete love – purely for "the sake of Heaven" – if such achievements remain disconnected from one's own being, hopelessly "external" in their very essence?

There is one way out of this paradox. There is one thing that makes it possible to act out of love, that allows for a will truly for the sake of heaven. That one thing is *Lech-Lecha*. God's proclamation of *Lech-Lecha* grants ultimate significance to individual existence. It makes the objective of service consistent with the love of life, the *Ḥesed*, which must be the motivation of service.

It behooves us to remember that man's only legitimate end in life is to finish God's work – to bring to full growth the capacities and talents implanted in us.

ERIC HOFFER[15]

Lech-Lecha is magnificent! For there is *one* – only *one* – achievement that is *not* external to your existence; one achievement for which you are truly indispensable; one achievement which is existentially beyond God Himself: yourself.[14] It is for this singular and absolutely unique accomplishment that the world exists.

> It is required of every single individual to say: The universe was created for me.
>
> SANHEDRIN, 37a

כל אחד ואחד חייב לומר,
בשבילי נברא העולם.
סנהדרין פרק ד משנה ה

The motivation and objective are one: the love of life expressed in every act drives the very act which allows that life to become fulfilled. *Lech-Lecha*, Go for you, "for your own satisfaction and benefit," indeed.

The deepest love is expressed in the most beautiful and meaningful gift imaginable – the only gift we can give to the One who has everything: To become fully and wholly ourselves, blessed with every conceivable blessing, grown into all the excellence towards which creation strives. Could there be a more deeply shared "for the sake of Heaven"? Could there be any other?

Lech-Lecha inoculated Avraham and his nation against the ravages of the selfish religiosity that destroys the service of God. *Lech-Lecha* protected those who embraced it from the hateful destructiveness to which such religion inevitably leads. *Lech-Lecha* created a tradition of *Ḥesed* based only on love of life and safeguarded a people from the dangerous lie of selflessness which seeks to destroy all the meaning of Creation.

Lech-Lecha opens with a request for a small gift, one tiny item that God asks in return for dreaming the universe:

> *Go for you – away from your land, from your birthplace, and from the home of your father, to the land that I will show you. I will make you into a great nation, and I will bless you and make you famous – and be a blessing.* (12:1-2)

> This means *be a blessing* to God, so that *God should rejoice in His acts (Tehillim 104:31)*. . . .[16]
>
> Said God, "Be a blessing to *Me*" – by growing in awareness and becoming whole. . . .
>
> SEFORNO, 12:2

והיה ברכה, ברכת השם היא שישמח
השם במעשיו כמו שאמרו רז"ל
ישמעאל בני ברכני...אמר אם כן
היה לי ברכה במה שתתבונן
ותקנה שלמות....

ספורנו

1 Avot, 5:3, and dozens of midrashic sources, including Shemot Rabba, 15:27; 44:4; Bamidbar Rabba, 14:10; *Tanḥuma, Lech-Lecha*, 18; *Pirkei Rabi Eliezer*, 26:1.

2 *Tanḥuma, Lech-Lecha*, 3.

3 Cf. Rashi, *Bamidbar* 22:21.

4 This explains something which, on the surface, appears utterly outrageous: *Please claim that you are my sister, so that they will be good to me because of you. . . .(12:13)*. Comments Rashi: So that they will give me gifts! And indeed, *They were good to Avraham because of her, and he came to possess sheep, cattle, donkeys, servants, maids, mules, and camels (12:16)*.

5 Malkizedek is *Shem*, שם, son of Noaḥ (Bereishit Rabba, 56:10). *Shem* actually translates as "fame," the very word used in the promise to Avraham: *va'agadla shem-echa*, שמיך.

6 13:14-17; 15:18-21; 17:8.

7 S.v. *Lima'an*, ד״ה למען.

8 *Sefer haBahir*, 86.

9 "On the Spirit of Gravity," *Thus Spoke Zarathustra*, 3, trans. Walter Kaufmann. I found it hard to resist quoting such a fabulous contrast to the nature of Avraham's "self-love" enabling the care of others rather than tolerance of self, and leading directly to the "roaming" of *Lech-Lecha*.

10 My dictionary defines *ulterior* as "lying beyond or outside of some specified boundary".

11 Or, in the literal translation of Rambam's דבר בעולם, "something in the world."

12 *The Clod and the Pebble* in *Songs of Experience*.

13 As pure farce, this paradox makes wonderful show business in Gilbert and Sullivan's musical *Patience*, in which the heroine cannot marry the man she loves, it being so pleasant to love him that it violates the tenet that "true love must single-hearted be/ from every selfish fancy free/ no idle thought of gain or joy/ a maiden's fancy should employ/ – true love must be without alloy."

14 This is why Rambam must add to "...he simply does Truth because it is Truth," the words, *"and the benefits will follow in its wake*, eventually. . . ."

15 "Brotherhood," in *The Ordeal of Change*, (New York: Harper & Row, 1963), 95.

16 Seforno's use of this particular verse is a beautiful allusion to the concept implicit in it, as analyzed in Ḥullin, 60a: God only "rejoices" in Creation when it acts independently. The reference there is to the independent decision of the plants to maintain genetic integrity.

IV Vayera
וירא

Milah, Medicine, and Murder

Avram and Sarai, transformed into Avraham and Sara, begin here a new life in a new era of Covenant. *Vayera* opens immediately following circumcision and renaming, as God visits the elderly convalescing *Av* with a healing vision of renaissance: The first child to be born into the fresh Covenant will be the first child born into the renewed youth of Avraham and Sara.

Vayera traces the transition to the second *Av,* Yitzḥak—first to be circumcised at birth, first product of *brith* (covenant). The novel world-view of *brith* is evident in a changed relationship between God and Avraham right at the opening of the parasha, a change that redefines the character of the Jewish people. *Milah, Medicine and Murder* examines circumcision's restatement of Man's relationship to God and its implications for Man's place in nature.

MILAH, MEDICINE, AND MURDER

Some recent court decisions focused my attention on the opening of *Parashat Vayera*. In Boston, David and Ginger Twitchell were found guilty of manslaughter in the death of their two year old son, Robyn. In Sarasota, Florida, William and Christine Hermanson were convicted of third degree murder in the death of their seven year old daughter, Amy. Typical cases of child abuse? Hardly. Both cases involved loving parents who refused to call a physician to treat their child's straightforward medical problem. Instead, they sat for days with their children, watching in anguish as the situation worsened: from fever...to agony... to delirium...to convulsions...to death.

Both these children could still have been saved – even after the days of delay – until just hours before the end.[1] However, instead of seeking medical assistance – instead of turning to mortal man – these parents turned to the True Doctor. With perfect faith, they relied on prayer. They were secure in their knowledge that they did all they could for their children. In five cases over two years, the courts did not see it that way at all. They affixed another name to the love and faith offered these children: *Murder.*

What is the Torah's judgment? To the mere suggestion that there might be an advantage to prayer over medicine, the Talmud retorts:

> One should not say such a thing, for...we are commanded, *And he must surely provide medical care (Shemot 21:19)*, which teaches us that to the physician is given the authorization to heal.
>
> BERACHOT, 60a

Vayera raises some intriguing points relevant to this controversy. In fact, the halachic volume *Yoreh De'ah* introduces the entire chapter of *Laws of Medical Treatment*[2] using *Vayera* as paradigm.

Vayera opens as Avraham sits in the sun, recuperating from his circumcision which was performed three days earlier. God comes to him "to visit the ill."[3] In this first biblical account of illness, one of three messengers sent by God heals Avraham.[4] Yet, despite the *divine* nature of Avraham's recovery from circumcision, the laws covering medical care – *human* therapeutic interference – are centered precisely and prominently within the Talmudic chapter delineating circumcision (the noted chapter, *Rabi Eliezer d'Mila*[5]). It would seem that we must view the interrelationship of the divine and human medical roles as deriving from this curious example of circumcision, in which humans play the sculpting role of God, and God takes on the bedside manners of a physician "visiting the ill," despite the angelic therapy.

If medicine could have saved him, I wish I had turned to it....
DAVID TWITCHELL

This whole quandary of prayer *vs.* medicine involves issues far more serious than church–state separation. It raises a broader paradox sometimes waffled by assorted religious doctrines. Religion presumably encourages faith and trust in God, but how do we draw the line between what we must do for ourselves and what faith demands that we leave in God's hands? What is the association between the efforts invested by man and Divine providence? Where does *hishtadlut* – human effort – end and *bitaḥon* – faith – begin?

Illness provides an acid test for doctrinal resolution to this problem. The stricken father of Robyn Twitchell poignantly voiced his misgivings: "If medicine could have saved him, I wish I had turned to it." The words reveal his suspicions that he was betrayed by his own Christian Science doctrine, rooted in early Christian myths emphasizing miraculous cures. Even today, evangelist meetings (electronic or in-the-flesh) routinely solicit an "I believe..." response meant to climax dramatically in an exuberant repudiation of wheelchair or crutches.[6] Jewish tradition, though, has always venerated medicine (quite aside from "my son, the doctor"). In fact, *halacha* even prohibits residing in a city which lacks medical services,[7] no matter how impressive the synagogue services. How do these disparate traditions reflect upon the broader conundrum: the human and the struggle vs. the divine and the providential?

"God helps those who help themselves," said seventeenth-century Philip Sidney, and so the saying goes nowadays among the conscientious in the sophisticated West. We cannot expect miracles if we are not willing to do the work ourselves. Examine this truism more carefully and it soon begins to look frivolous – a facile way of dodging an issue that lies at the heart of one's lifework and world view.

Did Sir Philip mean to say that God begrudges the time helping us unless we really work hard? How can he be so sure? Perhaps God helps those who *trust* in Him the most, those willing to forgo any belief in man? Besides, he skirts the main problem by assuming that we indeed *do* "help ourselves." In what way can we "help ourselves" if everything is up to the Lord – I thought that was the whole point! Or is life a little play in which we spend our days acting, *pretending* to help ourselves, so that God can hide while He helps us? This kind of superficial thinking is inappropriate to an issue of fundamental concern, an issue whose every nuance must eventually burst into practical significance.

I have a rather skeptical hunch that this Western carelessness is a result of wholesome intuition. It comes of a subliminal sense that since the whole thing is basically unsolvable it should be sensibly ignored. This battle between faith and self-help is essentially as intractable as the rest of the tortuous wrestling over monastery and world, sin and body, love and desire, and all the other dilemmas of "faith" and Last Temptations. *All* these issues are sensibly ignored until they are resoundingly propelled to the forefront by something as outrageous as treating diabetes with prayer. Then they are safely agonized over in the guise of simpler issues, like "separation of church and state," and everyone can get complacently back to "helping themselves," undoubtedly to allow God to do the *real* work.

The surprising, and fundamentally different, view of the Torah is expressed in the relationship we noted between *milah* and medicine. This correspondence is highlighted by what appears to be a nonsensical explanation of the order of the *berachot* of the *Amida*, the silent blessings of the Jewish daily prayer service:

ומה ראו לומר רפואה בשמינית?
אמר רבי אחא, מתוך שנתנה מילה
בשמינית שצריכה רפואה, לפיכך
קבעוה בשמינית.
מגילה יז:

> On what basis did they [the Sages] establish the prayer for healing as the eighth benediction [of the eighteen (*shemona esrei) berachot*]? Because *milah* was given on the eighth day, and it requires healing. That is why they made healing the eighth benediction....
>
> MEGILLA, 17b

As if circumcision were our greatest medical problem! There is no escaping the inference of a fundamental association between *milah* and medicine, a conceptual and intuitively evident relationship.

Consider how *milah* has long aroused the ire of those who reject human interference in a putatively pristine Nature: Nature is an expression of God's works and so must be perfect. The human form is as perfect as anything else in Nature, they argue, so how can the Torah insist that only in mutilating his body could Avraham *"be perfect" (Bereishit 17:1)?* Here is an early tale of contention over this issue, that continues to resonate within the modern anti-circumcision movement:

> Turnus Rufus once asked Rabbi Akiva, "Which is preferable – the works of God or the works of man?"
>
> ...Rabbi Akiva brought him wheat kernels and braided loaves, saying, "These are the works of God, and these the works of man. Are the works of man not preferable to these raw kernels?"
>
> Said Turnus Rufus, "But if God wanted us circumcised, why didn't He make babies that way – complete?"
>
> Said Rabbi Akiva, "And why do babies come 'complete' with an umbilical cord that requires cutting and tying?"
>
> TANHUMA, TAZRIA, 5:1

An elementary conception[8] of *milah* lies embedded in this story. *Milah* is seen here as the imperative to go beyond the givens of nature – on the *eighth* day we begin where Creation's seven days left off. *Milah* reflects the story of a nation seeking fulfillment through the acts of man – through life acting upon itself. To medically attend is to act upon nature; to cure is to act upon destiny. We accept diabetes in an organism no more than we accept a foreskin in an organ:

> If *milah*, which affects only one organ of the body, overrides Shabbat, then certainly medical care, which affects all the organs of the body, overrides Shabbat.
>
> SHABBAT, 136a

To deny medicine is to deny the meaning and significance of circumcision.

This argument is fine as far as it goes, confirming the crucial legitimacy of the acts of men. But it leaves the broader question untouched – what truly is the *affiliation* between the struggles of man and the deeds of Divine providence? After all, that eighth benediction calls for healing from God, not from a doctor.

Look again to *Parashat Vayera* and, this time, to the most astonishing of the parallels between *milah* and healing. The parasha opens with an historical event – for the first time the *Shechina*, the Divine Presence, rests freely upon a human being:

> Before his *milah*, Avraham could not stand up in the presence of the *Shechina*, as it says, *And he fell on his face, and God spoke to him....* (*Bereishit* 17:3). After his *milah*, he could even remain seated while God stood over him.
>
> PIRKEI RABI ELIEZER, 29

Now it happens that the new relationship with the *Shechina* takes place in the context of illness. You would think, however, that surely this is just a coincidence, a by-product of the proximity of the *milah*. After all, the real issue here must be circumcision and the newfound ability to be close to God. But it turns out, amazingly enough, that *every* illness recreates *Vayera*! Every illness draws the same *Shechina* to rest on the convalescent:

> It is prohibited to sit on a chair in the presence of the sick, because the *Shechina* rests above the head of the sick, as it says, *God will nourish him on his bed of pain* (*Tehillim* 41:4).
>
> SHABBAT, 12b

הנכנס לבקר את החולה לא ישב
לא על גבי מטה ולא על גבי כסא,
אלא מתעטף ויושב לפניו מפני ששכינה
למעלה מראשותיו של חולה שנאמר
השם יסעדנו על ערש דוי.
ואמר רבא אמר רבין מנין שהקדוש ברוך
הוא זן את החולה?
שנאמר השם יסעדנו על ערש דוי.
שבת יב:

To say that there exists a special relationship between *milah* as the Covenant and the Divine Presence makes sense. But what sense is there in *this*, the ultimate healing/*milah* parallel?

Herein lies the denouement of our story, the deepest connection between medicine and our identity as *B'nei Brith* – Members of the

Covenant. Ask yourself *why* the *Shechina* rests upon the ill, and all becomes clear. Health, until it is lost, is just part of nature, the way things are. We all have our vision, we all have our hearing, we all have our ability to move about freely – health is generic, as long as you have it. But healing is the most individual, special, and personal of things. No one can share the inside world of the patient whose kidneys are failing, whose blood sugar is gyrating, who is in agony from a tumor. To be cured is not merely to be restored, to be as everyone else. To be cured is not merely to learn to appreciate blessings. To be cured is to have what no one else on earth has, a unique and personal relationship, a gift of joyous life all one's own. The special relationship to the individual spells the difference between *Nature* and *Shechina*.

We are not sensible of the most perfect health, as we are of the least sickness.
MONTAIGNE

Nature proclaims no specific directions, no teleological mechanism for Creation and evolution. Nature's dynamics and beauty are movingly impersonal, poignantly reminding us that we are visitors to a panorama of Life. Nature simply *is*. That is why, for all its fabulous galaxies and stunning mountains, for all its intricacies of atomic structure and mind-bending mathematics, Nature is not where the Presence is to be found. God is to be found holding the hand of the sick child, wiping the brow of the old woman struggling for breath, breathing the breath of life into an *individual*. This is not some maudlin sentiment, but a strict definition: the Presence exists only within relationship, within the sanctity of the individual. That is the secret of the Covenant of *Milah*: Creation itself is complete only with the individual *self*, only with the one thing that God cannot create on His own.

התהלך לפני והיה תמים
Walk in front of Me and become whole. (Bereishit 17:1)

The Covenant tells a story of Life challenged to assert its own creativity. It proclaims that Creation as achieved by God alone cannot be whole, for it lacks still its own selfhood, its own individuality, its own creativity. The willingness to go beyond nature is much more than accepting the need to act. It is a restatement of the entire nature of Creation[9] and human existence, a recognition that Creation can only

Men who are occupied in the restoration of health...partake of divinity....
VOLTAIRE

"be whole" when man "walks in front of God," and acts independently. The Covenant makes us partners in Creation:

> God said to Avraham, "You and I are enough for the universe."
>
> BEREISHIT RABBA, 46:3

The Christian Science of Mary Baker Eddy has come up with a new explanation for imperfection in the world: it does not exist. God is perfect and mankind is God's creation, therefore mankind is perfect. Death and disease are mirages, illusions that can be overcome by realizing God's perfect nature. The church's official text says, "Man is not matter. He is not made of brain, blood, bones, and other material elements." It follows that there is no place for medicine in a perfect world.

How beautifully different is the *brith basar*, the covenant of flesh. The world cannot be perfect unless it becomes so through the actions of the individual human being.

והיה תמים
...and become whole.

It was not only Avraham who became whole at that moment. In that crucial relationship, Creation itself was vindicated.[10] The universe became whole, the *Shechina* became whole. The eighth day is the heart of creation.

Man's destiny lies half within himself, half without. To advance either half at the expense of the other is literally insane.

PHILIP WYLIE

We exist not as spectators to the drama of Life, nor as squatters on a stage with the scenery predefined for petty seekers of afterlife. We are here *to work the garden and to keep it (Bereishit 2:15)*, accomplices in a cosmic symbiosis called Creation. That is the real meaning of the relationship between the acts of man and the acts of God.

Hishtadlut, human effort, is the outgrowth of that command. *Hishtadlut* is not a cheap game which can be won by purchasing a lottery ticket just to give God a chance to send the cash. It is an existential mandate for creativity and achievement, encompassing all the demands physically symbolized in *milah*: love, fruition, sensitivity and integrity.

Medicine is a deep symbiosis, working within nature to provide more than nature would provide. But medicine only begins the healing, and each procedure must virtually end with a prayer. Renewal comes as the *Shechina* rests over the patient, nourishing, nurturing, sustaining, hand–in–hand with man. That is a deeper presence than can ever abide within miraculous cures. The *Brith* lives poetically and powerfully in medicine, confirming our work in the garden, affirming that we truly keep and cherish it.

To deny medicine is to deny the Presence of God.

1 Edward Dolnick, "Murder by Faith," *In Health*, volume 4, number 1, p. 58.

2 *Tur, Yoreh De'ah*, 335-339: הלכות בקור חולים ורפואה.

3 Rashi, *Bereishit* 18:1, s.v. *Vayera*, ד״ה וירא אליו; Bava Metzia, 86b; Sotah, 14a.

4 Bava Metzia, 86b; Rashi, 18:2.

5 Tractate *Shabbat*, Chapter Nineteen, folios 130a-137b.

6 An interesting Midrashic perspective on faith healing:

> Do we not often see people going to idolatrous worship who walk out healed of their lameness or blindness? These people were at the natural endpoint of their illness – just because the fool misbehaves should not nature take its course?
>
> MIDRASH ASERET HADIBROT, II, s.v. *Amar*, דיבור שני ד״ה אמר לו

7 Rambam, *Mishne Torah, Hilchot De'ot* 4:23.

8 *Sefer Haḥinuch*, 2.

9 Cf. Ḥullin, 60a, for the beautiful story of God's joy at Creation's independent functioning through maintaining genetic integrity for small plants.

10 Cf. Nedarim 31b; *Tanḥuma, Bereishit*, 19.

IV Vayera

וירא

He Who Laughs Last

Vayera begins with the impending birth of Yitzḥak and ends with the near sacrifice of Yitzḥak. This span encompasses the growth of a new *Av,* from conception to the singular event that stamped his life and his character forever: the *Akeida* on the altar.

That event became the symbol of Yitzḥak, the second of the *Avot*/archetypes imprinted upon the identity of Yisrael. Yet there is no denying that the parasha seems focused on *Avraham:* his inability to prevent the destruction of Sodom, his journey to the Philistines—even the *Akeida* itself is presented as the trial of the father, not of the son. The development of Yitzḥak proceeds hand in hand with profound changes in the character of Avraham. In the repeatedly underscored words of the Torah: *The two of them progressed as one* (22:6,8).

In *Vayera,* Avraham and Yitzḥak are adjoined. *He Who Laughs Last* seeks the conceptual glue that binds these utterly different father-and-son archetypes and connects the beginning of the parasha to its end. Bring along a sense of humor.

HE WHO LAUGHS LAST

Vayera revolutionizes the foundations of Jewish thought and transforms Avraham in the process. The ruthlessness of the *Akeida* challenges all the suppositions upon which Avraham based his existence: the search for kinship, the commitment to kindness, the absolute reverence for life expressed as *Ḥesed*. The parasha that brings us the *Akeida* also recasts *Avraham, the one who loves* God (*Isaiah* 41:8) in his new role: Avraham, the one who *fears God* (22:12).

Vayera begins with Avraham's warmth to his guests. It ends with Avraham's knife poised over his son's neck. *Vayera* opens as Avraham seeks to satisfy his guests' every need and luxury:

> He served each of his three guests an entire tongue in mustard sauce....
>
> RASHI, 18:7[1]

And *Vayera* concludes as Avraham seeks to find any and every way to sacrifice Yitzḥak – at least a *little*:

> *God's messenger called to him from heaven and said, "Avraham! Avraham!"*
>
> Avraham said, "Let me at least choke him...."
>
> *"Lay not your* hand *upon the lad...."*
>
> "Then let me just spill a drop of his blood...."
>
> *"...neither do* anything *at all to him!"* (22:12)
>
> BEREISHIT RABBA, 56:7

In the previous parasha[2] we met Avraham as the man who dedicated his life to the supreme value of the individual and to the principle that

> Every single individual must say: The universe was created for me.
>
> SANHEDRIN, 37a

But by the end of this week's parasha, as he binds his son on Mount Moriah, he seems unconvinced even of the individual's right to *exist*, not to mention his value. The exuberant and giving *Ḥesed* of Avraham appears to fade into the remote, exacting, judgmatic probing of Yitzḥak, the father of *Din* ("Judgment").

> Yitzḥak...from where all *Din* in the world is aroused.
>
> ZOHAR, II:257a

Vayera introduces Yitzḥak and *Din*[3] – Yitzḥak who neither gives nor takes something for nothing, who accepts upon the altar that only Life's Creator can have any legitimate claims on life.[4] It is here that Avraham first struggles with *Din* – and with God – when Sodom is threatened by *Din*:

> *"Would You actually wipe out the innocent together with the guilty....*
> *"Would the Judge of the whole world not act fairly!?"* (18:23,25)
>
> [Said Avraham to the Holy One:] If You want a world, forget about *Din*. If You want *Din*, forget about a world. You're pulling the rope from both ends – You want a world and You want *Din*. You've got to let go of one end!
>
> BEREISHIT RABBA, 39:6

השופט כל הארץ לא יעשה משפט!
אם עולם אתה מבקש אין דין,
ואם דין אתה מבקש אין עולם!
ומה אתה תופש חבל בתרין ראשין!
את בעי עלמא ובעי דינא!
סב לך חדא מנייהו ואם לית את
מוותיר ציבחר לית עלמא יכול קאים
א"ל הקדוש ברוך הוא: אברהם, אהבת צדק
ותשנא רשע...מחבריך. מהו מחבריך!
מנח ועד אצלך עשרה דורות, ומכלם לא
דברתי עם אחד מהם אלא עמך:

בראשית רבה

And in this parasha, Avraham *himself* is invested with *Din*. For though at first Avraham contests *Din*, he becomes at last its executioner. He and Yitzḥak walk to the *Akeida as one* (22:7).

> Why is the *Akeida* presented as a test to *Avraham* [as opposed to Yitzḥak]?
> Because it was *Avraham* who needed to be included in *Din*,
> Avraham who until that moment had no *Din* at all....
> Avraham was not complete until now,
> When he became invested with the power to execute *Din*!
>
> ZOHAR, I:119b

Clearly, successive archetypes of one nation cannot be ontological contradictions, so we would expect a smooth conceptual transition between them. *Vayera* is the parasha of that transition – but it is neither smooth nor conceptual. The traumatic *Akeida* is the dramatic catalyst of *Din*'s seminal development in both Yitzḥak and Avraham,[5] and the drama leaves us in a conceptual fog. What two concepts could be further apart than *Ḥesed* and *Din*? What could possibly link the giving man of kindness, *Ḥesed* incarnate,[6] with the scrutinizing man of *Din*? Most importantly, what did Avraham himself perceive that allowed him to span the impossible distance between absolute belief in Life and complete partnership in Death?

The key lies in what seems to be history's prize-winning misnomer: the name "*Yitzḥak*." It seems preposterous that this very unfunny *Av* who was created out of the anguish of the *Akeida* should be called "Laugh" (*zḥok*, צחוק). It is not just a question of his name – the important moments in his life involve laughter in all its subtlety. His birth evokes nuances of laughter – and contention over laughter between God, Sara, and Avraham.

> *Avraham fell on his face and laughed....* (17:17)[7]
>
> *But your wife Sara will bear you a son and you shall call him Yitzḥak, "Laughter."* (17:19)
>
> *Sara laughed within....* (18:12)
>
> *"...Why did Sara laugh?"*
>
> *"...I did* not *laugh!"*
>
> *"But you* did *laugh!"* (18:13,15)

After he is born, Sara's reaction is again laughter.

> *Sara said, "God has made* **laughter** *for me–whoever hears of it will* **laugh** *for me."* (21:6)[8]

The challenge of Yishma'el, so much a part of modern history, is expressed here at the source in an overtone of laughter.

> *Sara saw the son that Hagar had born to Avraham* **laughing**, *and she said to Avraham, "Expel this slave together with her son...."* (21:9,10)

Even Yitzḥak's deepest relationship is defined by laughter – though nowhere else is coitus referred to as "laughter."[9]

> *Yitzḥak was laughing with Rivka his wife.* (26:8)

There is no help for it – the Torah intimates that in Din's deepest recesses it is a real...laugh. Yet few things seem so singularly lacking in humor as the *Akeida*. We need to better understand laughter in order to understand Din.

Laughter is our response to the incongruous, to unexpected transpositions. The more sensitive the awareness of inappropriateness, the more subtle is the sense of humor – ranging from trivial slapstick to delicate paradox. And the birth of Yitzḥak was absurd, impossible, ridiculous by any standard.

> Our mother Sara was an *ailonit*,[10] for it says *Sara was barren* [and adds redundantly] *she had no child (11:30)*. This implies that she had not even the *place* (uterus) for a child!
>
> YEVAMOT, 64b

Yitzḥak's mother was not only barren, she was essentially sexless!

Humor is the only test of gravity, and gravity of humor.
ARISTOTLE

The bizarre news of Sara's forthcoming motherhood-at-ninety after a life of infertility overwhelmed both parents-to-be, astonished them to the point of outright laughter. The more outlandish the event, the greater the surprise: *Avraham and Sara were old (18:11)* is added here as yet another biological handicap in a history of barrenness and reproductive dysfunction, each obstacle another ingredient in the resultant shock, surprise, and laughter.

> *Avraham fell on his face and laughed....*
>
> Avraham fell on his face and was astonished....
>
> TARGUM YERUSHALMI, 17:17
>
> This was certainly something to laugh about: it was totally astonishing.
>
> RAMBAN[11]

Good humor is a paradox. The unexpected juxtaposition of the reasonable next to the unreasonable.
HELITZER

Din is the ultimate arbiter of appropriateness. In its finesse of judgment, it detects the slightest deviation from what properly fits the situation. In the simplest sense, *Din* adjudicates assets, ownership and "possessions," be they cash, bonds, home, children, health, appearance or whatever. At all times *Din* seeks to assert what is fitting and just; to restore the appropriate. *Din* relentlessly swallows the undeserved and replaces the inappropriate by way of an exquisite sensitivity to incongruity – that is, a sensitivity to humor. The authoritative, decisive and judicious power of *Din* is born of the keen perception of the tragicomic and farcical. *Din*'s power derives from nothing other than a definitively discriminating sense of humor!

We are able to identify certain simple elements of humor in justice, if only through our own experience. A good example would be the irony of poetic justice which can certainly bring a wry smile to perceptive lips – and at times even a good laugh to the most discerning.

> How ironic was the laughter which *Middat haDin* laughed over the inhabitants of Sodom….
>
> TANHUMA, AHAREI MOT, I

However, there is a vastly more profound humor that escapes our complacent lives. There is the humor of ultimate and utter astonishment at the outrageous incongruity of existence itself. This is the humor derived from our perception of the infinite surprise of Life. Such is the humor of Yitzḥak himself, the man formed by the *Akeida*. No other person in history ever experienced the apparently capricious and arbitrary command of his Creator, the Source of life and significance, to be slaughtered – to be snuffed out unquestioningly by the human father who had given the gift of biological life.

He was born with a gift of laughter and a sense that the world was mad. And that was all his patrimony.

SABATINI

The flagrant inconsistency and unfairness of God's command was part of the very essence of the *Akeida*. To Yitzḥak, the *Akeida* was infinitely more than an acid test of obedience. It was a completely new consciousness, an icy stab to the heart of our most cherished assumption: that our right to existence is somehow an absolute. It left Yitzḥak shattered on the altar, never to return home again. This is why the Torah portrays Avraham returning home from Moriah alone:

Humour simultaneously wounds and heals, indicts and pardons, diminishes and enlarges.

LOUIS KRONENBERGER

> *Avraham returned to his servants…to Be'er Sheva.* (22:19)

In every psychological and spiritual sense, Yitzḥak remained behind, burned on the altar.

> When they returned from Babylon…how did they know the precise location of the altar?
> They saw the ashes of Yitzḥak lying on that spot.
>
> ZEVAḤIM, 62a

This became the power of Yitzḥak. In recognizing that existence itself can never be justified, that life will always be the most astonishing surprise of all, he became Master of *Din*. All the incongruities of the human condition, all the absurdity of Man, arouse Yitzḥak to the spontaneous laughter of freedom from the *need* to justify.

What counts to Yitzḥak are not the blessings of life we try so desperately to clasp, for what has been *given* can never be truly ours. Nor is it transient life itself, for that can never be justified and so *surely* can never be ours. What matters to Yitzḥak is only what one *does* with life, the *opportunities* presented by life to become oneself. All of the suffering, pain and loss in life, all the absurd contrast to the wonder and measureless beauty of which life is capable, are to Yitzḥak a brilliant vision of the freedom of having nothing left to lose but opportunity – and *everything* to gain.

A paradox, a paradox,
A most ingenious paradox...
Ha! ha! ha!
Ho! ho! ho!
THE PIRATES OF PENZANCE

The literal meaning of '*yitzḥak*' is not 'laughter' but 'he *will* laugh', and Yitzḥak really *does* get the last laugh. Yitzḥak's vision of life becomes the great, final laugh, with God Himself awaiting the grand gesture of the concluding repartee!

> Why does it say, *For you are our father, because Avraham did not acknowledge us, and Yisrael refused to recognize us.... (Isaiah 63:16)*?
>
> On that future day [of the final *Din*], the Holy One will say to Avraham, "Your children have sinned."
>
> And Avraham answers, "Master of the Universe, wipe them out to sanctify Your Name!"
>
> So God thinks: Let Me try Ya'akov. He suffered raising children, perhaps he will pray for them. So He tells Ya'akov, "Your children have sinned."
>
> And Ya'akov answers, "Master of the Universe, wipe them out to sanctify Your Name!"
>
> So God thinks: Old men [like Avraham] have no sense, and youngsters [like Ya'akov] have no good counsel. He goes to Yitzḥak and says, "Your children have sinned."
>
> And Yitzḥak says: "Master of the Universe, *my* children and not *Your* children? You called them *Yisrael My firstborn (Shemot 4:22)* and all of a sudden they are *my* children?!
>
> "Besides, how much could they possibly have sinned? How long do they live, anyway – figure seventy years? Subtract the first twenty, when they are too immature to be punished, and they are left with fifty. Then figure about twenty-five off for nights, and they are left with twenty-five. Now, take off

> another twelve-and-a-half for praying, eating, time in the bathroom and they're left with twelve-and-a-half years to sin in! If You can handle that on Your own, fine. If not, how about we split it? And if You insist that I take it all myself – well, I *did* sacrifice myself to You!"
>
> Then all Yisrael burst out, "*You* [Yitzḥak] *are our father....*"
>
> SHABBAT, 89b

God was waiting here for Yitzḥak's rejoinder: What can You possibly demand in return for that which cannot ever be justified – for that from which Your children can preserve nothing for themselves? When You sent me to the *Akeida* I considered it eminently reasonable – but in the same spirit, You cannot demand their remittance for what was never their own. You granted them only opportunities and they have become Yours, and that is all that counts. Life to Yitzḥak is most meaningful when it is most laughable – *because* it is laughable.

Certainly there is a paradoxical relationship between *Ḥesed* and *Din*, between Avraham and Yitzḥak. Providing for life is the essence of Avraham's work, and every loss – even the loss of pitiless Sodom – is a rip in the fabric of universal existence. Making the universe a playing field[12] for life is the work of Yitzḥak, and the obstacles on the course are the best part of the game.[13] How does Avraham come to span the void between life's boundless potential and the tragedy that dogs its concrete experience?

Unless a man or woman has experienced the darkness of the soul, he or she can know nothing of that transforming laughter without which no hint of the ultimate reality of the opposites can be fairly intuited.

HELEN LUKE

Consider one of the most mysterious elements of the parasha: Avraham laughs when told about Yitzḥak, and God takes this laughter as the child's name.

> *Avraham fell upon his face and laughed. He said to himself, "Will a hundred-year-old man have a child?! Shall Sara who is a woman of ninety give birth?"* (17:17)

Yet when Sara laughs after she is told about Yitzḥak, God becomes annoyed at her.[14]

> *Sara laughed within herself saying, "After I have grown old could I become supple again, and my husband is old!?"*

God said to Avraham, "Why did Sara laugh, saying, 'Will I, who am old, indeed bear a child?' Is anything beyond the Lord?" (18:12-14)

This is so striking a problem, that the Talmud tells how the seventy (actually, seventy-two) translators of the Septuagint fabricated a word to avoid attack on the Bible.

> They changed "*Sara laughed within herself* (*bekirba*, בקרבה)" to "*Sara laughed among her relatives* (*bekroveha*, בקרוביה)"!
>
> MEGILLA, 9A

If we were able to distinguish between the respective reactions, we might learn the secret of Avraham's new vision.

There *is* one simple but crucial difference. Sara speaks of herself, "*within herself*": '*I am old*'; '*Shall I become supple*'. Avraham's response is about universals. He speaks not of himself, but of wonder: '*A man of a hundred*'; '*A woman of ninety*'. That universality is what makes all the difference in the world.

Laughter can be mocking, doubting, cynically expressive of the pain of absurdity. Laughter can be noble, lifting one beyond pettiness to see a whole picture from a new perspective. The former is crushing and bitter, but the latter is exuberant and free. The man who has learned such aware laughter lives an exquisite balance. In his moments of greatest honor, he knows that he is but a step away from foolish embarrassments. In his moments of greatest shame, he knows that nothing can touch the significance that is his. This was the laughter of Avraham. It was the kind of laughter that bridges paradox.

Humor exists within the dawning surprise of perceiving that contradictions can be true, that antitheses *need* each other! That is why even the simplest joke cannot be *explained* – one needs to *see* the harmony of paradox, to go beyond abstract explanations, to gain a new and transcendent perspective. Laughter is the balance, the sensitivity to the hairbreadth difference that lies between sobbing over our heartache and rejoicing in our madcap adventure of living, tears of joy mingling with tears of sadness. We move so easily from one to another, our laughing becoming crying and our crying, laughing – they are nearly identical physiologically and psychologically, emerging from the same inner wellspring.

Humor spans the paradox of a life with infinite meaning, a meaning that comes only through the struggle of what *we* make of it. Humor spans a life that is both endlessly precious and hopelessly transient. We are creatures of eternity playing in the moment. In such laughter resides the uttermost transcendence of Man, his deepest similarity to God.

> The Holy One laughs...*with* His creations, never *at* them.
>
> AVODA ZARA, 3B

Vayera opens with the very same laughter achieved at its conclusion. For while the laughter at Yitzḥak's birth is laughter at the surprise and wonder of a single impossible birth, Yitzḥak himself laughs at the surprise and wonder of a singular impossible birth – the birth of Creation, of the universe, of existence itself. In a certain sense, Avraham laughs his way from the birth of Yitzḥak all the way to the *Akeida,* as *Vayera* grows from the seeds planted at its inception.

The laughter of *Din* gives us the perspective that creates opportunity, the vision to see opportunity, and the freedom to use opportunity. Real life was invented for the true children of he who laughs last – and best:

> *The boy grew and was weaned, and Avraham made a great celebration on the day Yitzḥak was weaned.* (21:8)
>
> The Holy One is going to make a party for the Just on the day His *Ḥesed* is weaned for the children of Yitzḥak.
>
> PESAḤIM, 119b

1 Bava Metzia, 86b.

2 See previous parasha's essay, *For One Who Has Everything*.

3 This is why we are introduced here to the shofar of Rosh haShana, the Day of *Din*.

> Avraham asked, "What is this 'shofar'?"
> God told him, "Turn around!"
> At that moment, *Avraham lifted his eyes and he saw there a ram caught by its horns. . . .*(22:13)
>
> TANḤUMA, VAYERA 23

4 See my *Patterns in Time* (Jerusalem: Feldheim Publishers, 1988), volume 1, for an extensive treatment of Yitzḥak and *Din*.

5 Actually, every last story in *Vayera* is another conceptual step towards *Din*. But that is a topic that deserves an essay to itself.

6 *Sefer haBahir*, 86; cf. Micha 7:20.

7 As per *Targum haShiv'im* and Abravanel. Cf. *Onkelus*, Sa'adia Ga'on, and Rashi here, and Ramban who explains how they are identical.

8 It is important to note that "laughter" (*zḥk*) is never used to mean simply "joy." There are ten words for nuances of joy in Hebrew, and this is not one of them (see the list in *Shir haShirim Rabba*, 1:29). In the entire twenty-four books of the Torah there are only four other references to laughter!

9 In Bereishit 39:14,17, *rape* is referred to by the same word, implying 'cheapened, laughed *at*'.

10 Literally "like a ram" as per Ketuvot, 11a. Mannish, lacking secondary sexual characteristics (Yevamot, 80b).

11 17:17, s.v. *Vayitzḥak*, ד"ה ויצחק.

12 Cf. Pesaḥim, 88a.

13 This accounts for the other spelling of the name of Yitzḥak: ישחק, (*sḥk*), which means "to play." See Yermiah 33:26 and Tehillim 105:9.

14 Many explanations have been offered for this contradiction, but what is supported by the plain meaning of the text?

V Ḥayei Sara
חיי שרה

For the Love of a Woman

Ḥayei Sara, 'The *Life* of Sara', opens, ironically, with the *death* of Sara and her burial in Hebron. Avraham's intense reaction to her death adds poignancy to irony, for he exposes feelings that remained unexpressed during Sara's lifetime, becoming so bereft that he ages dramatically. Life and the parasha move quickly on, and Sara's death seems soon forgotten in the marriage of Yitzḥak to Rivka—and in Avraham's own remarriage to Ketura. But at parasha's end we find ourselves standing again at Sara's gravesite, as Avraham is laid to rest next to the woman he loved in the only piece of property he ever owned in the land he loved.

The juxtaposition of love and burial, marriage and property, is thematic here. Two profusely detailed *parashot* in *Ḥayei Sara* accentuate this motif: the opening section describes the haggling over the purchase of Sara's burial place; the next section portrays the marriage of Yitzḥak against the wordy backdrop of negotiations with Rivka's family.

For the Love of a Woman examines elements of love, ownership, and connectedness, touching intimate zones of the Jewish claim to the Land of Israel.

FOR THE LOVE OF A WOMAN

. . . *These were the years of Sara's life – and Sara died in Kiryat Arba, known as Ḥebron, in the land of Cana'an, and Avraham came to eulogize Sara and to weep for her.* (23:1,2)

How often we appreciate the full magnitude of a relationship's importance only in retrospect. Avraham's most passionate feelings for his wife find expression for the first time at her death.[1] He weeps over her loss and it affects him so profoundly[2] that he composes the lyrical poem *Aishet Ḥayil*[3] in her memory, reviewing with each stanza another episode in their long life together.[4]

There is another special relationship that realizes full expression here, along with the love of Sara. In fulfillment of his dedication to Sara, Avraham is moved to accomplish something of which he had surely often dreamed[5]: he purchases the very first portion of *Eretz Yisrael*. The Cave of Machpela, *Me'arat haMachpela,* becomes in *Ḥayei Sara* a Jewish heritage, in which Avraham himself will later be buried alongside his beloved wife.

> This section is written to teach of the advantages of the Land of Israel over all other lands for the living and the dead – and also to keep the promise of God to Avraham that he would personally have an inheritance therein.
>
> IBN EZRA, 23:19[6]

Such singular love of the Land of Israel as a final resting place was introduced in *Ḥayei Sara*, and has since become an expression of the most primal connection to *Eretz Yisrael*. So many who did not own in their lifetimes any of the Land, who never even *beheld* the land, dreamed and prayed over one small possession – a final plot of land.

> Why does Yisrael merit all the [coming] grandeur? Through the merit of dwelling in the Land of Israel: they would dwell

> in anguish [for her] among the nations of the world. So too do you encounter with the forefathers the intensity with which they agonized over burial in the land. . . .
>
> PESIKTA RABBATI, 1:6

In these moments of new fulfillment, the Avraham who until this point seemed almost an abstraction is now exposed in all his human vibrancy, brimming with personality. He is filled with renewed personal aspirations, which find expression in his negotiations for the *Me'arat haMachpela*. One of the striking subtleties to emerge from Avraham's carefully chosen words is that he wants this land *personally*, not as God's representative or as a symbol of a nation-to-be. He rejects the offer made him as "Prince of God,"

> *The people of Ḥeth replied to Avraham, telling him, "Listen to us, Sire. You are a prince of God in our midst. Take our best burial site ...not one among us would deny you his own grave to bury your dead!"* (23:5,6)

אשת חיל עטרת בעלה [משלי יב]:
זה אברהם שהיה מקונן על שרה.
מה כתיב למעלה מן הענין? ותמת שרה...
התחיל אברהם לבכות עליה ולומר
אשת חיל מי ימצא בטח בה לב בעלה...

תנחומא, חיי שרה ד

and insists on purchasing this land as any other individual, so that it become his very own. "*Listen to me*...carefully," he implores.

> *Avraham rose and bowed low to the people of the land, the Ḥittites. He spoke to them and said, "If you could find it within yourselves to allow me to bury my dead...then listen to me – and speak up for me to Efron....Let him sell me the Machpela Cave...let him* **sell it to me** *for its full price in your presence...."* (23:7-9)

The Torah is careful to state the outcome of the negotiations twice – once to define the Machpela Cave as a national heritage, the other to make it clear that it belongs to Avraham, the man.

> *Thus was elevated the field of Efron in Machpela...to be the* **property** *of Avraham....*(23:17,18)
>
> *Thus was elevated the field and the cave within to be the* **heritage** *of Avraham....*(23:20)

שרה היתה אשת פרעה, מאהבתו אותה
כתב לה בשטר כתובתה כל ממונו בין כסף
בין זהב בין עבדים וקרקעות וכתב לה
את ארץ גושן לאחוזה. לפיכך ישבו בני
ישראל בארץ גושן בארץ שרה אמם...

פרקי רבי אליעזר, כו

Avraham's connection to the Land of Israel seems to draw from the depths of his relationship with Sara. Indeed, the land of Israel is not the only territory that becomes a heritage through Sara. There is one other place that is called an inheritance of the Children of Israel – and it too is ours through Sara.

Yisrael settled in the land of Egypt, in the land of Goshen – they inherited it and their population increased rapidly. (*Bereishit* 47:27)

Pharaoh, out of his intense love for Sara, gave her the land of Goshen as an inheritance. That is why the Children of Israel settled in the land of Goshen – it was the land of their mother, Sara.

PIRKEI RABI ELIEZER, 26

The relationship with Sara underlies Avraham's possession of land. In coming to a consuming awareness of what Sara means to him, he is able to achieve an awareness of what connectedness means to him – that he can be attached to the earth itself, and come to possess it. The parasha describes Avraham's life in all its wholeness, concluding with the legacy of the Land of Israel and a final dispensation of his physical and spiritual property.[7] Sara seems so to catalyze the expansion and integration of the life of Avraham that the entire period is named after the "*Life* of Sara."

The woman is the embodiment and the content of "place"... Sarah is a medium and instrument of connectivity to possessed ground...

ERIC J. LEED[8]
THE MIND OF THE TRAVELER

But with this insight, the remainder of the parasha becomes troubling. Sara's death is rapidly and somewhat inappropriately forgotten in the negotiations with Efron for a burial plot, and Avraham moves on to a new marriage and family, fathering six children even as Yitzḥak founds his own home. What is the conceptual theme of this parasha and its overall relationship to Sara? *Ḥayei Sara* seems to be but the inside cover of the family Bible – a family history of marriages and burials.

I believe that *Ḥayei Sara*'s theme involves precisely that curious juxtaposition: marriage and burial. The parasha highlights the importance of three marriages – Avraham and Sara, Yitzḥak and Rivka, Avraham and Ketura, and three burials – Sara, Avraham, and Yishma'el. Actually, there were four burials:

Avraham came to eulogize Sara and to weep for her.

– From where did he "come"? From the burial of Teraḥ [his father].

BEREISHIT RABBA, 58:5

The main body of the parasha describes Yitzḥak's marriage to a woman whose name is an anagram of the Hebrew word for burial: *rvkh* is *kvrh*.

רבקה=קברה

But the clincher is a sober principle from the opening of Kiddushin, the Talmudic tractate which elucidates the marital *halachot* and their sources:

> How do we know that the state of marriage is established through a transfer of value? We learn it from [the common use of the word] "*take*," [as used here and again the word] "*take*" as it appears in regards to the field of Efron:
> It says here, *If a man* take *a wife... (Devarim 24:1)*;
> It says there, *[He spoke to Efron in hearing of all the people saying, "If only you would hear me –] I give you the money for the field,* take *it from me (Bereishit 23:13)!"*
>
> KIDDUSHIN, 2a

There is, of course, a difference between what one seizes and what one really possesses.
PEARL S. BUCK

Consider what is happening here. The parasha that consistently juxtaposes marriage and burial just happens to provide – within a story describing the purchase of a plot of land for burial! – the source for the very formulation of marriage as an *institution*, a subject matter not even considered in the parasha! A remarkable coincidence.

By linking the acquisition of fields with marriage, the Torah brings us to see the unique sense of *belonging* applied to the earth and to woman, which is entirely different than being *owned*. A car or a toaster oven can be "owned." But the word "own" has no bearing on the unique relationship between human and the field that must outlive him, forever. The word "own" has no place in the special relationship between man and woman. *Belonging* has the different meaning of "suitability" and "association" which comes closer to the connotations of the words "*take*" and "*take*" used to link marriage and earth.

But it is not just any field that is the object of Avraham's acquisition and the parasha's juxtaposition – it is a *burial* field. And it is not just any woman who is the object of Avraham's love, but his unique wife, Sara. There is a primal juxtaposition of these two, *wife* and *burial*, in the Garden of Eden.

> *To the woman He said: "... Your longing*[9] *will be to your husband, and he will dominate you." (Bereishit 3:16)*

To the man He said: "...Finally, you will return to the earth for you were taken from her. For you are dust, and to dust you will return." (Bereishit 3:19)

God did not inform Man of mortality *per se*, but of *burial*: *to dust you will return*. It was the underlying relationship with the earth that needed to be restored. That relationship, as with woman herself, lies not in *use*, but in the deep connection we mean by "place."

The more unique and specific the connection, the deeper the acquisition. It is because we were "*taken from her*" in the first place, that we are able to "*return to the earth*" and find peace.

> God collected the dust for man's creation from the four corners of the earth, so that wherever he would die he would find his place for burial.
>
> TANḤUMA, PEKUDEI, 3

The earth, *adama*, is the name of our species, *adam*, just as "human" is drawn from *humus*, meaning "earth." If we lose sight of that, as Adam did, we lose all connection to ourselves and to life. Burial is a restoration of that connection, and the deepest relationships are reflected therein.

> *Ya'akov kissed Rachel, then lifted his voice in weeping.... (29:11)*
>
> – Why did he cry? He perceived that he would not be buried with her.
>
> BEREISHIT RABBA, 70:12

With the Cave of Machpela, Avraham discovered them all: the intensity of his love for Sara, the depth of his roots in the earth, and his own need to remain rooted – connected and caring and *belonging*.

> R. Bena'ah was engaged in marking gravesites. When he came to mark the Cave of Machpela, he met Eliezer the servant of Avraham at the doorway. "What is Avraham doing right now?" he asked Eliezer.
>
> Answered he, "He is lying between Sara's arms, and she is caressing his head."
>
> BAVA BATHRA, 58a

Along with the *Me'arat haMachpela*, Avraham discovered himself, and so came at last to inherit the Land of Israel, a land as uniquely and specifically "his" as Sara was uniquely and specifically "his."

If he grew weary in the day he laid himself into a furrow, and there, with the good warmth of his own land against his flesh, slept.

PEARL S. BUCK

To be rooted is perhaps the most important and the least recognized need of the human soul.

SIMONE WEIL

נגלה הקב"ה עליו אמר לו: אברהם!
אין אתה יודע שהיית לך שרה
ראויה לאשה ממעי אמה והיא
חברתך ואשת בריתך.
לא נקראת שרה שפחה אלא אשתך;
לא נקראת הגר אשתך אלא שפחתך...
פרקי רבי אליעזר כט

> Avraham! Sara was meant to be your wife from the moment of conception – she is your friend and the wife of your youth. . . .
>
> PIRKEI RABI ELIEZER, 29:1

This is why only now is Avraham ready to *assert* his rights to the land as rightful owner:

> *I am an immigrant and a resident in your midst – give me a burial plot among you. . . .* (23:4)
>
> If you cooperate, then I am an "immigrant." But if you refuse, then I will be a "resident" and take it by right, for God promised me, *to your children will I give this land* (12:7). (—Rashi[10])

Now, did not Avraham break up earlier with Lot over precisely the issue of prematurely exercising the "rights" to *Eretz Yisrael*?[11]

Land is one's flesh and blood.
PEARL S. BUCK

> *. . . They could no longer live together. There was a quarrel between the shepherds of Avram's sheep and the shepherds of Lot's sheep – and the Prizi were then living in the land.* (13:6,7)
>
> Lot's shepherds would allow his animals to graze in land belonging to others, and Avram's shepherds admonished them. They responded: the land was given by God to Avram and Lot is his heir. That is why the verse concludes, "*The Prizi were then living in the land,*" because Avram had not yet acquired it. (—Rashi[12])

But there is no contradiction here. Indeed, "*the Prizi were then living in the land.*" But they had rights of *usage*, not the deeper rights of specific *belonging*. The Land of Israel can be rightfully *used* by others, even for many centuries. Avraham respected those rights; he would not allow Lot to strip the Canaanites of what they had rightfully grown from the land. Yet the Canaanites were only sojourners; the land could never become *theirs* in the sense of belonging. Were the Sons of Ḥeth to deny Avraham a place for *burial* – the deeper entitlement from which acquisition itself is ultimately derived – then Avraham could and would have taken what was his by right.

The children of Yishma'el also have rights.

> Because of the circumcision of Yishma'el, his children were given the right to dominate the Holy Land when she is empty, for a very long period. . . .

> But then they will prevent the Children of Israel from returning to their rightful place, until at last the merit of Yishma'el's *milah* will be depleted....
>
> ZOHAR, II:32a

But those rights are merely of *usage*, and they cannot stand in the way of the deeper inheritance of the Land of Israel by her true lovers when their time has come to love again.[13]

The first acquisition of *Eretz Yisrael* was an act of love, an act which set the stamp of Avraham and Sara on the Land for all its future. It was an act of love sealed in the city of Ḥebron, which translates literally as "bonding,"[14] in the *Me'arat haMachpela,* literally, "the doubled cave."

> Why was it called "doubled"? Because it was doubled with couples....in *Kiryat Arba,* [literally] the "Town of Four" couples: Adam and Ḥava, Avraham and Sara, Yitzḥak and Rivka, Ya'akov and Leah.
>
> EIRUVIN, 53a

Only connect! That was the whole of her sermon.

E.M. FORSTER

The bond to *Eretz Yisrael* cannot be based on petty nationalism. It is a bond of coevolution that penetrates deeper than any tribal rights to land or ethnic demands for political entities, a uniquely *personal* bond. As geopolitical forces focus on the nature of our attachment to the Land of Israel and demand of us soul-searching reconsideration, we need to remember that it became ours first and last through the love of a woman – the very *Life of Sara,* indeed.

1 Cf. R. Baḥya, introduction to *Ḥayei Sara*, based on Kohelet 7:1.

2 *Tanḥuma*, ibid.

3 Mishlei, 31:10 through end.

4 Cf. Midrash Tehillim, 112:1 and ibid.

5 *Tanḥuma*, ibid., *Kedoshim*, 13.

6 Cf. also R. Baḥya, 23:2.

7 25:5-6, and Rashi.

8 Leed, Eric J. *The Mind of the Traveler* (New York: Basic Books, 1991), 118-119.

9 Compare 'be-*longing*'.

10 S.v. *Ger vetoshav*, ד״ה גר ותושב.

11 *Ḥizkuni*, 23:4, attempts to answer this contradiction by pointing out that only now does Avraham have the "*seed*" to whom the land was promised, whereas before only Lot was his heir. This answer runs counter to Bereishit Rabba, 41:5.

12 13:7, s.v. *Vayhi riv*, ד״ה ויהי ריב.

13 The difference is stressed with one beautiful word here in *Ḥayei Sara*. When Machpela is purchased by Avraham, the Torah refers to "elevation":

> *Thus was* elevated *the field of Efron in Machpela. . . .* (23:17,18)
> *Thus was* elevated *the field and the cave within to be the heritage of Avraham. . . .* (23:20)

But when Yishma'el settles the land, the Torah refers to "decline":

> ...*On the face of all his brethren he* fell. (25:18)

14 From *ḥvr*, חבר, 'friend', 'connection'.

V Ḥayei Sara

חיי שרה

The Invention of Old Age

Ḥayei Sara, 'The Life of Sara', opens with the death of Sara and a quick review of her life; it concludes with the deaths of Avraham and Yishma'el and a wrap-up of their lives. It is a parasha of transition between the era of Avraham and the era of his son Yitzḥak, tracing the changing of the guard as the old generation fades away and the new begins its journey. The state called "old age" appears here for the first time in the Torah, and it is central to *Ḥayei Sara* and to an understanding of its transitions.

The Invention of Old Age contrasts Western attitudes towards senescence with that of the Torah, and discovers—along with some spirited perspectives for aging—the vital relationship of youth to elder.

THE INVENTION OF OLD AGE

The name *Ḥayei Sara*, 'Sara's Life', evokes the bittersweet ambiance of the many partings recounted in this parasha. Avraham returns from the burial of his father Teraḥ[1] to bury his wife Sara; Avraham himself grows old and dies; Yishma'el changes and passes on, and the focus of events shifts to a new age and a new cast – the generation of Yitzḥak.

> *So it was after the death of Avraham that God blessed Yitzḥak....* (25:11)

The *haftara* plays variations on the same theme, telling of the last days of the aged King David and the shift of focus to a new phase of Jewish history and monarchy. *Ḥayei Sara* is the parasha of aging:

> We find no mention of old age in the Torah until now.[2]
>
> BEREISHIT RABBA, 65:9

Dramatic changes in life expectancy, population patterns, and birth rates give this parasha a contemporary flavor, for we too live in a demographically and historically unique period of partings and transition.

We are increasingly likely to come face to face in our everyday lives with the effects of global demographic shift: within the next twenty years, the population of the entire United States will look the way Florida's does today.[3] With all the best intentions and attitudes, this shift presents a serious social, economic, family, and personal problem. The burning problem of providing care to so many people is only the tip of an iceberg that extends beyond painful, possibly cataclysmic, economic dislocation. The more fundamental issues involve the relationship to the aged – and to aging itself.

Sometime within the next decade or two, almost everyone reading these words will face some of the heartache and anguish involved in changing family roles. Within your family or business circumstances, or both, you will likely experience elements of the resentment, alienation, and apprehension involved in the metamorphosis of interpersonal dynamics and self-perception associated with aging and role reversal.

And sometime within the next decade or three, nearly everyone reading these words will be made profoundly and inescapably aware of his or her own slide away from domination and independence, towards dependency and senescence. But Western culture is in love with youth, obsessed with youth; to be consuming and young is to be alive, and to be old is to be almost dead. Either the prevailing attitudes to old age will critically change, or there will be many more mid-life casualties of crises and self-loathing. *Ḥayei Sara* speaks directly to these concerns that touch some of the most sensitive and vulnerable areas of our psyche: mortality, aging, senescence, and their effect on ourselves and our loved ones.

I knew quite well that some day
I must go down this road;
but I had never thought that
some day would be today.
I.W. FURUKAMI

The hallmarks of aging are easy to spot in our parasha. They occur one after another. The story opens with aging's familiar spur: the death of Avraham's lifetime partner changes him, ages him.[4] Sara's death focuses him on preparation for his own demise.

Then, Avraham finds himself too feeble to actively pursue the search for a match for Yitzḥak.[5] He becomes dependent on the quest of his trusted servant, himself now "*the aged.*"[6]

The reversal of roles begins as Yitzḥak, now called "*The Master,*"[7] comes to possess "*everything Avraham owned.*"[8] How achingly familiar are Yitzḥak's efforts to encourage Avraham to become involved again.

The final inversion is dramatically accentuated by contrast: the parasha which began with Avraham's search for a wife for Yitzḥak ends with Yitzḥak's presentation of a wife to Avraham.[9]

> *Yitzḥak was coming from Be'er Laḥai Ro'i. . . .* (24:62)
>
> He had gone there to bring Hagar to Avraham to remarry. (—Rashi)

Yet the familiar accentuates a certain strangeness. All the stages seem familiar enough, but they lack the emotive context we have come to assume in our own lives. There is no angst here, not in the parasha and not in the *haftara* – no trauma, none of the psychological upheaval we expect as par for the course. Even more confounding to our sensibilities is the approach of the midrash, teaching that old age was not merely *acceptable* to Avraham, but that he actually invented it.

> Avraham demanded old age. He said, "Master of the Universe, a man might enter a room together with his son and no one would know which to respect. If You would crown him with old age people would know whom to respect!"
>
> Said the Holy One to him, "By your life! That's a very good idea – let it start with you...."
>
> This is why it says, *And Avraham was old, coming along in days....* (24:1).
>
> BEREISHIT RABBA, 65:9

כיון שמתה קפצה זקנה על אברהם,
מה כתיב אחריו ואברהם זקן....
תנחומא, חיי שרה, ד

Nonetheless, despite a presentation so different from what we would expect under similar circumstances in our own lives, we somehow accept as almost natural that the characters here should assume their new roles with the same assuredness and simple clarity they exhibited in their previous roles. Transported into the Torah's mind-set, so fraught with subtle background,[10] we begin intuitively to grasp an alternative vision, a different existential map of aging more compelling than theory.

Attitudes towards aging, internal or external, play an undeniably consequential role in the process itself. It is important, therefore, to recognize the changes in perspective that the parasha suggests. Aging in the West is associated with meaninglessness, ennui, boredom and the games played to avoid them. "Whiling away" the time – endless card games, golf, retirement villages, travel for those of means, and attempts to maintain vigor and activity into our nineties, as if the problem were one of activity. But the end is the same: no position, no significance – no *future*. We are conditioned to view aging as a destructive process – perhaps it is more accurate to say a deconstructive process. A research psychologist puts it like this: "One of the fundamental accomplishments in life is to develop a sense of self. Those who live long enough get to partake of a last stage in adult development – deconstruction of the self."[11] Isolation and the loss of friends, of society, of identification,[12] of productivity, of a sense of usefulness – all these erase the cues that mark the path of relationship and connection to reality.

Ḥayei Sara introduces old age with a curious definition – one with precisely the opposite connotation: *Abraham was old, come into days (24:1).* The *haftara* opens with the same words: *The king, David was old, come into days (Melachim I, 1:1).* What could the phrase "*come into days*" possibly add to the straightforward word "*old*"? The Zohar supplies a moving interpretation:

ווי לההוא בר נש דגרע יומוי קמי
מלכא קדישא ולא שביק לעילא יומין
לאתעטרא בהו בההוא עלמא ולאתקרבא
בהדייהו קמי מלכא קדישא.
ת"ח כד קריבו אינון יומין קמי מלכא
קדישא אי הוא זכאה האי בר נש דנפיק
מעלמא סליק ועאל באינון יומין ואינון
לבושי יקר דמתלבשא ביה נשמתיה
ואינון יומין הוו דזכה בהו ולא חב בהו.
ווי לההוא דגרע יומוי לעילא דכד בעאן
לאלבשא ליה ביומוי אינון יומין דפגים
איהו בחובוי חסרין מההוא לבושא
ואתלבש במנא חסרא כ"ש אי סגיאין
אינון ולא להוי ליה לב"נ במה דאתלבש
בההוא עלמא כדין ווי ליה ווי לנפשיה...

זוהר, ויחי רכד

All the days of a person's life are laid out above,
one by one they come soaring into this world. . . .
If a person leaving the world merits,
he comes into those days of his life,
they become a luminous garment. . . .
Woe to one who cheapened his days above!
As he comes to be clothed in the days of his life,
the ruined days are missing,
and he wears a tattered garment.
The worst is if there are many ruined days,
then he will have nothing to wear!
Avraham who was pure, what is written of him? "*Come into days...*"
He came into the days of his very own life and put them on to wear!
Nothing was missing from that precious garment:
That is *come into days*!

ZOHAR, 1:224a

Avraham was only able to come into those days in old age,
So too David, as it says, "*The king, David was old,*"
And only then "*come into days*" *(Melachim I, 1:1)*.

ZOHAR, 1:129b

Old age allows us to "wear the days of our life" as a single garment – a totality, integrated and complete. In this perspective, aging is precisely the opposite of deconstruction of the self. It is a process of internalization, integration, consolidation, and reconciliation. The details, experiences, and memories of a lifetime come to be seen in context, and the broadened perspective helps resolve former pain and contradictions.

> Happy is our old age that cleanses our youth.
>
> SUCCA, 53a

Avraham uses this stage of his life for definition, reconciliation, and disbursement in a process of culling and sifting. He remarries Hagar[13] forty years after the painful breakup. He settles the relationship of his *children by concubines* (25:6) to Yitzḥak. He gives away the gifts he received from Pharaoh on behalf of Sara[14] (they are not his own accomplishment). And at last he draws Yishma'el back home.

Old Age in the Torah is the process of construction not of deconstruction. The word for elder, *zaken* (זקן), is seen in the Talmud as a contraction of *ze kana* (זה קנה), meaning "this one *has* it."[15] This adds a delightful twist to the famous dictum:

> סתירת זקנים בנין
>
> *De*construction by the aged is actually construction.
>
> MEGILLA, 31b

What is the great added value of age? Perhaps it is only that the early part of adulthood is often lived externally, focused on a success that is measured by its trappings or by the response of others – parent, public, or boss. In old age, however, the accumulated experiences of a lifetime can be consolidated and internalized into a whole personality with no need to prove anything.[16] Success is defined not by money or approval ratings, but by humanness, by making life work. Life itself takes on new reverence and dignity, by virtue of the internalization alone.

> Rav Yoḥanan would stand in the presence of the elderly, even heathens, saying, "Imagine the experiences these lives must contain!"
>
> KIDDUSHIN, 33a

The problem is that it is age itself and not attitudes that Rav Yoḥanan respects here. In which case our contrast between the hollowness of externalized youth and the internalization of old age is oversimplified.

For apparently even fools still age in terms that Rav Yoḥanan could respect. And, to him, youth would be merely youth even when seriously focused on genuine standards. There must, then, be a more critical distinction that is an outgrowth of youthfulness and aging *per se*.

Maybe youth's focus on *becoming*, the quintessence of youthfulness, is in conflict with the *being* which is the achievement of old age. To youth, life is an extensive investment in the present in the hope of vindication by the future. *Today* may be profoundly dissatisfying, but it is worthwhile for the achievement towards which it leads. The joy of being may remain tantalizingly out of reach to a person whose life must focus on achievement, whose life is addicted to the future. Whereas to the aged, the future cannot serve as justification for anything. Life in the present is either meaningful as is, or it is altogether meaningless.[17] Old age's integration and sufficiency is a function of *presence*.

He that would pass the latter part of life with honor and decency must, when he is young, consider that he shall one day be old; and remember, when he is old, that he has once been young.
SAMUEL JOHNSON

Listen as Tolstoy masterfully portrays the perspective of such presence, as he describes Prince Andrew's reaction to the old general, Kutuzov.

> The more he realized the absence of all personal motive in that old man – in whom there seemed to remain only the habit of passions, and in place of an intellect (grouping events and drawing conclusions) only the capacity calmly to contemplate the course of events – the more reassured he was that everything would be as it should. "...He will not devise or undertake anything," thought Prince Andrew, "but he will hear everything, remember everything, and put everything in its place...he understands that there is something stronger and more important than his own will. . . ."
>
> WAR AND PEACE, BOOK TEN

A terminally ill patient may become "aged" in the Torah sense through achieving presence: "I've stopped scheming, prearranging, preparing. I haven't lost the future; I've found today."[18]

The most amazing contrast in attitude between our own assumptions and the parasha, though, is yet to come: Avraham does not ask for the purely *psychological* aspects of aging. He specifically wants to *look* old!

> God told Avraham, "You are the most beautiful of humans...."
>
> Said Avraham, "You call it beautiful when I look as young as my son?" He woke up the next morning to find he had turned white...God told him, *White hair is a beautiful crown (Mishlei 16:31).*
>
> TANḤUMA, BEREISHIT, 1 (CONDENSED)

התחיל משבחו ואמר לו יפיפית
מבני אדם, אמר לו אי זה היופי שלי?
אני ובני נכנסין לעיר ואין בני אדם
מכירין בין האב לבן? אמר אברהם,
רבש"ע! צריך אתה להפריש בין האב
לבן ובין נער לזקן שיתכבד הזקן בנער.
אמר לו הקדוש ברוך הוא חייך! ממך
אני מתחיל! הלך ולן באותה הלילה ועמד
בבקר כיון שעמד ראה שהלבין שער ראשו
וזקנו, אמר לפניו, רבש"ע עשיתני דוגמא!
אמר לו, עטרת תפארת שיבה (משלי טז),
והדר זקנים שיבה (שם כ).
לכך נאמר ואברהם זקן.

תנחומא, חיי שרה, א

A society that spends billions on looking young – that performs hundreds of thousands of facelifts, tummy tucks, dermabrasions, and liposuctions every year – can scarcely begin to fathom Avraham's request.

Avraham is saying that to be *recognized* as old is important. This implies that the process and achievement of aging cannot be seen as something limited to inner life, but must be part of an externalized relationship. Somehow, appearances and relationship are actual components of the attainments and fulfillment of age. In the famous teaching quoted in the Passover Haggada, eighteen-year-old R. Elazar ben Azaria[19] refers to his graying *appearance* as if it were a meaningful measure of age.

> I am as one of seventy years, yet I have been unable to prove that the Exodus must be mentioned in the evening *Shema*...
>
> BERACHOT, 12b

Clearly, the perception of age, the bond to others as *they* distinguish age, is central to the reality of Age.

I think we come to the core issue here. The substance of the parasha's message is that neither the perspective of youth nor the vision of age is viable in itself. It is the Life Cycle which we must address – the nexus of youth and old age. There *is* a tension between being and becoming, and in the full and continual awareness of the polar phases of life, one lives and participates in both. Only the new perspective of life that comes of the contact between youth and age allows realism and joy.

Avraham asked for the appearance of old age when it came time to defer to the future, to pass *"to Yitzḥak all that he possessed."* R. Elazar ben Azaria needed his "age" only when he was appointed the *nassi*, the president. For age *per se* is not the point – the point is Elderhood, the true translation of the Hebrew *zaken*: 'elder', no matter what the age. To achieve selfhood through the provision for life itself instead of through dreams of personal participation in the future – that is the perspective and service of the Elder.

It is a privilege for us all to be a part of the perennial Circle of Life, extant only because youth, in *becoming*, builds a continuum. It is a privilege for the elder to bring significance and presence into the struggles of that youthfulness; to channel the tranquility and the perspective of totality into the lives of those who must, for now, be the generators.

> *The crown of elders is children's children,*
> *The glory of children is their parents.* (Mishlei 17:6)

It is the elder who teaches youth that the glorious days of young life are not a rehearsal for tomorrow – they are the real thing.

For the complete life, the perfect pattern includes old age as well as youth and maturity.
SOMERSET MAUGHAM

No wonder we are in such trouble with our beliefs of "deconstruction." We break the great "*knot of life*"[20] by severing the bonds between youth and age. We have nearly expunged the very concept "elder" from our children's vocabulary. In shielding ourselves and our children from the old as from disease we succeed merely in camouflaging life itself.

When "Old Man" becomes the equivalent of "antiquated" and "passé," it is not only the old man who is cheated of the chance to live within his own profound contribution to the life cycle. It is we and the future who are cheated, victimized into believing that success and life lie only in a future that may never come, beguiled into working endlessly for "retirement," as if in dormancy there awaits the great secret of life, as if in leisure there lies fulfillment.

What then can we say when crisis hits at midlife with the ghastly suspicion that, "this is about the way it is going to be for the rest of my life." What then can we say when we have lived by the dictum that regards limits on the future as being limits to meaning? On that day when our youth discover in the core of their being that there is no longer a future, they will feel cheated, meaningless, lost, detached, and hopeless.

Fear of aging cheats us of youth. There are two sides to the coin of life, and without both life is terminally one dimensional. The elder vindicates Life itself, makes its moments real, its memories significant, re-*membered* into a whole and glorious tapestry we call a human life. *Ḥayei Sara*, the *Life of Sara,* indeed, even as she awaits burial.

The two sides to the coin of life were literally minted by Avraham and Sara, visionaries of old age:

> The coinage of our Father Avraham was engraved with an old man and woman on the obverse, and a youth and maiden on the reverse.
>
> BAVA KAMA, 97b

1 Bereishit Rabba, 58:5.

2 Previous mentions in Bereishit 18:11 are explained in Bereishit Rabba, 48:19.

3 *Aging*, U .S. Department of Health and Human Services, Winter-Spring 1992, p. 54.

4 *Tanḥuma*, Bereishit 4:1 and Shemini 2:1; *Aggadat Bereishit*, 34:1.

5 Cf. *Ḥizkuni* and *Seforno* 24:1.

6 Bereishit 24:2.

7 Bereishit 24:65.

8 Bereishit 25:5.

9 Bereishit Rabba, 60:14; Rashi, Bereishit 24:62, s.v. *Mebo*, ד״ה מבוא.

10 See Erich Auerbach, *Mimesis: The Representation of Reality in Western Literature* (Princeton University Press, 1953), Chapter 1, for extraordinary insight into the nature of the Torah narrative.

11 David Kahn, Ph.D., quoted in *Psychology Today*, volume 25, number 1, February 1992.

12 Cf. Ramban's poignant and innovative explanation of באים בימים in 18:11.

13 Rashi, Bereishit 25:1, s.v. *Ketora*, ד״ה קטורה, and Rashi, Bereishit 24:62, s.v. *Mebo*, ד״ה מבוא, from Bereishit Rabba, 1:5.

14 Rashi, s.v. *Natan*, ד״ה נתן.

15 Vayikra 19:32; Kiddushin, 32b, and note Rashi, s.v. *Ein zaken*, ד״ה אין זקן.

16 An allusion to this idea here in the parasha: Eliezer the trusted servant is referred to (24:2) as זקן ביתו, "the aged of his home who mastered all that he had." The unusual *zaken* implies that mastery is the essence of *zikna*.

17 We could hold a mirror to Robert Browning, and say:

> Grow old along with me,
> The best is never *yet* to be,
> But only just to Be.

18 Jane Mayer, *Newsweek*, May 11. 1992, p. 14.

19 Berachot, 28a.

20 Shmuel I, 25:29.

VI Toledot
תּוֹלְדוֹת

Jews and Traitors

The lives of Yitzḥak, of Rivka his wife, and of their children, Ya'akov and Eisav, unfold here in context of the momentous theme of the parasha: *Toledot* means 'progeny', and the parasha defines the makeup of Yitzḥak's spiritual heirs, the nature of the future nation Yisrael. It is here that the historic and fundamental split between Ya'akov and Eisav evolves. The entire opening of the parasha is contrived, by sacrificing chronological order, to provide the essential background for that later development, beginning with the prophecy to Rivka that *Two nations are in your womb— two civilizations will divide from within you. . . .* (25:23), and continuing with the story of Ya'akov's "purchase" of the "birthright" from Eisav.

The selection of Ya'akov over Eisav raises questions about the nature of culture, integrity, and identity that are as contemporary as this morning's paper and as provoking as the legend of Judas. *Jews and Traitors* examines Jewish identity in light of the multiple elements of *'toleda'*, and formulates the core of the inescapable destiny that drives Yisrael.

JEWS AND TRAITORS

The commotion raised not long ago by the cinquecentennial of America's politically-incorrect "discovery" has soured the Thanksgiving turkey for some. The anniversary stirred up quite a tempest, blustering a slew of politically correct words and challenging us with obscure concepts, unnamed just a few ignorant years ago.[1] All national and cultural definitions touch upon the tension between nature and nurture, genetic inheritance and environment, intuition and education. But whereas defining "American" is a newly fashionable concern, the politico-religious question of "Who is a Jew?" raises a long-standing and bitter controversy involving religion and culture, past and future, the special and the universal. It is a question as contemporary as this morning's newspaper and as old as the Jewish people. Yitzḥak the *Av* struggled with it as well. He nearly came to the wrong conclusion.

Parashat Toledot addresses the complex interplay of factors involved in defining genuine Jewish identity – in defining "Yisrael." That is how the parasha got its name: *Toledot*, an expansive word referring to every aspect of that intricate interaction. A parasha is not named mindlessly and indiscriminately after its opening words. As a matter of fact, this is not even the first weekly Torah portion to begin with the words, *Eleh toledot* ("*These are the descendants....*"). An earlier portion, *Parashat Noaḥ*, begins the same way. It would have made as much sense – more, if we are partial to openers – to have given *Parashat Noaḥ* the name *Toledot*, and to have called this week's portion "*Yitzḥak*." The truth is, however, that this parasha is *Toledot* par excellence. It focuses entirely and definitively on the *toleda* relationship.

Over fifty diverse and conspicuous references to congenital associations occur in this parasha. Almost all of these references seem superfluous, at times even absurdly repetitive. What are we to make of statements like, *Yitzḥak the son of Avraham, Avraham fathered Yitzḥak (25:19)*? Three of the most flagrant redundancies are addressed by Rashi.[2] He manages to explain two of them with a midrash, but he throws up his hands at the astonishing re-identification – at the very end of the story! – of its central character:

> . . . *Rivka the mother of Ya'akov and Eisav.* (28:5)
>
> I have no idea what this is meant to teach us. (—Rashi[3])

But there is nothing surprising about the overall focus on such relationships here in *Toledot*. Clearly the divergence of Ya'akov and Eisav – both children of Yitzḥak – mandates a more subtle definition of "*toleda*" than simply "progeny."

In a sense, this is the moment we have been waiting for since Creation:

> "*In the beginning*" implies *for the First*, i.e. for Yisrael who are called *First* (*Yermiah* 2:3).
>
> RASHI[4]

But what defines this "Yisrael"? Only *Toledot* will tell.

The content of the Torah until this point was put in writing[5] in order to assert, warrant, and vindicate the *birthright* of a distinctive nation to a distinctive land.[6]

> *In the beginning God created the heaven and the earth. . . .* (1:1)
>
> The Torah ought actually to have begun, *This month is to you the head of all months . . .* (*Shemot* 12:2), which is the first mitzvah given to Yisrael [as a nation], Why, then, did it begin with *Bereishit*?
>
> For *The power of His works He declared to His people, to grant them the heritage of nations* (*Tehillim* 111:6). [To vindicate their inheritance of Eretz Yisrael].
>
> If the nations of the world were to claim, "You are imperialists, usurping the territory of the Seven States (of Cana'an)!" they can now be answered, "All the earth belongs to the Holy One – He created it and bequeaths it to whomever He sees fit. . . ." (—Rashi[7])

But what defines this distinctive nation? Only *Toledot* will tell.

After twenty-one generations of careful selection starting from Adam, we finally discover exactly to whom God referred when He promised

Avraham: *to your* issue *I will give this land* (*Bereishit* 12:7). It was never clear: just who *are* these bona fide inheritors of the land-as-*inheritance* (15:7)?

"Land-as-inheritance" was a concept which Avraham himself found difficult to accept. He too wondered about the deeper reality of "*your issue,*" about the impact his genes and breeding could have on a culture centuries in the future. He questioned the nature of Yisrael's underlying identity, and rejected the notion that his heirs would warrant the land of Israel just by virtue of being his biological "issue."

> *"How can I know that I will have it as an inheritance?"* (15:8)
>
> By what account will my progeny retain it? (—Rashi)
>
> Avraham said, "Master of the Universe! Perhaps Yisrael will sin before You...How can I know?"
>
> TA'ANIT, 27b

Defining what God meant by "*your issue*" is not always as straightforward as you might think. When it came to determining, for instance, whether Yishma'el was "issue of Avraham,"[8] the criterion was simple enough, and purely genetic: A child born to a non-Jewish mother is not halachically pedigreed to its Jewish father. The child from the *amah* (maidservant), Hagar, was not considered "seed of Avraham."[9] The Torah only recognizes Avraham's progeny from the *wife,* Sara, as his true descendant: *in Yitzhak shall be defined "your seed"* (21:12). But the situation here in *Toledot* is different. What criteria apply in defining which of two children with identical pedigree – twins – is the genuine *toleda*? What criteria apply to choose a Ya'akov over an Eisav?

Consider a case where the child *is* pedigreed to the father. A non-Jewish couple have children and the father later converts. The technical pedigree stands, but the father is not *related* to these children in the eyes of halacha – there are no biblically[10] mandated incest restrictions on their intimacy. Now is such a convert bound by mitzvah (*be fruitful and multiply*) to procreate as a Jew? Certainly. Any children born to him as a non-Jew cannot count towards the offspring required to satisfy the mitzvah. Suppose, now, that the child also converts – at that point the father *has* discharged his mitzvah though the child remains "unrelated" to him![11]

Now, might this imply that *toledah* is a philosophical affiliation in the sense of "spiritual heir" ("affiliation" in the Latin, from *filius*, means literally "to adopt as heir")?[12] No. The Torah goes out of its way to reject just such an interpretation. Avraham's supplication for a *toleda* is accompanied with an embittered rejection of an already extant spiritual heir, a veritable clone of Avraham, molded in his own image and master of his entire teaching.[13]

> *Lord God, what can You offer me if I have no offspring, if Damesek Eliezer...is to inherit me! (15:2,3)*
>
> "Damesek," (דמשק), implies that he [Eliezer] could draw his master's wisdom and pour (*doleh* דו׳לה + *mashke* משק׳ה) it out to others.
>
> *Eliezer...who ruled all that was his [Avraham's]. (24:2)*
>
> This teaches that Eliezer mastered all of Avraham's Torah.
>
> YOMA, 28b

Toledot helps resolve the fundamental question of "Who is a Yisrael?" It actually sets up a contest for a winning definition of *toleda*.

The competition between Ya'akov and Eisav for both the *bechora* (בכורה), primogeniture, and for the *beracha* (ברכה), blessing, was a competition for *toleda* primacy.[14] Yitzḥak's blessings reflect on a lifetime relationship, on care and on service: *Prepare me delicacies...so that I may bless you (27:4)*. The entire context in which the blessings are placed establishes them as testament and legacy of biological father to son.

Yet these blessings are also part of a historical transmission, beginning with God's blessings to Avraham, and they impact the entire future of history. They must also involve intense questions of philosophical and emotional affinity, as emphasized throughout the entire story of the Ya'akov-Eisav bifurcation, beginning in the womb.

> *Two nations are in your womb – two civilizations will divide from within you.... (25:23)*

It is not only the *beracha* but also the *bechora* that involves an affinity of sorts, a psychological cathexis beyond mere impregnation. Primogeniture is not defined exclusively by biology.

The first of his vigor . . . (Devarim 21:17)

Only a child to whom a father's heart would naturally respond is a *bechor*... (excepting mutants).

NIDDAH, 23b

Yitzḥak was closer to Eisav than to Ya'akov. Yitzḥak saw Eisav as the object of *beracha* and *bechora* for more than reasons of genetics, cathexis, service, or religion. He considered Eisav his true successor.[15]

Eisav was of the same nature as Yitzḥak . . . This is why *Yitzḥak loved Eisav* more than Ya'akov, for likes attract.

ZOHAR, I:137b[16]

Yitzḥak even poignantly blamed himself for the shattering disappointment in Eisav:

As for you, what can I do, my son! (27:37)

Why "*my son*"? Yitzḥak was saying, "It is all my fault, because you are *my* son. I affected you this way..."

ZOHAR, I:145a

Yet all along Yitzḥak was wrong – subtly but spectacularly wrong.

Biology (זרע), pedigree (יחוס), incest restriction (ערוה), cathexis (דוה), character (איש תם), religion (יושב אהלים),[17] similarity (בני) – all these are factors that the Torah considers in determining the bona fide heir, but no single factor is definitive. Even among contemporary proponents of the various (somewhat stupefying) arguments regarding nature versus nurture and sociobiology versus culture, it is difficult to find any serious believer in true dichotomy. It is more a matter of fixing a mediating principle within the various components of the synergetic system we call "culture."[18] If even after considering all these recognized elements, Yitzḥak still believed that Eisav was the man, then what is the mystery ingredient?

It is as if the Torah created here a controlled experiment to discover the missing component, eliminating the effect of all the known factors. We study twins who shared the same womb, who experienced equivalent nurture, who won similar blessings,[19] and who represent historical and cultural parallels.

Two nations ("goyim," גויים) in your womb (25:23)

Read this [not "two nations" but] "two aristocrats," ("*gayim*," גאים):

Adrianus in Rome,
Shelomo in Israel;
Antoninus in Rome,
Rebbi [Yehuda haNassi] in Israel;
You have fairs and markets,
he has fairs and markets;
You have your etiquette,
he has his etiquette.

BERACHOT, 57b; BEREISHIT RABBA, 63:7

They were certainly similar enough to confuse Yitzḥak, yet one is heir and the other anti-heir.

Does the parasha finally give us a clue as to the nature of the mediating element? It does indeed, and in a mind-boggling historical irony, it is the very element with which Eisav has chosen to brand Yisrael for *rejection*: the Jew as Judas, a nation of traitors, in a new contest wherein Eisav sees himself as victorious! Consider what moves Yitzḥak at last to actually deliver the *berachot* into the hands of Ya'akov:

He smelled the odor of his clothes and he blessed him. (27:27)

But what could smell worse than goat hides?

Read it then not as "*clothes*" (*begadav*, בגדיו), but as "*traitors*" (*bogedav*, בגדיו). Thus he sensed the future presence of Ya'akov's renegades and then he blessed him.

"*Traitors*" such as Yosef Meshitha. When the Romans wanted to enter the Temple Mount, they said, "Let a Jew go in first, and whatever he takes out he can keep." Yosef went in and walked out with the golden menorah.

The scandalized Romans said, "This is something that no commoner ought to use – go in again and anything you take will be yours." He refused.

They threw in a three year tax break, but he still refused, saying, "It is bad enough to have angered my Creator once – should I do it again?"

וירח את ריח בגדיו ויברכהו:
כגון יוסף משיתא ויקום איש צרורות.
יוסף משיתא, בשעה שבקשו שונאים
להכנס להר הבית אמרו, יכנס מהם
ובהם תחלה! אמרין ליה, עול, ומה
דאת מפיק דידך. נכנס והוציא מנורה
של זהב. אמרו לו, אין דרכו של הדיוט
להשתמש בזו! אלא עול זמן תנינות,
ומה דאת מפיק דידך. ולא קיבל עליו.
א"ר פנחס, נתנו לו מכס שלש שנים
ולא קיבל עליו. אמר, לא דיי שהכעסתי
לאלהי פעם אחת אלא שאכעיסנו פעם
שניה! מה עשו לו! נתנו אותו בחמור
של חרשים והיו מנסרים בו. היה מצווח
ואומר, ווי! אוי אוי שהכעסתי לבוראי!
ויקום איש צרורות היה בן אחותו של
רבי יוסי בן יועזר איש צרידה והוה
רכיב סוסיא בשבתא. אזל קומי שריתא
למצטבלא. א"ל, חמי סוסי דארכבי מרי,
וחמי סוסך דארכבך מרך! א"ל, אם כך
למכעיסיו ק"ו לעושי רצונו!
א"ל, עשה אדם רצונו יותר ממך!
אמר לו, ואם כך לעושי רצונו קל וחומר
למכעיסיו! נכנס בו הדבר כארס של עכנא.
הלך וקיים בעצמו ארבע מיתות בית דין,
סקילה שריפה הרג וחנק. מה עשה! הביא
קורה, נעצה בארץ, וקשר בה נימא וערך
העצים והקיפן גדר של אבנים ועשה מדורה
לפניה ונעץ את החרב באמצע והצית האור
תחת העצים מתחת האבנים ונתלה בקורה
ונחנק קדמתו האש נפסקה הנימה, נפל לאש
קדמתו חרב ונפל עליו גדר ונשרף.
נתנמנם יוסי בן יועזר איש צרידה וראה
מטתו פרחה באויר. אמר, בשעה קלה
קדמני זה לגן עדן!

בראשית רבה

> So they trussed him up on a carpenter's bench and started sawing off pieces of his body, and he just kept sobbing, "Oh, how I upset my Creator! Oh!"
>
> SANHEDRIN, 37a; BEREISHIT RABBA, 65:22

Even as the Temple stood at the verge of destruction, the turncoat Yosef Meshitha so repudiated his Jewishness that he became the enthusiastic Roman lackey to demoralize and debase all reverence for the sanctity of Jewish symbols. Yet with a single and sudden insight he became a paradigm of reverence and care.

This exposes a subliminal cultural connection in the descendants of Ya'akov that can survive purposeful attempts at uprooting, to leap into awareness only at moments of trauma. The existence of this connection was enough to persuade Yitzḥak to bless Ya'akov, even though it was a trait that would become evident only in the distant future of Ya'akov's progeny. Somehow this connection became more important to Yitzḥak than a lifetime of the here and now.

Snakes, in my heart-blood warm'd, that sting my heart! Three Judases, each one thrice worse than Judas!
RICHARD THE SECOND, III,2

The definition of *bechora* involves the same enigma. Though primogeniture requires "a child to whom a father's heart would respond," such responsiveness is subliminal – almost theoretical – and possibly in strong conflict with current emotions. The laws of *bechora* prohibit a father from attempting a transposition of primogeniture on the parochial basis of his subjective awareness of current love and hate:

> *He cannot choose the son of his beloved over the son of his despised wife, who is the* bechor. *(Devarim 21:16)*

Why would the definition of Yisrael – The First, the *bechor* of Creation, *My firstborn son, Yisrael (Shemot 4:22)* – rest on something so subtle? Why should this trait of traitors, so deeply repressed, be more important than an aware and clear-cut philosophical identification in the present? I believe that it is because Creation can be served by nothing less. No philosophy, religion, culture, or achievement can embrace the wholeness of Creation; it is an ongoing saga subsuming all the dynamic change and interplay of factors held within the wholeness of existence itself. There is nothing so changeable as the present, nothing so fickle as love, nothing so malleable as culture, nothing so variable as religiosity – as Avraham himself exclaims:

> *"How can I know that I will have it as an inheritance?"* (15:8)
>
> Avraham said, "Master of the Universe! Perhaps Yisrael will sin before You...How can I know?"
>
> TA'ANIT, 27b

The one who won the *toleda* contest was the *whole man* (25:27), Ya'akov. For there *is* no single missing mystery ingredient that defines Yisrael – it is wholeness itself that defines Yisrael. More than any individual factor, it is the openness to the full dialectical interrelationship of biology, pedigree, tradition, cathexis, history, character, vision, culture, religion, family, past and future that define Creation and must come to define Yisrael, Creation's *First*.

Ya'akov bequeathed Yisrael a psyche tortured by anything less than full integration of the elements of *toleda*-of-Creation. It is this psyche that drives the alienated Jew to *teshuva* or to the forefront of every mad cultural, social, and religious experiment in a never ending search for a lost wholeness. It is this psyche that will not be denied, that punishes with "Jewish guilt" and self-doubt all who ignore her. It is this psyche that accepts no substitute for achievement, that can lead the hopelessly complacent Jew to heroism.

True *toleda* reflects upon basal identity, defining the foundation and essence of a trans-cultural Jewish self, making it possible for a profoundly alienated Yosef Meshitha to rediscover his Jewishness and for a father and son to rediscover each other.[20] *Toleda* defines areas we do not think *about*, but think *with*, such that our deepest subconscious, unchallenged, and unsuspected presuppositions are defined by it – ready to pop into consciousness when conditions demand, no matter how little we may consider ourselves to be in sympathy with our own past, family, culture, or religion. Ya'akov's finest achievement is to be found within the traits of his traitors,[21] driven by their search for life beyond themselves.

How did Yitzḥak see all this? How did he catch a whiff of this traitor's trait in Ya'akov? It was all in the test he had essentially created himself, a test that would confirm the drive to wholeness in the psyche of a potential *toleda*. Incredibly, he detected it in the way that his two children presented their *'delicacies'*.

> Ya'akov spoke to Yitzḥak with consideration and care, *Please arise....* (27:19);
> Eisav spoke with disdain, *My father will rise....* (27:31).
>
> RASHI, 27:22[22]

The difference here, I believe, is the distinction between recognition and gratitude. Eisav gave enormous honor to his father, and would even wait on him wearing only royal attire.[23]

> No one in history honored his father to the extent that Eisav honored his father.
>
> ZOHAR, 1:146b[24]

But this honor was discharge of debt. Eisav developed no love relationship at all with his father, and spoke to him and of him[25] without feeling or care. It was the debt of gratitude that moved him, for nothing is more burdensome than gratitude unpaid. Eisav's approach to his father was similar to his approach to God – "How do I tithe salt," he would ask,[26] believing that tithing is a matter of procuring rights, paying his way, rather than sharing in the achievements of creation.

But Ya'akov spoke softly with love and care. He experienced not debts of gratitude, but *hakarat tova* – "recognition of good." Gratitude asks, "What do I owe?" Recognition asks, "What has become part of my existence?" Where gratitude is oppressive, recognition is liberating. Where gratitude is an attitude, recognition is an awareness. Gratitude is owed only in exchange for a conscious and unselfish act; recognition applies regardless.[27]

Such recognition is profoundly existential, involving an intense awareness of what I have come to be; it speaks of what is inherently mine – my *inheritance*. It is an appreciation of roots and all they imply, far beyond simple personal history and psychology.[28] Such recognition is the root of wholeness, the intuitive insight that to be fully oneself one must be *fully* oneself, incorporating the dreams and the deeds of the past with the hopes and potential of the future, incorporating as much

Distrbute; pay the Lord His tithe...
As you from all and each expect,
For all and each thy love direct,
And render as you reap.

CHRISTOPHER SMART

There are minds so impatient of inferiority that their gratitude is a species of revenge, and they return benefits, not because recompense is a pleasure but because obligation is a pain.

SAMUEL JOHNSON

as possible within a single lifetime the themes of Creation from *the beginning (1:1)* – for Yisrael[29] – to the end.

> To save a single individual of Yisrael is to save an entire universe.
>
> BAVA BATHRA, 11a

Anything less than full recognition, full identity, cannot satisfy the firstborn of a full Creation.[30]

It is the *"whole, simple"* Ya'akov, יעקב איש תם, who thus assures the underlying Jewishness of his most alienated descendants. The Land of Israel is to these distant Jews as real an inheritance as spawning grounds are to salmon. That is the beauty and necessity of the historical irony of secular Zionism – it is the astonishing and profound answer to Avraham's *how can I know – what if my progeny will sin?* The answer is that *it will make no difference*. That same sinning progeny will search endlessly for ways to reach the same achievements no matter how tortuous the path may turn out to be. Meanwhile the Land is served even more than by the parochially or consciously religious.

> *I don't ask for your understanding.... Just for your recognition of me in you....*
> TENNESSEE WILLIAMS, SWEET BIRD OF YOUTH

Let us turn back to the parasha now, and trace the theme of *toleda* in the sections that seem unrelated. *Parashat Toledot* is an achievement of Yitzḥak, for it is his life that most fully expresses the concept of *hakarat tova* recognition, it is his being that demonstrates the self that can exist only in a wholesome and complete context of past and future. This is the powerful theme of the only section that might appear to be irrelevant to the theme of *toleda*: the section describing the famine and Yitzḥak's visit with the Pelishtim (Philistines).

Yitzḥak's activities are synopsized here to reveal a curious pattern: he seems to completely relive the life of his own father, Avraham.

> *And there was a famine in the land–besides the original famine that took place in the days of Avraham...And God appeared to him and said, "Do not go down to Egypt...." (26:1,2)*
>
> He had wanted to go to Egypt just as his father had during the famine. (—Rashi[31])

He then proceeds to go to Avimelech, his father's second choice. There he attempts the same stratagem his father used: he describes his wife as his sister (only Avimelech was smarter the second time around!).

Then

> *Yitzhak went back and re-dug the wells of water which had been dug in the days of his father....*
>
> *And he gave them names as the names that his father had given them.* (26:18)

Afterwards, Avimelech the king and his royal entourage went to Yitzḥak asking for a treaty.

> *We have seen, yes seen – that God is with you....*
>
> We have seen in your father and now have seen in you. (—Rashi[32])
>
> *Let there be an oath between us – let it be between us and you.* (26:28)
>
> The oath which is between us from the days of your father, *let it be between us and you.* (—Rashi[33])

All this takes place in Be'er Sheva, the location of the treaty devised between Avraham and Avimelech before Yitzḥak was even born – a treaty which provides the city's name:

> *Therefore they called the name of the place Be'er Sheva, for that is where they both [Avraham and Avimelech] swore.* (21:31)

But a full lifetime later when Yitzḥak recreates the treaty, we are informed, incredibly,

> *He called it Shiv'a, which is why the city is called Be'er Sheva till this very day.* (26:33)

What you have inherited from your fathers, earn over again for yourselves or it will not be yours.

GOETHE

Yitzḥak's life did continue a family vision, but so independent and fresh was his approach, so inimitably his own were his techniques, that the city could be renamed with the same name and yet the name would be uniquely his own![34] Yitzḥak lived the maxim,

> A person should not deviate from his own vocation or the vocation of his forefathers....
>
> ARACHIN, 16b

Does that sound limiting? It all depends on whether your point of view is Ya'akov's or Eisav's. In *Toledot*, Yitzḥak discovered Ya'akov.

Ya'akov, the *whole man (25:27)*, would never allow life to be a balance sheet. It was in his *hakarat tova* that he formed a whole and wholesome self, orchestrating, conducting and never denying the immensity of his *bechora* inheritance. It was Ya'akov who bequeathed us an exquisite sensitivity to roots and to *yiḥus* (pedigree); Ya'akov who provided us a world-view that could fulfill tradition and custom – and Creation itself – along with the presently manifest. He was a living legacy of *the Beginning*.

I am a living legacy to the leader of the band.
DAN FOGELBERG

The horror Yitzḥak felt at the moment he recognized his own mistaken definition[35] reflected his understanding of how close he had come to devastating the link of true *toleda*. In focusing on the immediate, on affinities, on philosophy, he had been willing to dedicate his own future to one who could hardly wait for him to expire.[36] And he had nearly turned away from one who viewed his own life as a poem to Yitzḥak and his vision.

It has become fashionable to believe that Jewish identity, and certainly "Jewish education," is contemporarily definable. We must remember that each and every one of us serves as a miniature Yitzḥak to our own progeny, disburse similar blessings, and must similarly recognize the nature of Yisrael. If we concentrate only on the details and the elements, on the intellectual, the emotional, the cultural, the immediate, then we may thoughtlessly create arrogant, self-contained, and unwholesome mini-Eisavs whose traitor's traits have been expunged. We may end up cheating our children of the most vital and relevant aspect of their inheritance and identity. We may persuade them that only the separate factors count, not the Ya'akov-like *whole man*. We may be cheating them of the roots called *toledot* – and that might just cost them their survival as Jews, no matter the quality of their nature – or their nurture.

1 Among the more serious (buzzwords notwithstanding) are concerns regarding heredity and culture (*are 'Afro-Americans' part of American tradition and culture? etc.*), ethnicity and diversity (*identifying common 'family values' and standards, etc.*), roots and education (*'Afro-Centrism' as alternative to classical education, 'cultural bias' in testing, 'Latinos' and English instruction, etc.*), cultural chauvinism (*Only DWEMs* [Dead White European Males to the uninitiated] *could "discover" inhabited continents! etc.*), and citizenship (*the status of 'indigenous peoples', etc.*).

2 Op. cit. s.v. *Em,* ד״ה אם יעקב ועשו, however cf. Rome edition and Ramban here. The others are in Rashi, 25:19, s.v. *Avraham,* ד״ה אברהם; Rashi, 25:20, s.v. *Bat,* ד״ה בת.

3 S.v. *Em,* ד״ה אם יעקב ועשו.

4 Cf. Vayikra Rabba, 36:4.

5 Cf. Ramban, 1:1 s.v. Bereishit, ד״ה בראשית.

6 Cf. *Yalkut Shim'oni, Shemot, 187.*

7 Cf. Bereishit Rabba, 1:3; *Tanḥuma Yashan, Bereishit* 11; *Yalkut Shim'oni, Bo,* 187; Ramban, 1:1, s.v. *Bereishit,* ד״ה בראשית.

8 This determination has contemporary significance in establishing whether the children of Yishma'el require circumcision as descendants of Avraham. See *Mishne Torah, Hilchot Melachim,* 10:7.

9 Though he is certainly Avraham's personal "seed." See 21:13.

10 The Rabbis did extend the incest prohibitions to include even such technical non-relatives, but only so that the convert should not begin to discount the holiness of having become a Jew. See Yevamot, 22a.

11 *Mishne Torah, Hilchot Ishut,* 15:6; *Shulḥan Aruch, Even haEzer,* 1:7; Yevamot, 62a; *Minḥat Ḥinuch,* 1:10,13.

12 See *Moreh Nevuchim*, Section I, Chapter 7, for examples of just such use of the word הולדה.

13 Bereishit Rabba, 59:8.

14 See Bava Bathra, 123a for the connection of *toleda* to primogeniture.

15 Both share the attribute of דינא קשיא and Eisav is seen as the full-blown outgrowth of unchecked *Din*. Cf. Zohar here. This explains Yitzḥak's positive view of Eisav's mode of speech (27:22), and questions (in Bereishit Rabba, 63:10).

16 Cf. also Bereishit Rabba, 78:3.

17 25:27; see Rashi and Bereishit Rabba, 63:10.

18 Cf. the suggestions of Stephen Jay Gould, "Nurturing Nature," in *An Urchin in the Storm*, (New York: W.W. Norton, 1987).

19 To Ya'akov: *God will give you of the dew of heaven and the fat of the earth* (27:28). To Eisav: *Behold, your abode shall be of the fat of the earth and of the dew of heaven* (27:39).

20 Cf. *Malachi* 3:25 – the closing words of the Prophets.

21 In one of those odd etymological coincidences that seem to be part of the nature of language as carrier of the subconscious, the word "traitor" shares its roots with "tradition."

22 S.v. *Kol*, ד״ה קול.

23 Pesikta Rabbati, 24:65.

24 Cf. Targum Yonatan, 32:12; also a personal note in Devarim Rabba, 1:15.

25 Verse 27:41.

26 Bereishit Rabba, 63:10; Rashi 25:28.

27 Moshe cannot even smite the sand to which he owed his life. Cf. Shemot 8:12, Rashi; Shemot Rabba, 10:7.

28 The operative alternative to recognition is not gratitude, but denial. Denial that where I come from has significance; denial that my life is only truly mine when I live it in context. Denial brings with it a rootless restlessness that is never satisfied; a commitment to a literal *pursuit* of happiness so that the faster one runs, the farther away the dreams he pursues become. This is the life of Eisav who, instead of gaining broader identity, becomes a *non-nation (Devarim 32:21)*, a non-identity. Cf. Rashi, Devarim 32:21, s.v. *Belo*, ד״ה בלא עם.

29 Vayikra Rabba, 36:1.

30 A beautiful story by Y.L. Peretz encapsulates the inner and simple Yisrael awareness and commitment to creation as a whole:

> The innkeeper's appealing little boy with his jerky movements and his curls, full of feathers, still haunts me. Now he stands before my eyes with a scallion in hand and he wails, he wants another; or I hear him at evening prayer saying the kaddish in such a childlike, plaintively earnest manner that it pierces my very heart. . . .
>
> Hopping on one little foot he stretches his face upward to the moon; he sighs.
>
> Has he seen a star fall?
>
> No.
>
> "Oh," he says. "How I wish the Messiah would come!"
>
> What?
>
> "I want the moon to become bigger already. It's such a pity on her. True, she sinned, but to suffer so much ... we are already living in the sixth millennium."
>
> Altogether two requests: From his father on earth, another scallion, and from his father in heaven, that the moon become bigger.
>
> A wild impulse seized me to tell him, "Enough! Your father, down here, will soon get married again, soon you will have a stepmother, soon you will become a stepchild, and will have to wail for a piece of bread.... Forget about the moon!"

from "Rayze Bilder: a Yingl," trans. Helena Frank, "Travel Pictures: A little Boy" in *Stories and Pictures* (Philadelphia: private, 1906), 256-259.

31 S.v. *Al tered*, ד״ה אל תרד מצרימה.

32 S.v. *Re'oh*, ד״ה ראו ראינו.

33 S.v. *Tehi*, ד״ה תהי נא.

34 In a marvelous short story (that I find myself quoting often in these essays), *Pierre Menard, Author of the Quixote*, Jorge Luis Borges describes an author who completely rewrites *Don Quixote*, word for word as the original. He then proceeds to do a comparative review of the two books, showing how the exact same words have totally different meanings in the contexts of the respective cultures that produced them. Though Menard's deconstructionism is cynical, the application here is not.

35 Bereishit Rabba, 67:1,2; *Tanḥuma*, 11.

36 See 27:41.

VI Toledot
תוֹלְדוֹת

Motherhood

With its opening words, *Toledot* presents itself as the parasha of "Father Yitzḥak": *These are the descendants of Yitzḥak the son of Avraham. . . .* Here Yitzḥak raises his two children, Ya'akov and Eisav, here he becomes independently wealthy, seals a treaty with the Pelishtim, and grows old and blind. But *Toledot* is focused mainly on the cardinal event of Yitzḥak's twilight years: the passing of the torch to Ya'akov. True to its name, *Toledot*, which means 'progeny', formulates the makeup of the spiritual heirs of Yitzḥak. The selection of Ya'akov over Eisav here is a definitive determination of the nature of Yisrael and the course of history.

One individual stands at the center of this saga, and it is not Yitzḥak. It is Mother Rivka who holds the key to the future and turns it Ya'akov's way. *Motherhood* examines the notion of personal and national 'motherhood', the better to appreciate Rivka's pivotal role as mother of her people.

MOTHERHOOD

It is hard to rightly translate "*Toledot.*" It is a complex word that can be roughly rendered "progeny," but the archaic "begotten," connoting something generated as an effect, is closer. We can understand it best as incorporating both literal progeny – biological children, and figurative ones – developments,[1] implications,[2] history,[3] and achievements.[4] The introductory verse, "*These are the* toledot *of Yitzḥak...*" implies then that the topic here is not only Yitzḥak's children, but his entire future.

The spotlight, however, shifts immediately to Rivka. Though the parasha's opening words ostensibly introduce the story of *Yitzḥak's* life, from the outset his wife is presented as the moving force. She stands behind the events of the parasha and the entire life of Yitzḥak, whose real future begins only at this moment, after his marriage to Rivka:

> *These are the* toledot *of Yitzḥak... Yitzḥak was forty years old when he took Rivka... as his wife* (25:19-20).

The parasha continues with the story of Rivka – her infertility and the problems of her eventual pregnancy. But we miss the point entirely if we consider the opening as mere biological background for the *toledot* of Yitzḥak. *Toledot* goes beyond biology – and I believe *that* is the point.

The parasha sets out to demonstrate that the profoundly personal bond implied by "*toledot*" requires a unique relationship between man and woman. Biology generates babies, not *toledot*. The difference is highlighted by a flagrant redundancy in the opening verse:

ואלה תולדות יצחק בן אברהם—אברהם הוליד את יצחק...

> *These are the* toledot *of Yitzḥak the son of Avraham – Avraham begat* [*'hld'* 'ה'ל'ד', *as in 'tldh'* 'ת'ל'ד'ה'] *Yitzḥak.* (25:19)
>
> – Because above [in *Parashat Vayera*] it mentioned *Yishma'el the son of Avraham* (25:12), from his union with Hagar, it was necessary to clarify that Yitzḥak was the *authentic* child of

> Avraham because he was a *toledah*, through his authentic wife (Sara)....
>
> RASHBAM[5]

In this new context of *toledot* it is no coincidence that the marriage of Yitzḥak and Rivka outshines the earlier relationships described in the Torah. Remember how Avraham was delighted to have fathered Yishma'el by Hagar, his concubine? When he was subsequently told that his *wife* Sara would bear him a child, he responded, *If only Yishma'el would live before You (17:18)*. Sara articulated the pain his detachment caused her:

> *It is you I blame for the hurt done me.... (16:5)*
>
> – When you prayed to God [for a child] you prayed only for yourself! You should have pleaded for us *both*, and then I too would have been given a child.... (—Rashi[6])

In marked contrast, Yitzḥak's whole focus in prayer was entirely on his wife.

> *His wife was sterile, and Yitzḥak pleaded with God for her sake.... (25:21)*
>
> – He prayed, "Master of the Universe! Any children that You give me should please come only from this exalted woman!"
>
> BEREISHIT RABBA, 63:5

לנכח אשתו- מלמד שהיה יצחק שטוח כאן והיא שטוחה כאן ואומר: רבש"ע כל בנים שאתה נותן לי יהיו מן הצדקת הזו.

בראשית רבה

What a difference! And the change was triggered by this new cognizance of *toledah*.

The rest of *Toledot* also revolves around Rivka. *She*, and only she, is the one who is informed that the future of civilization will be determined by the two children in her womb.

> *Two nations are in your womb,*
> *Two civilizations will divide from within you....*

And *she* is the one who understands that there can be no compromise solution – one child can develop only at the expense of the other.

> *And the upper hand will go from one civilization[7] to the other.... (25:23)*
>
> – If one is fulfilled, then the other is in ruins....
>
> MEGILLA, 6a

She is the one who recognizes the significance of the different behavior patterns developing in her children, and selects accordingly.

> *The boys grew up. Eisav became a man expert at trapping, a man of the field. Ya'akov was a wholesome and scholarly man. Yitzḥak loved Eisav...but Rivka loved Ya'akov.* (25:27-28)

She is the one who knows how devastating a mistaken selection could prove to be – and she is the one who ensures that Yitzḥak makes no mistake.

> *"Bring it to your father and let him eat, so that he will bless you before he dies."* (27:10)

She is the one who prepares the food for Ya'akov's ruse in receiving the blessings from Yitzḥak.

> *His mother told him, "Let your curse fall upon me – just listen to me and go bring it to me!" He went and took it and brought it to his mother, and she prepared it as his father liked best.* (27:13-14)

She is the one who understands the dangers to Ya'akov.

> *"Now look – Eisav your brother is planning to murder you. Now, my son, listen to me and run away to my brother Lavan...."* (27:42-43)

She sees to it that Yitzḥak sends him away – to *her* family.

> *Rivka said to Yitzḥak, "I am disgusted with life because of those Ḥittite women. If Ya'akov marries such a Ḥittite girl, from the local population, why should I go on living?"* (27:46)
>
> *Yitzḥak sent Ya'akov on his way...to Padan Aram, to Lavan...the brother of Rivka....*(28:5)

And Rivka does not even make Yitzḥak privy to her superior knowledge, because she does not believe that he will act upon it, whereas she sees need for action.

> Apparently, Rivka never informed Yitzḥak of the prophecy that was told her...and she did not want to tell him now because he would...just leave it in God's hands.
>
> RAMBAN, 27:4

The entire future of the nation of Israel was determined here wholly through Rivka, and Yitzḥak proceeded along the course set by her. Rivka became the ultimate *Em* (אם, *matriarch*), the true mother of her country. She is the one who consciously evaluated, conscientiously planned, and autonomously orchestrated the unfolding of history.

But Rivka's centrality goes much deeper than her active interference in the course of events. The most important bifurcation in history – the division between Ya'akov and Eisav that forms the essence of *Toledot* – seems itself to be a consequence of the relationship between Rivka and her children. Ya'akov related to both parents, but Eisav, who fabulously honored his father,[8] totally disregarded his mother, Rivka.

When Rivka expresses her horror at the Canaanite wives of Eisav, *"I am disgusted with life because of those Hittite women,"* it matters not at all to him. But when, many years after his first marriages, his *father's* opinion became clear, Eisav immediately sets out to find a wife from within the family.

> *Eisav saw that Canaanite girls were immoral* in the eyes of his father Yitzḥak. *(28:8)*

Ya'akov, on the other hand, even while responding to his father's direct instructions, takes into consideration his *mother's* feelings:

> *Eisav saw that Yitzḥak had blessed Ya'akov, and sent him to Padan Aram to find a wife...[and that] Ya'akov heeded* his father and mother, *and went to Padan Aram. (28:6,7)*

Everyone was saying: Rivka has two sons, Lavan has two daughters— elder for elder, younger for younger!
RASHI 29:17

Yes, Eisav saw that the only acceptable marriage was to be found in Padan Aram. Nonetheless, he not only disregards his mother's opinion, not only ignores the mental anguish (26:35) that his Ḥittite marriages cause her, but even as he makes an attempt to mollify Yitzḥak with a more suitable marriage he refuses to have anything to do with his mother's brother in Padan Aram (though all and sundry assumed his marriage to Leah to be a forgone conclusion)! Instead, he chooses to marry a daughter of his father's brother:

> *Eisav therefore went to Yishma'el and married Maḥlat, daughter of Avraham's son Yishma'el.... (28:9)*

Eisav's hatred of his mother was legendary.

> Eisav yearned to murder his mother....
>
> TANḤUMA, KI-TEZEI, 10

His hatred was not a *response* to Rivka personally, for it *antedated* his adolescence and even his childhood. It was a loathing that extended beyond Rivka the individual – it was *motherhood* that he hated.

> At birth, Eisav tore out his mother's fallopian tubes.[9]
>
> IBID., 4[10]

> Eisav stood on the road like *an enraged bear (Mishlei 17:12)* to *murder mother and child (Bereishit 32:12).*
>
> PIRKEI RABI ELIEZER, 38

If Caesar had stabbed their mothers, they would have done no less.

JULIUS CAESAR, I,II

Eisav's exploitation of women and abuse of marriage reflected his aberration.

> For forty years Eisav lured married women away from their husbands and raped them....
>
> BEREISHIT RABBA, 65:1

Though his mother repelled him, Eisav was attracted to his father's orientation in life. He modeled himself on Yitzḥak's commitment to independence and autonomy, to finding one's own way.

> Eisav was of the same nature as Yitzḥak.... This is why *Yitzḥak loved Eisav* more than Ya'akov, for likes attract.
>
> ZOHAR, I:137b[11]

Yitzḥak recognized this, and poignantly blamed himself for Eisav's failures.

> *As for you, what can I do – my son! (27:37)*
>
> Why mention "My son"? Yitzḥak was saying in essence: "It is all my fault, because you are indeed my son – I affected you this way...."
>
> ZOHAR, I:145a

Eisav paid his respects to his father, and served him grandly:

> When Eisav would serve his father, he would wear royal garments.
>
> PESIKTA RABBATI, 24:55

> No one in history ever served his father as Eisav did....
>
> ZOHAR, I:146b

But Eisav corrupted his father's dedication to earning his own way. He turned it into a sweeping detestation of commitment to relationship. Motherhood represented to him a crushing dependency which he loathed. He was born *eisav*, which means "fully formed."[12] From the beginning he had no need for the bonding of infancy and childhood – he was free even of the dependency on nursing:

> *They called him 'Eisav'.* (25:25)
>
> Because he was born with full head and facial hair, and incisors and molars.
>
> TARGUM YONATAN, 25:25

His service to his father reflected not love, but duty – *paying* his respects. The *relationship* was non-existent, and he could hardly wait until his father was out of the way:

> *"Soon enough the days to mourn my father will be here – then I will be able to kill my brother, Ya'akov!"* (27:41)

Even in his service, there was no tenderness:

> *"My father shall sit up and eat his son's venison, so that your soul may bless me."* (27:31)
>
> – Eisav spoke harshly. (—Rashi[13])

Contrast his attitude to the care evinced by Ya'akov throughout. Even as Ya'akov presents his deceptive meal to Yitzḥak, he betrays himself through his care!

> *"Please, now, sit up and eat from my meat...."*
>
> *He [Yitzḥak] said, "The voice is the voice of Ya'akov...."* (27:20,22)
>
> For he speaks with tenderness! (—Rashi[14])
>
> Ya'akov is roused [here] to closeness with Yitzḥak, and becomes bonded to him. He attends him, and Yitzḥak eats. They become completely tied to one another...[Yitzḥak] then becomes joyful, and filled with compassion....
>
> ZOHAR, II:100a

What Yitzḥak tastes is the love brought to him by Ya'akov – through the food prepared by Ya'akov's mother, Rivka. At that moment he recognizes his genuine *toledah* – and asserts it, despite the ruse, even in the face of Eisav's desperate protests:

"...*May he indeed be blessed!*" (27:33)

The closeness Ya'akov reached with his father was achieved through his mother – her vision, her planning, her love, and even her cooking. But Eisav, whose entire life was philosophically associated with his father, was incapable of real connection – because he had no relationship with his mother. *Toledah* is defined entirely by the depth of connection to mother.

Yitzḥak was in a unique position to establish *toledot* and appreciate his own connection to his wife Rivka, because he himself was the first real *toledah*. He was the product of the maturation of the relationship between Avraham and Sara.

God said [to Avraham], "But Sara **your wife** *is going to bear you a son whom you shall name 'Yitzḥak'!"* (17:20)

God told him: Avraham! Don't you know that Sara was
meant to be your wife from the moment she was conceived –
she is your friend, the wife of your youth.
Sara is *not* your maid – and Hagar is *not* your wife!

PIRKEI RABI ELIEZER, 29:1

The relationship Yitzḥak had established with *his* mother is what inspired the flourishing of his love of Rivka.

Yitzḥak brought her to the tent, his mother Sara....

He brought her to the tent and found that she was similar to his mother Sara, i.e. she **was** "*his mother Sara.*" (—Rashi[15])

and Yitzḥak was consoled for the loss of his mother. (24:67)

As long as a man's mother is alive, he is attached to her.
When she dies he is comforted in his wife. (—Rashi[16])

When Yitzḥak blesses his son, Ya'akov, he stresses the relationships defined through a mother.

The children of your mother shall bow to you....(27:29)

"Motherhood" here takes on a meaning that extends beyond biology and beyond relationship to child. We speak of mother as source, origin,

As long as Sara was alive
a lamp burned all the week long,
good fortune filled the dough,
and a glow lay over the tent.
When she died, they died with her.
And when Rivka arrived,
they reappeared.

RASHI 24:67

and wellspring: the "mother" of invention. The Hebrew word for mother, *em*, אם, connotes all of that[17] with the additional implication of "essence."[18] The breadth of new possibilities is opened through this sense of "motherhood," intuiting the essence of a thing without being limited to its specific form or its current behavior. "Mother" means acceptance, the ability to see beyond the horrors of a child's corruption, to touch an essence that is still visible to her – still pristine and full of potential. "Mother" means faith, the vision of an essence capable still of perfection, of rebirth.

Even as Rivka speaks of Eisav's murderous intent, even as she warns Ya'akov that he must escape, her heart is torn – equally! – over Eisav who might also be killed in the duel with Ya'akov:

> *Your brother Eisav is planning to kill you...set out and flee....*
> *Why should I lose you* **both** *on the same day!* (27:42-45)

Heard, have you? what? they have told you he never repented his sin.
How do they know it? are they his mother? are you of his kin?...
And if he be lost–but to save my soul, that is all your desire–
Do you think that I care for my soul if my boy be gone to the fire?
I have been with God in the dark–go, go, you may leave me alone–
You have never borne a child–you are just as hard as stone.
TENNYSON

Eisav himself is torn over the relationship with his mother – in his heart he knows that there is no one else in the world he can trust:

> *Rivka took the valuable clothes of Eisav her older son that she had with her in the house....*(27:15)
>
> – He had so many wives but leaves his clothes with his mother?! But he *knew* what his wives were really like....
>
> BEREISHIT RABBA, 65:16

"Mother" implies the ability to see beyond a man's single-minded[19] expression of his own energies and potential. She nurtures his *essence*, enabling it to take new form in future generations. Through her acceptance, husband and child may come to finally accept and appreciate themselves. They can be transformed through her, becoming aware of new possibilities and new relationships.

Rivka is not limited to being the mother of potential in the biological sense. She becomes here nurturer, planner, and executor. Rivka is "mother" in the most primal sense, the ultimate wellspring of selfhood and identity, both personal and national. She is mother earth herself:

> His mother told him, "*Let your curse fall upon me....*"
> She said, "When Adam sinned, was it not his mother who was

> cursed: *Cursed be the* earth *because of you....* (*Bereishit* 3:17)? You, too, if you will be cursed, '*Your curse will fall upon me!*'"
>
> BEREISHIT RABBA, 65:15

Rivka's motherhood defines the essence of everything she touches. Without her, Eisav becomes a parody of his father: Yitzḥak to a fault. With her, Ya'akov becomes most himself – and a nation discovers its own identity. Eisav, who rejects the sensitivity of motherhood, can absorb nothing from the two prodigious personalities with whom he lived.

> Eisav lived between two righteous people, and did not learn from them....
>
> YOMA, 38b

Rivka, the paradigm of motherhood, is capable of absorbing all the valuable essence from the family of Avraham's father where she grew up while seeing beyond their personal perversions and failures.

> *Rivka the daughter of Be'tuel the Aramean of Padan Aram...sister of Lavan the Aramean....*(25:20)
>
> [Her lineage is repeated here] to teach us that though she was the daughter of an evildoer, the sister of an evildoer, and from a city of evildoers, she did not learn from their actions. (—Rashi[20])

Parashat Toledot interprets all relationships through the presence of "*Em*," through new insight into their roots. This is what accounts for a consistent and otherwise unfathomable repetition of relationships that are established and well known:

> *His son, Eisav...* (27:1)
> *Her son, Ya'akov...* (27:6)
> *Eisav, your brother...* (ibid.)
> *Eisav, her older son...* (27:15)
> *Ya'akov, her younger son...* (ibid.)
> *Ya'akov, her son...* (27:17)
> *Ya'akov, my brother...* (27:41)
> *Eisav, her older son...* (27:42)
> *Ya'akov, her younger son...* (ibid.)
> *Be'tuel, your mother's father...* (28:2)
> *Lavan, your mother's brother...* (ibid.)

The most striking repetition of all is so outrageous that the great commentator Rashi throws up his hands in despair. After an entire parasha that speaks in detail about Rivka and her children, the Torah suddenly identifies Rivka again:

> *Rivka – the mother of Ya'akov and Eisav* (28:5)
>
> I do not know what this is meant to teach us. (—Rashi[21])

I find this 'redundancy' the most poignant moment of all. Until the very end, even after Ya'akov has been forced to leave her, alone, brooding over the murderous intentions of her older son, nursing her loss and pain at the breakup of her family, she remains *Rivka – the mother of* both *Ya'akov and Eisav.*

Rivka's ability to bridge polar realities, to harness the drives of two worlds pulling in opposite directions and further creation with a team of contradictions, is the essence expressed in her name: רבקה.

> *rivka*, n. f., a device for harnessing two or more animals together for work in common.
>
> EVEN SHOSHAN, HAMILON HA'IVRI HAMERUCAZ (ESSENTIAL HEBREW DICTIONARY)[22]

One woman – the mother of the furthermost limits, of the contradictory extremes, of civilization's potential. She was the fountainhead, who literally embodied within herself the essence of all our contradictory culture. She teaches the meaning of *Em* as applied to the nation,[22] a full counterpart to all that is achieved by the *Avot*. She teaches the meaning of motherhood.

1 Cf. Mishlei 27:1; Yoma, 54b.

2 E.g. Bava Kama, 2a ff.; Shabbat, 2a ff.

3 See Ibn Ezra and Radak, Bereishit 6:9; cf. Sanhedrin, 38b. Seforno actually translates "*toledot*" *here* as "history."

4 Bereishit Rabba, 30:6.

5 See the analysis by *Kli Yakar* here, and cf. Sa'adia Ga'on.

6 Cf. Bereishit Rabba, 45:5.

7 Cf. Avoda Zara, 2b.

8 "No one in history honored his father to the extent that Eisav honored his father." Zohar, I:146b, and more—see infra.

9 Fascinating that the kings of Edom, leaders of Eisav, would become synonymous with the procedure of tearing through the mother to retrieve the fetus: caesarian section, named for Caesar. Cf. Avoda Zara, 10b, Tosafot s.v. *Kol*, who writes:

> ...one who originally managed to grab control of power was an individual whose mother had died in labor, her stomach was torn open and the child was found alive, eventually becoming king. They called him "Caesar," which means "torn," and all future kings were named "Caesar" after him.

A further curiosity is the Latin etymology of "Caesar": the hairy one. This is precisely the reason that Eisav was given *his* name:

> *The first one emerged reddish, coated with hair and they called his name Eisav* עשו, (25:25) – He was so called because his hair was complete (*eisuy,* עשוי) [at birth] as if he were fully matured. (Rashi s.v. *Vayikre'u*, ד״ה ויקראו).

At certain times in the history of Rome, the position of Ceaser was inherited, such inheritance being determined entirely by father and *filius*. This accounts too for the preference for "*father*land."

10 Cf. also *Midrash Hagadol*, Bereishit 25:22; *Pesikta d'Rabi Kahane,* 3:47.

11 Cf. Bereishit Rabba, 78:3.

12 Rashi and Rashbam, 25:26.

13 27:22, s.v. *Kol Ya'akov*, ד״ה קול יעקב.

14 Ibid.

15 Bereishit Rabba, 60:16.

16 S.v. *Aḥarei*, ד״ה אחרי אמו.

17 In fact, the word "*em,*" אם also used for "uterus," is synonymous with "*mekor*" מקור, meaning both "source" and "wellspring."

18 Pesaḥim, 86b; Succa, 6b; Kritut, 17b, among others.

19 This is the real meaning of *nashim **da'atan** kalot* (Shabbat, 33b; Kiddushin, 80b): a woman's specific attachments are easily broken to see new possibilities.

Da'at דעת becomes unconfined through woman's added בינה, *bina yeteira* (Sotah, 35b, Niddah, 45b): "deeper intuition."

20 Cf. Bereishit Rabba, 63:4; Zohar, I:136b, II:132b, III:378b.

21 Interestingly, these words do not appear in the Rome edition of Rashi.

22 Cf. Pesaḥim, 26a; Gittin, 53a; Bava Metzia, 30a.

23 The word for nation is אומה, *umma,* rooted in *em,* אם.

VII Vayetze
ויצא

Sleeping Beauty

Through the previous parasha we met Ya'akov in his early years as a scholarly "man of tents" who earned Eisav's dangerous enmity in expropriating his birthright and blessing, and who avoided confrontation by fleeing to his mother's family in Padan Aram—there, perhaps, to find a wife among the daughters of Lavan, his mother's brother. *Vayetze* tells the story of a new and radically different phase of Ya'akov's life, beginning with his journey to Aram. Here, the scholar is transformed first into a hardworking shepherd, and finally into a wealthy rancher. Together with his two wives and two maidservants, Ya'akov raises a large and varied family who will be known one day as "*the Children of Yisrael*" (42:5). The unassuming and reserved Ya'akov grows into a formidable competitor to his manipulative uncle, Lavan. As *Vayetze* ends, Ya'akov is on the road again—this time towards his parents and a show-down with Eisav.

The transformation in Ya'akov must not be seen only as a slowly evolving outgrowth of his years with Lavan. Ya'akov arrived in Ḥaran a far more aggressive and robust individual than when he left Be'er Sheva. What catalyzed the dramatic change in Ya'akov—a change that redefines the nature of the nation he builds? The only information we have is embedded in the brief story of the journey to Ḥaran. *Sleeping Beauty* explores those few verses, and discovers a new and beautiful approach to living.

SLEEPING BEAUTY

Vayetze opens as an anxious, unsure and destitute[1] Ya'akov begins his flight from an outraged and threatening Eisav.

> *Ya'akov left from Be'er Sheva....* (28:10)
>
> He said, "What if Eisav faces me down now and accuses me, saying, 'Is this how you deceive me and misappropriate my blessings!' and I end up losing everything...."
>
> BEREISHIT RABBA, 68:7

The parasha concludes twenty years later, as a secure, assured and wealthy Ya'akov returns, able to face that same brother.

> Ya'akov told his messengers: Tell him [Eisav] that he better not accuse me of taking anything at all from home. Every last thing that I have here was purchased with my earnings, of my own power – *I crossed over this Jordan with my walking stick, and now I have grown into two encampments....* (32:11)
>
> BEREISHIT RABBA, 75:11

During the course of building his life in Padan Aram, Ya'akov not only became capable of confronting Eisav – he became capable of confronting the world. The "*simple*" Ya'akov (25:27) managed to fight his way all the way to the top among the world's most sophisticated and cunning businessmen.

> [Ya'akov told Eisav], "*I lived with Lavan*...(32:5) who is the master of deceit – and now I have him in my pocket. You will be no trouble at all!"
>
> BEREISHIT RABBA, 75:5

Two decades can change much in a person's life, so perhaps a metamorphosis such as this should not be so surprising. However, the Torah makes it clear that Ya'akov *arrived* in Ḥaran a changed man, already well prepared for his new life in Aram. He was aggressive and he was tough and he let everyone know it right at the beginning – from the local shepherds down to the girl who would one day become his wife.

He told them [the shepherds], "The day is still young...water those sheep and take them out to graze!"

They said, "We cannot – first all the flocks have to be rounded up, then the [massive] stone is rolled of the mouth of the well and we can water the sheep."

Now, as Ya'akov saw Rachel...and the sheep of Lavan...Ya'akov stepped up and popped[2] *that stone right off the well...and kissed Rachel.* (29:7-11)

The most striking turnabout, though, is in terms of sophistication. Before even meeting Lavan, "innocent"[3] Ya'akov was convinced that he could beat him at his own game.

Ya'akov told Rachel that he was her father's brother....(29:12)

But he was *not* his brother – he was his nephew! What it implies is that when Ya'akov asked Rachel to marry him, she said, "Yes, but it's not going to happen – my father is a cheat!"

Said he to her, "I am his soul-*brother* in deception!"

Rachel asked him, "But is it *permissible* for a righteous man to be a master of deceit?"

MEGILLA, 13b

This is the same Ya'akov whose personality at home was succinctly described as,

Ya'akov was a simple man, a tent dweller. (25:27)

"*Simple,*" implying that he was innocent and naive of all such manipulation – his heart was where his mouth was. Anyone who is guileless and unable to deceive is called "*simple.*" (—Rashi[4])

What accounts for the revolution in Ya'akov's personality?

It is not as if "*Ya'akov* left *Be'er Sheva*" in the sense of "leaving the past behind" completely, ready to take on a new personality the mirror-image of his own. Remember the one other element in his personality profile:

"*A tent dweller*" – This refers to two "tents," i.e. two centers of learning[5] – one run by Shem and one by Eiver.

BEREISHIT RABBA, 63:10

Though he had no choice but to leave his beloved study for the twenty years he spent with Lavan, he certainly did not leave his old self behind. As a matter of fact, after leaving home it took Ya'akov fourteen years to arrive at Ḥaran – because of his love of learning.

> How to account for the fourteen year discrepancy in the age of Ya'akov? He spent fourteen years studying in the house of Eiver while on his way to Lavan. (—Rashi[6])

This makes the sudden transformation of Ya'akov all the more difficult to understand. After all, he spent those fourteen years in yeshiva wholly immersed in Torah, in the atmosphere of dedicated spirituality he loved so much.

> Not once during the fourteen years that Ya'akov learned in the home of Eiver did he ever sleep at night!
>
> BEREISHIT RABBA, 68:11

Yet when he reaches Ḥaran just one day later, he is suddenly prepared to struggle in the fields or in the boardroom, far from his own sustaining environment. The servant of innocence overcomes the master of deceit. His sleepless nights poring over the words of Torah become sleepless nights standing guard in the fields. How?

It happened overnight – literally. The sleepless nights in yeshiva ended with one night of sleep in a very special place that changed Ya'akov forever.

> *He met the place, and stayed the night there because the sun had set… and he lay down to sleep in that place.* (28:11)[7]
>
> "*He lay down to sleep in* that *place,*" but for fourteen years that he spent with Eiver never once did he lie down to sleep.… (—Rashi[8])

So the change in Ya'akov begins with sleep – a night of sleep that is forced on him "*because the sun had set.*"

> It ought to have been phrased "The sun set, and he stayed the night.…" The implication of "*because the sun had set*" is that he was caught by a sudden early sunset brought *in order* that he should sleep there! (—Rashi[9])

For some unfathomable reason it was essential that Ya'akov should sleep – then and there, in "*The* Place," as the location of the future *Beit Mikdash* was known.[10]

> Ya'akov wanted to move on but found the world like a solid wall before him. . . .
>
> BEREISHIT RABBA, 68:10

> Ya'akov finished praying and wanted to continue on his way. Said the Holy One: Is this *tzaddik* going to come to My hotel and leave without staying the night?! At that moment, *the sun set.*
>
> ḤULLIN, 91b

But since when is the *Beit Mikdash* a "hotel"? It is prohibited to even enter the Temple for secular purpose, much less to sleep there! The angels who appear in Ya'akov's dream and find him fast asleep on the holiest spot on earth hardly seem happy.

> *Angels of the Lord were going up and down on it.* (28:12)
>
> – They wanted to harm Ya'akov. . . .
>
> IBID.

Ya'akov himself awakes with a start when he grasps what has happened.

> *"God is truly in this place," he said, "but I did not know!"* (28:16)
>
> – "If I had known, never would I have slept in this holy place!" (—Rashi[11])

Overcome by awe, Ya'akov realizes that this place is the center of man's relationship with God, and upon it one day the *Beit Mikdash* would stand.

> *He was frightened, and said, "How awesome this place is! It is nothing but the very house of God, and this is the gate to heaven!"* (28:17)

Why was it so important to God that Ya'akov *sleep* – completely inadvertently – in this awesome place, if Ya'akov himself understood it to be a sacrilege?

Maybe we ought to ask Ya'akov – because following his evident compunctions and his newfound awe, he does a most incredible thing:

he goes right back to sleep! After he was wakened in the middle of the night by his prophetic vision, the Torah tells us that he awoke again...

> *Ya'akov* woke up early in the morning, *and took the stone that he had placed under his head...saying, "Let this stone that I have set up as a pillar become a temple to God...." (28:18,22)*

Whatever it was that he was to have discovered through his sleep, he apparently learned it well – well enough to have changed his entire appreciation of what a "House of God" means, well enough to see, himself, that it must indeed be a...hotel.

The *Beit Mikdash* whose cornerstone was laid then by Ya'akov, becomes known in the future as "The Resting Place."

> *You have not come yet to the resting.... (Devarim 12:9)*
>
> – This refers to [the Temple in] Yerushalayim, as it says, *God has chosen Zion...."This is My resting place forever...." (Tehillim, 132:13,14).*
>
> ZEVAḤIM, 119a

And every pilgrim who visits that Resting Place on the annual holidays is not allowed to go home *unless he sleeps overnight* in Yerushalayim.

> Just as the holiday of Pesaḥ requires overnighting, so does the holiday of Succot require overnighting...as it says, *You may turn* in the morning *and go back to your tents (Devarim 16:7).*
>
> ROSH HASHANA, 5a

Sleep, then, is somehow the key to the new Ya'akov with his new blessings and new powers. During that one night of sleep, all of the Land of Israel was given to Ya'akov like a gift smuggled beneath the pillow of a sleeping child.

> *The land* upon which you are sleeping – *I will give it to you and to your children. (28:13)*
>
> This teaches that the Holy One folded the entire Land of Israel beneath Ya'akov....
>
> ḤULLIN, 91b

Ya'akov earned here a *boundless* gift that was never achieved by any *Av* before him.

Not like Avraham, to whom God promised only, "*Get up and walk the land* length and breadth, *for I will give it to you.*" *(Bereishit 13:17)*;

Not like Yitzḥak to whom was promised, "*To you and your children I will give all* these *lands. . . .*" *(ibid. 26:3)*;

But Ya'akov was promised here, "*You shall spread out to the west, to the east, to the north, and to the south. . . .*" *(28:14)*.

SHABBAT, 118b

From that night of sleep emerged a new Ya'akov, confident about the future, imbued with new vision, and filled with boundless energy to seize the moment and achieve what he must.

Ya'akov carried his feet. . . .(29:1)

His heart uplifted him and he became light on his feet. (—Rashi[12])

Sleep that knits up the ravelled sleave of care...
Chief nourisher in life's feast.
MACBETH II.2

It was sleep, *sweet* sleep, that gave him the gift of the land, paved the way for the *Beit Mikdash* – and saved him from Eisav and from Lavan.

Then you shall walk your way in safety and your foot shall not stumble: If you will lie down, then you will have no fear – when you lie down, your sleep will be sweet! (Mishlei 3:23,24)

This refers to Ya'akov:

"*Then you shall walk your way in safety,*" as it says, "*Ya'akov left Be'er Sheva.*"

And "*If you will lie down, then you will have no fear,*" of Eisav or of Lavan.

"*When you lie down, your sleep will be sweet,*" as it says of Ya'akov, "*. . .he lay down to sleep in that place.*"

BEREISHIT RABBA, 68:1

בשלום יחדו אשכבה ואישן
כי אתה השם לבדד
לבטח תושיבני.

תהלים ד:ט

Ya'akov learned here to touch upon the most primal cycle of life, a cycle that is mirrored on so many nested levels. Our circadian rhythms of wake\sleep, tied to the diurnal revolution of our planet; the annual cadence of spring\autumn; birth and death – all are linked to the work\rest cycle of Creation itself.

Heaven and earth, and all their components, were completed.
And God completed on the seventh day the work that He had done,
and He rested on the seventh day from all the work that He made.

> *God blessed the seventh day, and made it holy.... (Bereishit 2:1-3)*

"Rest" here is clearly not the absence of work. Rest is a *bona fide* component of Creation – at least as important as anything else that God created. Rest was *created* on the seventh day as an intrinsic and inescapable element of the act of creating:

> *God completed on the seventh day the work that He had done....*
>
> What was still missing [after the six days]? Rest! Came Shabbat, came rest – and with that, the "work" was completed. (—Rashi[13])

Rest is the only reason that the seventh day is holy!

> *Because in six days God made the heaven, the earth, the sea, and all that is in them, and He rested on the seventh day – therefore God blessed the Sabbath day and made it holy. (Shemot 20:11)*

Rest, then, is holy. Ya'akov was the Av who here learned the holiness of rest, the Av who became forever associated with the House of God, His 'resting place'.

> *Many nations shall go and say, "Come – let us go up...to the house of the God of Ya'akov...." (Isaiah 2:3)*[14]

And Ya'akov became the Av whose name was to be linked forever with resting on the Day of Rest:

> *A day of rest and holiness You gave Your nation:*
> *Avraham will revel,*
> *Yitzhak will rejoice,*
> Ya'akov and his sons *shall* rest *in it.*[15]
>
> SHABBAT MINḤA PRAYER

אף ערשנו רעננה, זה בית המקדש,
המד"א ואת מניקתו בחדר המטות...

שיר השירים רבה, א

Sleep itself, the sweet sleep Ya'akov discovered at The Place, is part of the delight and holiness of the Shabbat:

> One should not miss his regular afternoon nap on Shabbat, because it is a Shabbat delight for him.
>
> SHULḤAN ARUCH, ORAḤ ḤAYIM, RAMA, 290:1

For sleep is a primary expression of holiness.

Holiness is a function of special connection, of meaningful relationship. The holiness in creation derives from the day God rests – because there is a *deeper* relationship between Creator and creation on that day. If rest were only cessation and withdrawal, then God would be *less* present on that day. But rest, and especially sleep itself, imply an openness to relationship that no longer needs creating, working on, or performing. When people *literally* "sleep together" they engage not in a euphemism, but in a vitally important aspect of intimacy – an intimacy deeper in many ways than carnal attachment.

When we lay down our heads to sleep, we never sleep alone. The "sweetness" of sleep is its security, the acceptance of not needing to create, of not needing to do more now in life. It is the trust implicit in slipping away into the arms of mother earth, and if we are more fortunate, into the arms of the Shechina[16] herself: *"when you lie down, your sleep will be sweet."*

When God "rested" on Shabbat, He opened His arms to Creation and transformed the universe from a monument into a lover. Ya'akov and his children, the nation of Yisrael, are the ones who express that loving:

> Shabbat came before the Holy One and said: Master of the Universe! To all You gave a companion, but I have no companion!
>
> Said the Holy One to her: Yisrael is meant to be your mate. . . .[17]
>
> BEREISHIT RABBA, 11:8

When Ya'akov slept at The Place, he did not sleep alone. No sleep was ever sweeter, because no sleep ever so deeply touched the inmost realm of belonging. Ya'akov discovered that creation was meant to be the profound source of contact with God. This is why we learn a special lesson from the primal sleep of Ya'akov at The Place: how human beings must sleep when they are meant to be together.

> *"He met the place,"* implies that he touched it first, sensitively. It is not right for a bridegroom to come to the bride unless he first speaks to her softly, and only then does he *"stay the night."*
>
> And why *"because the sun had set – כי בא השמש"*? Read it not as *ki va* (כי בא) but *kiva* (כיבה)– that is, He "extinguished" the sun. From here we learn that one who is to be alone with his wife

> at night must extinguish the lights. Only then did Ya'akov *"lay down to sleep in that place."*
>
> ZOHAR, III:225b

For that Place was to be forever the intimate "bedroom" of Creation.

> *You, my beloved, are beautiful...and our bed is fresh. (Shir haShirim 1:16)*
>
> The *Mishkan* (Tabernacle) is called a 'bed' – as in, *Behold the bed of Shelomo (ibid. 3:7)*;
>
> The *Mikdash* (Temple) is also called a 'bed' – as it says regarding Yoash, *In the bedroom...within the House of God (Divrei haYamim II, 22:11,12)*. (—Rashi[18])

When Ya'akov slept at that Place, he became *"light on his feet,"* suffused with the meaning that he could now find in creation, with the fulfillment he could now find in the simplest of work. What had once appeared to him as estranged and hopelessly distant, became part of the journey home. He saw the universe as a vast hotel, providing a place for each individual and each moment, expanding out from *The* Place – the ultimate and most intimate hotel, the inmost Resting Place.

Just as the sleep of Shabbat empowers and justifies the *six days shall you work and perform all your own creativity (Shemot 20:9)*, sleep made it possible for Ya'akov to throw his heart and soul into every moment of life.

> *The worker's sleep is sweet....(Kohelet 5:11)*

That single sleep allowed Ya'akov to regard his two decades with Lavan as a long day full of creativity and life – far from sleep!

> *He slept in that place....*
>
> In *that* place he slept, but for the next twenty years with Lavan he did not sleep.[19]
>
> MIDRASH TEHILLIM, 124:1

From this moment on, Ya'akov's mental states could be expressed instantly in pure physicality. Joy and love became empowering, and his body responded to them just as his feet had carried him away to Ḥaran.

> *Now, as Ya'akov saw Rachel...Ya'akov stepped up and popped[20] that stone right off the well....*

For the sake of the man who focused his heart,
And popped the stone from upon the well….

PRAYER FOR RAIN, SIDDUR

The world, too, responded to Ya'akov. Even the stones that he set around his head desired to be close to him, wanted to *sleep with him*!

[First] It says, *He took* some stones *from the place*…. (28:11).
But then it says, *He took* the stone *which he had set around his head*…. (28:18)?
This teaches us that all the stones came to one place, and each one argued, "Let the *tzaddik* rest his head on *me*!" We are taught that they all were fused into one.

HULLIN, 91b

כתיב, ויקח מאבני המקום.
וכתיב, ויקח את האבן!
אמר רבי יצחק, מלמד
שנתקבצו כל אותן אבנים
למקום אחד, וכל אחת ואחת
אומרת, עלי יניח צדיק זה ראשו.
תנא, וכולן נבלעו באחד.

חולין, צא

This profound responsiveness is the deep-seated significance of the parasha's title, *Vayetze*.

Vayetze – Ya'akov left *Be'er Sheva*….

It would have been sufficient to tell us where Ya'akov was *going* – why was it necessary to tell us from where he *left*: why "*vayetze*"?
To teach us that when a *tzaddik* leaves a place, it *affects* the place.

As long as the *tzaddik* is in a city, he is its glory, he is its radiance, he is its beauty.
When he leaves – gone is its glory, gone is its radiance, gone is its beauty. (—Rashi[21])

This beauty is the hallmark of Ya'akov, the *Av* of *Tiferet* (beauty).[22] It is in Ya'akov that beauty and attraction are seen to be related at their source – in holiness. Reflections of such *tiferet* as Ya'akov can be glimpsed for fleeting moments as we peer into the heart of galaxies or into the structure of cells, as we feel the pounding of the surf, or watch – as Ya'akov did – the setting sun. We are brought face to face with the immanence of all Creation in every detail, and we catch our breath in knowing that we are meant to be attached to *it all*. The *Beit Mikdash* is called "the Beautiful,"[23] Shabbat is called "the Beautiful."

He wrapped the Day of Rest in Beauty….

SHABBAT PIYYUT, SIDDUR

The Beauty of greatness and crown of deliverance,
A day of rest and of holiness You gave Your people....

SHABBAT MINCHA PRAYER, SIDDUR

A crown of Beauty on his head You set....

SHABBAT MORNING PRAYER, SIDDUR

The deepest connection to life lies in the holiness granted by such beauty. In Ya'akov's sleep we find the most intense relationship, inconceivable to the ministering angels themselves.

Angels of the Lord were going up and down....

They would go up and find Ya'akov's picture (on the heavenly throne), and then come down and see his image! They wanted to hurt him. At that point,

Suddenly he saw God standing over him (28:13).

If the verse had not written it, we would have found it inconceivable: It implies that God stood as a father stands fanning his sleeping child!

ḤULLIN, 91b

This is the relationship available to those of Ya'akov's children who come to love Shabbat sleep, who come to understand with Whom they find rest:

A Rest of love and devotion,
A Rest of truth and faithfulness,
A Rest of peace and calm and silence and trust,
A Rest of wholeness, the kind that You want –
May Your children come to be aware and know,
That it is from You that they find rest,
And in their rest they will sanctify Your Name.

SHABBAT MINḤA PRAYER, SIDDUR

מנוחת אהבה ונדבה,
מנוחת אמת ואמונה,
מנוחת שלום ושלוה והשקט ובטחה,
מנוחה שלמה שאתה רוצה בה....

תפילת מנחה לשבת

This is the sleep that is meant for the true lovers for whom all Creation was dreamed:

So will He grant to his beloved, sleep! *(Tehillim, 127:2)*

1 Bereishit 32:11 and Bereishit Rabba, 70:12; Rashi 29:11.

2 Bereishit Rabba, 70:12; Rashi 29:10.

3 Rashi, 25:27.

4 S.v. *Tam,* ד״ה תם.

5 In English, as well, 'to dwell' can mean 'to contemplate' as in 'to dwell upon'. "Tents" in Hebrew connotes learning; see an early occurrence in Shemot 33:7-11.

6 Bereishit 28:9, s.v *Aḥot,* ד״ה אחות; cf. Megilla, 17a.

7 Cf. Sa'adiah Ga'on on שכב, *shachav,* 28:13.

8 S.v. *Vayishkav,* ד״ה וישכב.

9 S.v. *Ki,* ד״ה כי בא.

10 Bereishit 22:4. Cf. Ḥullin, 91b, and Rashi 28:11, s.v. *Vayifga,* ד״ה ויפגע.

11 S.v. *Va'anochi,* ד״ה ואנוכי.

12 S.v. *Vayisa Ya'akov,* ד״ה וישא יעקב רגליו.

13 S.v. *Vaychal,* ד״ה ויכל.

14 Cf. Pesaḥim, 88a.

15 Cf. also Shabbat, 118a-b.

16 Zohar, I:122 and Zohar Ḥadash, Bereishit, 23b. See also Berachot, 5a regarding Tehillim 31:6.

17 From here comes the dictum, "A gentile who keeps Shabbat is liable...." Sanhedrin, 58b. He invades the intimate relationship of Shabbat and Yisrael.

18 S.v. *Af,* ד״ה אף ערשנו. Cf. Shir haShirim Rabba, I:68.

19 So Ya'akov tells Lavan: *Sleep was snatched from my eyes—twenty years now I have worked for you.... (31:40,41).*

20 See note 2.

21 Cf. Bereishit Rabba, 68:6.

22 Cf. Divrei haYamim I, 29:11; Zohar, I:172a, II:276a, III:302a.

23 Succa, 51b; Mo'ed Kattan, 26a and many more.

VII Vayetze
ויצא
The Business of Faith

In *Vayetze,* the focus of the Torah turns to Ya'akov and his escape from Eisav to his mother's family in Ḥaran. Here Ya'akov undergoes the challenges and changes that will transform him into Yisrael, the father of a nation. Ya'akov, the *"ish tam,"* ingenuous man, must now learn to deal with a tough and deceitful business world, the world of Lavan, "master of duplicity." It is here that Ya'akov must display the faithfulness that is to be his hallmark. Instead, Ya'akov seems to show incongruous facets of both integrity and deceit in his business dealings, whether with Eisav or with Lavan.

The Business of Faith explores the relationship of faith and business, and finds in Ya'akov and his apparent contradictions the paradigm for Jewish dealings with the "real world."

THE BUSINESS OF FAITH

The Roaring Eighties of L.B.O.'s and fast-buck artists left a legacy of pain that lingers on. That decade bequeathed a crisis of faith in business-as-usual and the "me-generation" ethic, with far-reaching effects on nearly all the players in the global economy. In the political fallout the mighty were dethroned, and scandal penetrated the *sanctum sanctorum* of the business and banking worlds. The breakdown of the work ethic and of personal integrity finally caught up with us and it is no secret that Jewish names are prominent among the former high-fliers. We can continue to boycott the hapless dictionaries that dare define "Jew" as a verb,[1] but that won't change the track record behind the etymology.

In a way, the Jewish connection is hard to understand because the Torah tradition is suffused with concern for scrupulous honesty. *Parashat Vayetze* centers on business integrity and speaks highly of the work ethic:

> Labor is more precious than the merit of the forefathers.
> Merit safeguarded only money, as [Ya'akov told Lavan:] *"Were it not that the God of my father, the God of Avraham...were with me, you would have sent me away empty handed."*
> But labor protected life itself: *"God saw my travail and my labor, and reproved you last night!"* (31:42)
>
> BEREISHIT RABBA, 74:12

Ya'akov, the model of this midrash, was a victim – he needed to work seven additional years only because of Lavan's fraud. Nonetheless, he meticulously utilized every minute of his time and assumed full responsibility for any reverses.

> *Twenty years I've been with you now...I never brought to you anything clawed by a beast – I bore the loss myself, you always took it from my account, whether something was stolen by day or by night. There I was, exhausted by heat in the day, frozen at night, never able*

to sleep...though you changed our arrangements ten times over! (31:38-40)

Ya'akov was introduced in the previous parasha as the "*ish tam,*" the unaffected man "whose mouth was where his heart was,"[3] and his behavior here appears consistent with that sketch.

> You would expect a laborer to work for two or three hours with integrity and then start to get lazy. But here [with Ya'akov], just as the first years were wholehearted, so were the second [set of seven swindled] years wholehearted; just as the first years were served with integrity, so were the second seven served with integrity, as it says, *also to Rachel and loved also Rachel....* (29:30).
>
> BEREISHIT RABBA, 70:20

to Jew: verb colloquial, to cheat or overreach, in the way attributed to Jewish traders or usurers.
OXFORD ENGLISH DICTIONARY[2]

But there is a rather ironic twist to all this, of course: Ya'akov *Avinu* also appears to be quite a con man himself – maybe the original source of that dictionary *jew*! After all, the only reason he needed to hide in Lavan's home in the first place is because he defrauded Eisav of the *berachot*. The name "Ya'akov" (יעקב) actually *means* "cheating,"[4] (עקבה). *Ḥizkuni*[5] even suggests that Lavan made no overtures or agreements during the first month[6] because of Ya'akov's bad reputation – Lavan wanted to check him out first. Ya'akov appears to indict himself in his first meeting with Rachel:

> *And Ya'akov told Rachel that he was her father's* brother.... (39:12)
>
> But he was *not* a brother, he was a nephew! What it means is that when Ya'akov asked Rachel to marry him, she said, "Yes, but it won't happen – my father is a cheat."
>
> Said he to her, "I am his soul-*brother* in cheating!"
>
> MEGILLA, 13b

It is all too easy to relate to the contemporary tone of Eisav's comments on the *ish tam*, principled image of Ya'akov:

> "Come and see what Mr Innocent has done to *me*!"
>
> DEVARIM RABBA, 1:14

Yitzḥak himself characterized Ya'akov's behavior toward Eisav as *cunning*[7] – hardly what you would expect of the simplicity of an *ish tam*. Not to mention that by the end of the parasha Ya'akov indeed walks away with Lavan's riches and daughters – just as he promised Rachel.

We can afford no ambiguity in this issue because business integrity is not *a* moral issue, it is *the* moral issue – at least in the Torah. Whereas "faith" in Christianity refers to belief in God, in the Torah "faith," *emunah*, refers specifically to faithfulness in business:

> *And the faith of your moments* (אמונת עתיך)... *(Isaiah 33:6)*
>
> This refers to the six questions a person is asked when he stands before the heavenly court. The first is *faith*: Did you conduct business faithfully?
>
> SHABBAT, 31a

> Stealing an employer's time is no different than embezzlement, even to use the time for doing a mitzvah... [such a] mitzvah becomes a travesty, for God is interested only in *emunah*, faith, as it says, *God watches over the faithful (Tehillim 31:26)*, and *My eyes are on the faithful of the land (ibid. 101:6)*, and *Your eyes look to faith... (Yermiah 5:3)*.
>
> MESILAT YESHARIM[8]

Each and every one of those verses would be read by the church as a reference to faith in God. To the Jew, each refers to business integrity.

The Talmud traces the destruction of Jerusalem to a breakdown in faith – but what kind of faith?

> Yerushalayim was only destroyed when there were no men of faith left, as it says, *Search the streets of Jerusalem, see now and know, seek throughout her boulevards, if you can find one...seeking faith – I will forgive her (Yermiah 5:1)*.
> But do we not have a tradition that even in the breakdown of Yerushalayim there were always men of faith within her?... Indeed we do! But those were faithful in terms of Torah. What was missing was a man of faith in business!
>
> SHABBAT, 119b

All of the *mitzvot* stand on this one issue, as the Talmud tells us:

> Ḥabakkuk came and stood all the *mitzvot* on one:
>
> וצדיק באמונתו יחיה
>
> *The righteous will live by his own faith (Ḥabakkuk 2:4)*.
>
> MAKKOT, 24a

If *emunah* is the root of all *mitzvot*, then it must be fundamentally involved in the nature of Creation. Indeed, God Himself lives by faith.

The righteous will live by his own faith. (Ḥabakkuk 2:4)

Even the Eternal Righteous One above lives by His own faithfulness....

KOHELET RABBA, 3:12

All His works are achieved and vindicated by faithfulness:

With *Emunah*, I created the universe,
With *Emunah*, I guide the universe,
With *Emunah*, I will renew the universe!

OTIYOT D'RABI AKIVA, CHAPTER 26

Earnest as it sounds, it might be difficult in light of our own experiences to accept all this as more than old fashioned moralistic homiletics. We have become used to Western concepts of faith – mostly dogma oriented – stressing belief in the irrational. After all, if integrity were truly the *sine qua non* of Creation, how could Jews who are otherwise highly religious be lax about the core issue? Does not the ambiguous behavior of Ya'akov, father of the nation Yisrael, seem to imply that there is at least some room for winking at duplicity?

Let us make no mistake about it: the Torah considers Ya'akov to be *the* paradigm of truthfulness. As an *Av*, literally "prototype," he is allowed one and only one characteristic.[9] That characteristic is Truth – as expressed in the Jewish sense of faith:

זכר חסדו ואמונתו לבית ישראל

He has remembered His love and faith towards the house of Yisrael.... (Tehillim 98:3)

His love refers to Avraham;
His faith refers to Ya'akov, as is written,
Give Truth to Ya'akov,
Love to Avraham.... (Micha 7:20).

BEREISHIT RABBA, 73:2

But just how could Ya'akov represent Truth itself? What are we to make of his deceit when dealing with Eisav and Yitzḥak, his dubious requisitioning of Lavan's sheep? There must be an underlying consistency that explains how this individual who was a legend of reliability and conscientiousness could simultaneously engage in such dealings.

To find a clue, let us eavesdrop on the rest of that conversation between Ya'akov and Rachel:

> Rachel said to him, "But is it permissible for *tzaddikim* to be expert at deception?"
>
> "Absolutely," he answered, "for it says, *With the pure You act purely, and with the perverse You are subtle (Tehillim 18:26).*"
>
> MEGILLA, 13b

Consider for a moment the implications of this incredible interchange. Ya'akov has spent his entire life in Yeshiva.[10] He is about to meet the "Master of all cheats"[11] who has spent his life eating innocents alive. How does he have the temerity to suggest that he, with all his naïveté as *ish tam*, that he has what it takes to outthink and outmaneuver the Master? Surely there is a trick or two that he might not have picked up in his vast experience?

There is only one possible answer. Ya'akov never outthought or outmaneuvered anyone. As Truth, he simply mirrored them. He responded to them as *they* wanted to be. *With the pure You act purely, and with the perverse You are subtle.* Ya'akov won by *not* manipulating – he was a mental judoist who guided his opponent's energies, but never insinuated himself. His "business opportunities" were presented by others to whom he responded with perfect Truth: face yourself – this is what you were saying, here is what you wanted.

> Eisav was "utterly tired of it all."[12] He wanted the freedom to live this life fully, without the burden of morality. Ya'akov gave it to him.
>
> Yitzḥak wanted the chance to give the blessings to one with the care of Ya'akov and the capabilities of Eisav.[13] Ya'akov gave it to him.
>
> Lavan was looking for an opening to get away without paying Ya'akov a salary, to have him make his living from the genetic detritus of Lavan's flocks. Ya'akov gave it to him.

The Men of the Mark do not lie, and therefore they are not easily deceived.

J.R.R. TOLKIEN

Only the totally "simple," the uncomplicated and straightforward *ish tam,* can be totally aware of what the other desires, can be totally truthful and totally unmanipulative. The complex often see what they want to see and hear what they want to hear, thinking of ways to change a situation instead of dealing with it; the uncomplicated see and respond to things as they are. There is no greater or more fair advantage in business than the complete knowledge and full concern for the heart and mind of one's rival. The man limited by a definite agenda, a burning need and a closed mind has already lost – he cannot negotiate. Success requires understanding the man on the other side of the table better than he understands himself, and such subtlety is the fruit of a simple integrity. Ya'akov enjoyed that fruit by responding instantly as every opportunity was presented, often by others seeking their own advantage but betraying themselves – *with the pure, pure; with the perverse, subtle.*

But if you look for truthfullness,
You might as well be blind...
Honesty is such a lonely word.
BILLY JOEL

Integrity, Faith, and Truth do not imply the directness, frankness, or candor of "honesty." A parochial and naive frankness can devastate a transcendent truth. God Himself is dishonest,[14] though He is utterly Truthful.[15] Integrity and Faith, rather, connote the consistent assertion of an inclusive vision, a truth unswayed by convenience or mere opinion, responsive to reality as it is, not as it is wished to be. Integrity, from the Latin *integrare* meaning "whole," is defined[16] as "wholeness," "entireness," "completeness" – exactly what the *ish tam* and the *shalem,*[17] the "wholesomeness," of Ya'akov imply. This is precisely the way he lived, at enormous personal cost. There is nothing surreptitious or furtive about him, and what you see is what you get. But what you see is what you want to see, a mirror of your own desires.

> Eisav demanded, "What's the bottom line – what did Ya'akov feed you?"
> Answered Yitzḥak, "I don't really know...I was able to taste in it anything I wanted – bread, meat, fish.... "
>
> BEREISHIT RABBA, 67:2

There seems to be a dilemma here: if Ya'akov mirrors the inner desires of the other, then he will always be vilified by those who live in denial and delusion. But certainly an archetype must *project* his own fundamental characteristic – it is essential that all should be able to *perceive* his integrity. Even if we can justify Ya'akov's behavior, are appearances not of the essence for an *Av*? It is on the horns of this dilemma that Ya'akov's life becomes a metaphor for the struggle of the Jewish people throughout history and exile.

As long as society lives in illusion, Ya'akov and his Truth must be perceived as lies – how else may self-deception be maintained but through denial? This is why Ya'akov was forced to live with faithfulness in a counterfeit society, to be himself whatever the cost, until he could exact recognition of his own truth. To grow into Yisrael, Ya'akov needed to project his inner faithfulness as Truth and to project his vision as undeniable reality.

> *Your name shall no longer be called Ya'akov* יעקב *– Yisrael shall be your name, for you have struggled with god and man and have prevailed. (Bereishit 32:29)*
>
> That is, it will no longer be said that you took those *berachot* using deception and trickery (*'akov* – עקב), but rather openly.... (—Rashi[18])

Ya'akov led his life surrounded by misleading appearances and veneers, and won his way conscientiously within a world of duplicity, living with the master of deceit in a land of deception:

> Her father was a cheat, her brother a cheat, and the entire country was deceitful.
>
> BEREISHIT RABBA, 63:4

The usual trade and commerce is cheating all round by mutual consent.

THOMAS FULLER

Lavan's artifice coated his final confrontation with Ya'akov in delicious irony. The one time Ya'akov was in the *wrong* – albeit mistakenly – was the only time that Lavan was finally satisfied that he was in the right![19] But Ya'akov survived decades living with Lavan without compromising himself. Such was the message that Ya'akov sent to his brother Eisav:

> *I have been living* (גרתי) *with Lavan.... (Bereishit 32:5)*
>
> And I have kept the 613 (תריג) mitzvot. (—Rashi[20])

There is no way to hurry this process. Ya'akov's entire tenure in Ḥaran was necessary only that he be able to face his brother such that Eisav himself would see the truth and accept the sale of the *bechora*. It took Ya'akov twenty-two years to earn the name Yisrael, twenty-two years until Eisav would say, *"My brother, let what is yours be yours!"*[21]

Yet even then "Yisrael" was not fully his and he remained still, "Ya'akov." As long as the state of Yisrael is not fully perceived, it is not fully achieved, and Ya'akov's name throughout history oscillates between

"Ya'akov" and "Yisrael." The people of Yisrael, too, live with the same oscillations, and traverse the same worlds of deception. For the genuine assay, significance, and achievement of *emunah* cannot take place within a withdrawn, internal world, never to be tested and never to affect reality. The substantiation of a belief, of a vision of reality, lies in its practical consequence. Ya'akov had to live in the world of pretense and yet treat everything as if it were real because *emunah* ultimately would *make* it real, just as Ya'akov and his people *will* at last become Yisrael within that same counterfeit world.

There is no way to rush history, no way to exact recognition except through consistency amidst the force of events. This is why Ya'akov was willing to take the back-seat of history[22] for millennia. The only way to earn recognition as Yisrael is through the development of a civilization which fully reflects *emunah*. The vindication of Creation and of the faith of a Jew comes only through engaging, testing, and struggling in the contest implied by the very name Yisrael:

> *Your name shall no longer be called Ya'akov – Yisrael shall be your name, for you have struggled with God and man and have prevailed. (Bereishit 32:29)*

"It will no longer be said that you took those *berachot* using deception and trickery (*'akov*), but rather openly, through real contest (*sirara*)." And in winning that contest, your "faith" comes to define reality. Faithfulness has proven profoundly successful despite its rarity – or maybe because of it.

Being in business is not about making money. It is a way to become who you are.
PAUL HAWKEN, GROWING A BUSINESS

Emunah defines the way an individual's interconnectedness with his society and the world around him enlightens and refines. This explains why the word for "craftsman," אומן (*oman*), has the same root as *emunah*. They both imply a deep connection that lies behind excellence whether it be a way of relating to the strings on the violin or the grain of the sculptor's wood or the gears in the mechanism that makes them – and ourselves – sing and create together. God needs to have a similar *emunah* in Creation so that He and it can create together:

> *The God of Faith... (Devarim 32:4)*
>
> He had faith in the world and created it.
>
> SIFREI, HA'AZINU, 306

The vindication of this relationship is a process that has stretched over millennia and is still incomplete. There have been many changes and incredible growth, even unto contemporary developments in national concerns and morality undreamed of in the past.

Yet many loyal descendants of Ya'akov have come to believe that the "real world" is an utter contradiction to their own faith. They feel that they must either withdraw or succumb. They are convinced that within the world of business they face either loss of integrity or loss of money, and so surrender their vision and faith as they enter the office. But this is the same world of facade that Ya'akov punctured long ago, in which corruption cannot win over the long term and faith cannot lose over the long term.

The mistake of those Jews who leave their faithfulness behind when they come to Wall Street is their refusal to believe that the world seeped in deception is the one that tests and establishes Truth, the world of Yisrael's struggle. It's all a dog-eat-dog farce anyway, they say, so what does it matter how I behave? They are dichotomized, therefore they run no contest, bring no faith, instill no *emunah* in their dealings. But there can be no escape for the Jew, neither through withdrawal nor through splitting life into separate niches. Ultimately, that is why they lost.

The disillusionment handed down by the 1980's is just another step towards the discovery of the Jewish "real world." The real world to the Jew is the world of faithfulness and integrity functioning within a milieu that seems to require swindling and deception in order to succeed. "They will eat you alive out there, Ya'akov!" But he *won,* because a single individual with belief is more powerful than a society of those who have only delusion.

This above all: to thine own self be true,
And it must follow, as the night the day,
Thou canst not then be false to any man.

HAMLET, I, iii

The life of Ya'akov – and the life of every Jew – is a process of continually growing into Yisrael. Business is the most important vehicle of the relationship of *emunah* to life and its creativity, providing the means of interconnection of every member and need of society. Business is the ultimate experiment, critique and evaluation of vision, and that is why it is the fundamental measure of the integrity of each individual's selfhood and relationships. In a society built on *emunah*, business would be a true "bottom line" of societal responsiveness to vision. Every business is a vision of society and its needs, its future and its interconnections. In a society built on *emunah*, business would be a true "bottom line" of societal responsiveness to vision. There would be no illusive junk-bonds, no leveraged-buyout-pillaging of enterprises built over generations, no insider manipulations.

Such is the true business of faith and such is the true faith of business.

1 I refer to the recent outcry regarding putative anti-Semitism in the guise of dictionary definitions. The Webster's New World Dictionary (1959) defines, v.t. *jew,* to get the better of in bargaining, as by sharp practices. . . . Not bad, but consider the quote from the OED in the margin of page 174.

2 1971 edition.

3 Rashi 25:27, s.v. *Tam*, ד"ה תם.

4 Cf. Zohar, I:138a; Rashi, Bereishit 35:10.

5 Cf. *Ḥizkuni* 29:14.

6 Bereishit 29:14.

7 See Bereishit 27:35.

8 Rabbi Moshe Ḥaim Luzzato, *Mesilat Yesharim*, Chapter 11.

9 See essay on III *Lech-Lecha, Avraham and the Superconducting Super Collider.*

10 Megilla, 17a, Bereishit Rabba, 68:11; Rashi, Bereishit 28:9,11.

11 Bereishit Rabba, 75:5.

12 Cf. Bereishit 25:30.

13 Cf. Bereishit 27:22.

14 Yevamot, 65b; Bereishit 18:3.

15 Shabbat, 55a, Yoma, 69b.

16 Oxford English Dictionary, 1971.

17 Bereishit 33:18.

18 S.v. *Lo Ya'akov,* ד"ה לא יעקב.

19 Ya'akov's entourage had indeed stolen Lavan's totems, but Lavan never found them in his extensive search of Ya'akov's premises. See 31:19-43.

20 S.v. *Garti*, ד"ה גרתי.

21 Bereishit 33:9. See Bereishit Rabba, 78:11: Here Eisav agreed to the transfer of the blessings. Cf. Rashi loc. cit.

22 Cf. Bereishit 33:14; Devarim Rabba, 1-17; Avoda Zara, 8b; Zohar, I:172a.

VIII Vayishlaḥ

וישלח

Instant Gratification and the Pursuit of Happiness

In *Vayishlaḥ,* Ya'akov returns at last from the harshness of Padan Aram to Cana'an, settling in Shechem. But his troubled life continues: he faces a mysterious attacker; confronts the antipathy of his brother, Eisav; suffers the tragedy of the rape of his daughter, Dina; and mourns the death of his beloved wife, Rachel. Though Ya'akov does succeed in defeating Eisav's "guardian angel" and in securing his brother's forgiveness, the subtle and complex negotiations that conclude with Eisav's departure from the Land of Cana'an also concede a disastrous historical ascendancy to the civilization of Edom: Yisrael must accept a millennia-long postponement of its own fruition and triumph.

But these painful terms were not quite as coercive as one might believe. *Instant Gratification and the Pursuit of Happiness* finds in this "delay clause" of the Ya'akov-Eisav understanding a strangely thematic and definitive element central to the delineation of the issues that divide Yisrael and the West.

INSTANT GRATIFICATION AND THE PURSUIT OF HAPPINESS

It's Bill Gates yet again on the magazine cover – just another sign that the electronic cornucopia is at hand, soon to satisfy the primitive longing to have everything magically available at the flick of a laser wand. Food will be running *Windows*. Microwave meal containers already have plastic strips that turn blue when the food is hot, and we are promised better: strips that directly transmit cooking instructions to the oven, relieving any remaining necessity for thought. But fast food is more than a mere convenience, for these kinds of choices and rituals help shape and control daily life and human relationships.[1]

As a critical enactment of a scale of values and preferences, fast food is actually a powerful metaphor for a hallmark of modern Western civilization: infantile desire for instant gratification. We now have fast-food books, fast-food schools, fast-food news, and even fast-food Torah – all dishing out barely passable nourishment. Each day brings another bland, mediocre, but easy-to-digest product to satisfy the need for no-pain and no-exertion nourishment, entertainment, spirituality, and life itself.

Such is not the way of Yisrael, as Ya'akov *Avinu* compellingly illustrates. *Parashat Vayishlaḥ* describes Ya'akov's astounding acceptance of history's most delayed gratification. Despite his victory in a superhuman struggle with a mysterious angel,[2] Ya'akov chooses to appease his brother with a gift: the stage and spotlight of human civilization until the closing act of history.

> Eisav told Ya'akov, *Let us travel on, and I will walk as your counterpart.* (33:12)
> –Ya'akov, my brother! Let us walk together in this world as partners.

Ya'akov answered him, *Let my master pass on ahead.*
–You take the world first – *until I come to my master to Se'ir* (33:14).

But where does it say that Ya'akov ever went to Se'ir!? It must refer to the time when *the liberators will ... judge the mountain of Eisav (Ovadia 1:21)* – he could only be referring to the Messianic Era!

DEVARIM RABBA, 1:17, TANḤUMA, TERUMA, 9[3]

Within these short verses of *Vayishlaḥ,* Ya'akov established the framework of the entire painful history of the relationship of Yisrael and the West. Before embarking on diplomatic missions to Rome, Jewish ambassadors would study *Vayishlaḥ*,[4] and the Talmud traces historical events directly to this parasha:

For twenty-six years Rome kept her agreements with Yisrael, but then subjugated Yisrael. What changed?

At first, Rome expounded Eisav's offer: *Let us travel on, and I will walk as your counterpart.* But then they based themselves on Ya'akov's reply:

Let my master pass on ahead....יעבור נא אדוני לפני עבדו

AVODA ZARA, 8b

Seen in this context, Ya'akov's words are shattering: Ya'akov, as the embodiment of the nation Yisrael, proclaimed here his willingness to play second fiddle for millennia. His children are to watch from the sidelines for thousands of years as Western civilization thrives on the cutting edge of history. To perfect and vindicate all that Yisrael believes and lives, Ya'akov was willing to postpone his triumph for thousands of years. Now that is about as far from "fast food" as you can get.

But "fast food" is meant here as a lot more than metaphor – it was *literally* the catalyst of the initial clash between Ya'akov and Eisav. The coinage exchanged by Ya'akov for the *bechora* (primogeniture) was the ultimate fast-food dinner, bypassing even chewing!

"Pour[5] me on some of that red red stuff, because I'm tired of it all." (25:30)

Eisav stretched his mouth open like a camel and said, "I'll open my mouth and you just keep on pouring!"

BEREISHIT RABBA, 63:12

It was indeed Eisav's quick and easy attitude towards food that made Ya'akov suspect that the *bechora* might be for sale.

> When Eisav came in that day, he found Ya'akov standing over the stove cooking lentil stew, eyes tearing from the smoke.
> Said Eisav to him, "The rest of the world grabs any available food and you take the trouble to cook lentil stew?"
> Said Ya'akov to him, "If we aren't willing to invest in the future, how can we work towards the day when the just are rewarded?"
> Said Eisav, "You really believe in this *Olam Haba* business? You think the dead will live again?"
> Said Ya'akov, "If that's your attitude, what do you need this *bechora* for anyway? *Sell me today*... (25:31)."
>
> MIDRASH HAGADOL, BEREISHIT, 25:31

The greatest and sublimest power is simple patience.
HORACE BUSHNELL

The conflict between Ya'akov and Eisav here centers upon the competition for the *berachot* (blessings) bequeathed by Yitzḥak. But even those *berachot* differ mainly in the matter of delivery time – otherwise, they appear quite similar.

> To Ya'akov, the blessing begins: *God will give you of the dew of heaven and the fat of the earth* (27:28).
> Why did Yitzḥak begin with, "*God* **will** *give*...."? He meant to say, "*Eventually*, my son, when God is recognized as King...."
>
> To Eisav, however, the blessing begins: *Behold, your abode shall be of the fat of the earth and of the dew of heaven* (27:39).
> Why did Yitzḥak begin with "*Behold!*"? Because that implies: *immediately*.
>
> MIDRASH ZUTA, BEREISHIT 27:28[6]

There is another telling difference between the two *berachot*, a difference that emphasizes a crucial corollary to these differing attitudes. Ya'akov was committed to *earning*, to achieving, while Eisav was committed to *taking*, to owning. Eisav was the consummate consumer:

> To Ya'akov, the blessing begins: *God* (Elohim) *will give you*...
> – What is meant by *Elohim*? [This Divine name denotes] Justice, i.e. if it is appropriate that you should have, only then will God give you.

To Eisav, however, the blessing begins: *Behold, your abode shall be...*

– Whether Eisav is deserving or not.

TANḤUMA YASHAN, TOLEDOT[7]

Here we touch upon attitudes so fundamental to cultural disposition that the two brothers are even named for them: Yisrael means "grapple, struggle." Eisav translates as "already made"[8] – his byword of success is "I've got it *made*." Unlike Eisav, Ya'akov wanted nothing until he could identify with it, until he had struggled to make it his own:

Why did Ya'akov say, *Let my master pass on ahead...*?
Because Ya'akov did not even *want* those *berachot* at that time. As it says, *It is good for a man to bear a burden in his youth (Eicha 3:27)*, and, *She will laugh at the last day (Mishlei 31:25)*. Note how not one of his blessings has yet come about, for Ya'akov postponed them until the final days....

ZOHAR, I:172a

There are two main human sins from which all the others derive: impatience and indolence. It was because of impatience that they were expelled from Paradise, it is because of indolence that they do not return. Yet perhaps there is only one major sin: impatience. Because of impatience they were expelled, because of impatience they do not return.

FRANZ KAFKA

The Torah traces the eventual development of these two antipodal yet oddly similar brothers, these inverted images of human culture who produce in bifurcation both the slime of fascism and the glory of the millennium. But all these contrasts can be traced back to *Vayishlaḥ*, back to a simple yet critical distinction in the brothers' respective attitudes towards "fast food" living.

This implies that Western demand for instant gratification is not a side effect of recent technological innovation, but actually evolved from the roots of the civilization developed by Edom/Eisav. Pundits may consider the breakdown in the West a temporary "future shock" symptomatic of adjustment to the pace of change; the Torah sees it as an essential feature of Edom. In other words, shortcomings in education and discipline are not the source of the problem, nor are improvements in those areas sufficient solution of the problem. An actual cultural mythos is involved here, the mythos determining the underlying set of assumptions and beliefs about the nature of life for an entire society.

With consumption the focus of the fast-food society, achievement and distinction fall by the wayside. Education fails – why invest effort in a genuine education when what counts is the fast-food sheepskin?

Marriage fails – why invest the painful years needed to achieve success in long term relationships when simpler arrangements can be made? Morality fails – why invest in making an honest buck when there is so much for the taking?

It becomes politically impossible to enact the difficult measures required to deal with an unavoidable future. Demographic changes that threaten budgetary funding are ignored, entitlement programs that guarantee ultimate ruination are inviolate, and in the end society itself fails through mediocrity and irrelevance. All the marvelous potential of Eisav's blessings falls into a morass of drugs, crime, and ignorant, splintered egos leaving behind wrecked lives, "sweet dreams and flying machines in pieces on the ground." Though everyone knows that it cannot go on, there is always the hope of still one more tomorrow – and Eisav fiddles while America burns.

Ya'akov's insight into the psychology of Edom made it possible for him to ensure that Yisrael's development would be ignored and untouched by a dangerous fraternal antagonist. Beyond the bare appeal to Eisav's needs, Ya'akov devised a simple but subtle strategy. He presented himself as the antithesis to Eisav's search for the immediate.

Ya'akov projects this difference between them even as he first presents his gifts to his brother:

> *Please take my gift which has come to you....* (33:11)
>
> Ya'akov told him, "How I worked and toiled until I could afford all this. But to you – it has just *come to you.*"
>
> BEREISHIT RABBA, 88:12

"Master Eisav," he proclaims, surrendering to his brother the privileges of premature honors.

> *And these are the kings who reigned in the land of Edom before there reigned any king over the children of Yisrael....* (36:31)
>
> Said the Holy One to Ya'akov: Eight times you called Eisav, 'Master!', and eight kings from his descendants will reign before any of your children.
>
> BEREISHIT RABBA, 75:11

Eisav needs the immediate spotlight, needs to be on the cutting edge, and that is just what Ya'akov offers him.

> *Pass ahead, please, my master....* (33:14)
>
> Ya'akov said: You master civilization first...I will suffer your [Eisav's] *galut* (exile) until the time comes for me....
>
> ZOHAR, I:172a

On the other hand, nothing could be more distasteful to Eisav than toil, poverty, or shabbiness. Proximate power and instant fame, no matter how transitory, are Edom's flashy accouterments until today, his only sure definition of success. Ya'akov gave Eisav a sense of what would lie in store if they were really to become partners: no more Wall Street mergers, media fame, blinking marquees, fast cars, or late nights out away from family.

> *My master knows that the children are tender and the flocks and herds giving suck are a care for me. If I drive them too much even for a day, the sheep will die... I need to take it slow because of all the labor I have responsibility for, and the children....* (33:13,14)
>
> At that moment, Eisav, the "Guardian" of Ya'akov, decided it was time to get out, *So Eisav returned that day on his way to Se'ir* (33:16).
>
> ZOHAR, III:100b

Ya'akov needs only one thing more: *Eretz Yisrael.* But by the end of the parasha, Eisav senses the full import of Ya'akov's strategy and his own departure becomes a foregone conclusion. He wants the gain without the pain, is unwilling to suffer delay, and will accept no liabilities on his way to happiness – Eisav has no choice but to desert the Land of Israel for greener pastures.

ויען יצחק אביו ויאמר אליו
הנה משמני הארץ
יהיה מושבך ומטל
השמים מעל

> *And Eisav took...all his substance which he acquired in the land of Cana'an and moved to another country because of his brother Ya'akov.* (36:6)
>
> – Because of the liability that needed yet to be paid for the Land of Israel: *Your children will be strangers....* (*Bereishit* 15:13). Eisav said, "I would rather have no share in the gift of this land and not have to share in the liability."
>
> RASHI 36:6,[9] BEREISHIT RABBA, 82:12

It is Eisav's tragedy that his obsession with immediate results makes any long term investment unattractive – whether in money, relationships, or life. Such is indeed the more chilling ramification of the *beracha* to Eisav:

> *Behold, your abode shall be...* (27:39)
>
> "Behold" implies right now – but *only* now.[10] You can have what you see – but what you see is all will you get.
>
> There is the insinuation here that Eisav will atrophy and face extinction....
>
> RAMBAN 27:28[11]

But at least Eisav has fun while he can, you say wistfully? Then ask yourself how Ya'akov could have imagined that a gift worth at most a few dozen grand could buy off an incensed Eisav who has been literally 'stewing' for twenty-one years? Notice how Eisav at first politely declines the gift he eagerly accepts at the end? Now pay close attention to that dialogue, which encapsulates in just two words the opposing characteristics of Ya'akov and Eisav and shows us why Eisav will never be fulfilled.

> *And Eisav said, "I have plenty!"* (33:9)
>
> "*Plenty*" implies much, much more than I need. (—Rashi[12])
>
> *And Ya'akov said, "...and I have all..."* (33:10,11)
>
> "*All*" that I need. (—Rashi[13])

The man who thinks in terms of having "much, much more than I need" will never have enough. His possessions are external and his connection to them remains superficial. Ya'akov, the man to whom everything was really and truly his own, saw that Eisav would sell his soul for just a little more of what's out there – he wants it all, and he wants it now. Eisav got his instant gratification here all right – in the literal sense of 'bribe',[14] succumbing to his own overpowering urgency.

Eisav pursues enjoyment in indulgence and cheap pleasures, fast-food to senses that always crave more. Ya'akov, the man who truly does "have it all," experiences the joys and satisfactions of fulfillment rather than the pleasures of gratification. To Ya'akov, the connection and relationship are what count, not the actual possession. You can see this most

ויאמר עשו יש לי רב אחי יהי לך
אשר לך. ויאמר יעקב...
קח נא את ברכתי
אשר הבאת לך
כי חנני אלקים וכי יש לי כל.
ויפצר בו ויקח.

Thus happiness depends, as nature shows,
less on exterior things than most suppose.

WILLIAM COWPER

strikingly in the description of his attitude during another painful period of "delayed gratification": the seven years of toil before he was allowed to marry the woman he loved.

> *And Ya'akov served seven years for Rachel and they seemed to him like just a few days, so did he love her. (Bereishit 29:20)*

What a fabulously counter-intuitive statement: The *more* that he loved her, the *less* painful was the time he needed to wait to have her! Each moment of working for Rachel, every sheep that needed feeding, every post that needed pounding, was another act of love to Ya'akov. The investment itself was to him an act of love – fulfilling and satisfying in itself.

Because of his deep attachment to what became fully his own, Ya'akov was willing to risk his life even for the proverbial *pachim k'tanim*:

> *And Ya'akov remained behind, alone.... (32:25)*
>
> He stayed over for *pachim k'tanim* [small containers of little worth[15]].
>
> From here we learn that the tzaddik's money is more dear to him than his own body. Why? Because he would never touch anything that was not completely his own....
>
> HULLIN, 91a

מכאן לצדיקים שחביב עליהם ממונם יותר מגופם.

חולין צא.

Ya'akov cherishes, Eisav indulges. Ya'akov is fulfilled in love, Eisav can only pursue new conquests:

> Eisav would seduce women away from their husbands and rape them.
>
> BEREISHIT RABBA, 65:1, RASHI 26:34[16]

To Ya'akov, happiness is a consequence of fulfillment; to Eisav, happiness is a goal to be pursued. And in the terrifying and compulsive *pursuit* of happiness,[17] endlessly chasing after something that is only to be found within, Eisav and his society are doomed to a life of joyless pleasures. Those who have "much more than they need" are neither satisfied nor happy.

No two societies can be more different than those of Ya'akov and Eisav. On the surface they are so deeply alike that even Yitzḥak was fooled. But expose the mythos underlying the Western vision of life and you find the origins of a society addicted to addictions. Expose the mythos of Yisrael and you find the roots of a people who have spent millennia investing in life, and who have seen every moment of that investment as an act of love, of belief, and of deep faith. Yisrael will look back one day and say, as Ya'akov once did,

"It felt like just a few short days, so deep was the love...."

1 The *Korban Pesaḥ*, the Passover offering, demands advance planning of a meal which needs to take place from beginning to end in one pre-defined location and within a pre-defined group of people.

2 32:24-31.

3 Cf. also Zohar, I:172a; Bereishit Rabba, 78:14.

4 Bereishit Rabba, 78:15, Cf. also ibid. 75:5, 76:8 and 77:2; Avoda Zara, 25b.

5 The word used here for "pour" is *hal'itani*, the technical term for feeding camels, as in Shabbat, 155b. Cf. Rashi, s.v. *Hal'itani*, ד״ה הלעיטני.

6 Cf. Aggadat Bereishit 43:1, Malbim, *Sefer haCarmel*, entry הנה.

7 Cf. Rashi, Bereishit 27:28: Shlomo learned from this when he dedicated the *Beit Mikdash*. He prayed: Master of the Universe! If someone from Yisrael asks something of You here, if it is suitable for him, grant the request. But if he does not merit it, do not grant his request, *Give a man in accordance with all his ways (Melachim I, 8:39)*. Whereas if the non-Jew prays to You here, grant him everything he asks for, *And also to the gentile . . . just listen from the heavens (ibid. 41,43)*.

8 Rashi and Rashbam on Bereishit 25:25.

9 Appears in retrospective Rashi on 36:7, s.v. *Velo*, ד״ה ולא.

10 *Ohr haḤayim* 27:39.

11 A similar idea is expressed in the seventy oxen brought on Succot, starting with thirteen on the first day and then one less each day, a symbol of the gradual decline of the nations. Cf. Succa, 47a.

12 Rashi 33:11, s.v. *Yesh*, ד״ה יש לי כל.

13 Ibid.

14 *Oxford English Dictionary*, 1971, "*gratification*: n. something given to gain favor; in a bad sense, a bribe."

15 Cf. Rashi, op. cit., s.v. *Shenishtayer*, ד״ה שנשתייר.

16 S.v. *Ben*, ד״ה בן ארבעים שנה.

17 Of course, the "pursuit of happiness" of America's "Founding Fathers" refers to 'an occupation', not a 'chase'. Nonetheless, it is a curious double entendre.

VIII Vayishlaḥ
וישלח

The Joys of Tolerance

Vayishlaḥ continues the saga of the life of Ya'akov, mixing triumph with tragedy. Here, Ya'akov achieves a diplomatic accommodation with Eisav; here Ya'akov purchases a homesite in Shechem only to flee when the rape of his daughter triggers retaliation by his sons; here Ya'akov suffers the loss of his adored wife, the youthful Rachel, and celebrates the birth of his last son, Binyamin; here Ya'akov's intimate life is violated by his firstborn, Re'uven; here Ya'akov is reunited at last with his father, Yitzḥak, and learns of the death of his beloved mother, Rivka. But the most significant attainment of *Vayishlaḥ* is Ya'akov's maturation into a new identity with a new name: "Ya'akov" here becomes "Yisrael"–twice. Once, after his private struggle with the Guardian of his brother Eisav, when that angel is forced to concede Ya'akov's identity as Yisrael (32:29); and once again, after he returns to Beit El, when God informs him that Yisrael is meant to be his authentic name (35:10).

The repetition underscores the emphasis in *Vayishlaḥ* on formulating the relationship between the nascent Jewish people and the nations of the world. Ya'akov contends here that his new identity must be accepted by Eisav even before it is offered by God, and then goes on to establish new associations with Eisav and the Canaanites, relations that serve as historical models for generations to come. The parasha concludes with the severance of Eisav's ties to the Land of Israel and its people, as he leaves to start a new life in Se'ir.

The Joys of Tolerance examines the intricate and subtle negotiations that form the framework of the relationship between Yisrael and the nations, and makes some disturbing discoveries involving expediency, religion, and economics.

THE JOYS OF TOLERANCE

Hindsight's remarkable 20/20 vision often makes history painful to read: the opportunities lost, the mistaken judgments, the overlooked data – all the "if-onlys" that urge the future to shout out to the past. In one of the Torah's most frustrating historical moments, *Vayishlaḥ* opens as Ya'akov manages to snatch defeat from the jaws of victory.

After investing twenty years of hard labor preparing to meet Eisav, after besting Lavan on his own turf, after defeating even the guardian angel of Eisav himself,[1] after warning Eisav of the massive power that could be used against him,[2] Ya'akov suddenly seems to beat a miserable retreat:

> *Ya'akov...prostrated himself on the ground seven times as he approached his brother.* (33:3)
>
> He did not stop bowing, and then bowing again....
>
> BEREISHIT RABBA, 78:8

This made about the same impression on Eisav that Munich made on one of Eisav's unlamented descendants.

> When Eisav first received Ya'akov's [warning] message, he thought, "I will never be able to defeat him, so it's best that I reach a diplomatic settlement with him."
>
> But then, when Eisav saw that Ya'akov *prostrated himself on the ground seven times* and bowed and scraped before him, he decided, "If he really had the power he claims, he wouldn't be bowing to me!"
>
> ZOHAR, 1:167a

Now, there was a great deal of ambivalence on *both* sides of the fence here. It is by no means clear that Eisav was ever definitely committed to an open attack on Ya'akov. It was *Ya'akov* who jumped to the conclusion that Eisav intended to destroy him. In fact, his actual intention may have been very different.

The messengers returned to Ya'akov to report, "We came to your brother, Eisav, and he is heading towards you with four hundred men." Ya'akov became very frightened and distressed.... (32:7,8)

"*He is heading towards you...*" – to greet you in joy.

HIZKUNI, 32:7;

"*with four hundred men...*" – to do you honor!

RASHBAM, IBID.

Yet, despite his personal anxiety, Ya'akov was equally pained by the chance that *he* might hurt Eisav.[3]

Ya'akov became very frightened and distressed....

He was "frightened" that he might be killed, and "distressed" that he might kill.... (—Rashi, 32:8[4])

When Eisav does meet Ya'akov, the midrash senses the continuing ambivalence in ambiguous acts and double entendres:

Eisav ran to meet him, and hugged him, and fell on his neck and kissed him....(33:4)

There are dots in the Torah scroll above the word "kissed"....

Said R. Shimon: This indicates that for once Eisav kissed Ya'akov with all his heart.

Said R. Yannai: It teaches that Eisav's real intent had been not to kiss his neck (*neshika-* נשיקה) but to bite through it (*neshikha-* נשיכה).

BEREISHIT RABBA, 78:9

What, then, drove Ya'akov to a style of appeasement infamously associated with umbrellas? Even after Eisav made clear that he desired a warm and long-term relationship – nothing short of a historic collaboration – Ya'akov persisted in giving everything away:

He [Eisav] said, "Let us travel onwards together, and I will walk as your counterpart...." (33:12)

Eisav said, "Let's proceed together – we will divide this world and rule together!"

ZOHAR, 1:172a

Eisav told Ya'akov, "Ya'akov my brother! Let us walk together in this world as partners."

> But Ya'akov said, "*Pass ahead, please, my master*... (33:14) – You take your world first....I will take my time...."
>
> DEVARIM RABBA, 1:17

The result of this unfortunate encounter brought Eisav much more than he had hoped for. Here Ya'akov-as-archetype committed Yisrael to a secondary position in history. He left Eisav as the primary power and builder of world civilization.

יעבור נא אדוני לפני עבדו

Pass ahead, please, my master.... (33:14)

> Ya'akov said: Let Eisav master civilization first...I will have to suffer your [Eisav's] *galut* until the time comes for me to rule *the mountain of Eisav* (*Ovadia* 1:20).
>
> ZOHAR, 1:172a

Those five words of capitulation brought Israel thousands of years of suffering, and sanctioned the perception of Western Civilization as the custodian of knowledge, truth, culture and enlightenment.

> The Holy One said, "By your life, Ya'akov! We'll play it just as you say: Eisav is going to dominate you in this world."
>
> PIRKEI RABI ELIEZER, 36

The vision of foreign relations presented here by the father of the nation that now bears his new name, had an immense conscious and subconscious impact on the entire matrix of Jew-gentile relationships. *Vayishlaḥ* served as the Jewish model for official diplomatic contacts with Rome.

> R. Yehuda the *nassi* [president] once ordered R. Aphas, "Address a letter to our master, Caesar." He proceeded to write: From Yehuda, the president, to our master, Caesar Antoninus.
>
> R. Yehuda read the letter, tore it up, and ordered, "Write: From your *servant* Yehuda, to our master Caesar Antoninus...."
>
> Said R. Aphas to him, "Why is it necessary to abase your presidency in such a fashion?"
>
> Answered the *nassi*, "Am I better than my own grandfather – did he not say, '*So says your* servant *Ya'akov*....' (32:4)?"
>
> BEREISHIT RABBA, 75:5

The implications of Ya'akov's words have hardly been lost on the nations.

> For twenty-six years, Rome kept her treaties with Yisrael, but then turned and subjugated Yisrael....
>
> Originally, they followed the lesson of Eisav's first offer, "*Let us travel onwards together, and I will walk as your counterpart.... (33:12).*"
>
> But then they followed the lesson of Ya'akov's reply, "*Pass ahead, please, my master....(33:14).*"
>
> AVODA ZARA, 8b

The so-called "*galut*-mentality" has its roots here in *Vayishlaḥ*. It is not only the servility that came to be perceived – and resented by some – as the Jewish approach to the gentiles, but also the *shtadlanut*, the "smoothing" of the right channels with liberal applications of gifts. Or, more accurately, *bribery* – precisely what Ya'akov applies here to Eisav.[5]

> *He selected a tribute for his brother Eisav...200 female goats, 20 male goats, 200 ewes, 20 rams, 30 nursing camels and their young, 40 cows, 10 bulls, 20 female donkeys, 10 male donkeys...He said to his servants, "Get ahead of me, and keep a distance between one herd and the next...."* (32:14-17)
>
> He wanted to stun Eisav with the lavishness of his gift, to sate Eisav's lust. Eisav would be sure that the gift was complete – and then he would suddenly see another whole camp coming. Again he would be convinced that there could be no more – and up would come yet another one!
>
> BEREISHIT RABBA, 76:8
>
> The entire period that Ya'akov spent in Beit El, he would continuously honor Eisav with more tribute....
>
> BEREISHIT RABBA, 78:16

Call a thing immoral or ugly... a peril to the peace of the world or to the well being of future generations: as long as you have not shown it to be 'uneconomic' you have not really questioned its right to exist, grow, and prosper.
E.F. SCHMACHER

"Bribery" is a nasty word. What Ya'akov actually did here was enormously penetrating and had a far-reaching impact on the nature of the Jewish experience in exile. Ya'akov formulated the fundamental basis of Jewish survival among unfriendly nations: economic self-interest. A more sophisticated appreciation of Ya'akov's approach needed to await the late twentieth century when the entire basis of peaceful international relations became *consciously* economic in nature.

From this meeting between Ya'akov and Eisav was modeled international banking.[6] Jews became the currency dealers and money lenders of the world. They became the only group that could deal with all sides in circumstances of world conflict. Relationships of respect and trust grew up between "court Jews" and world leaders. Jewish survival was sustained through economic pragmatism.[7] Today, the same approach is being attempted in the Israeli-Palestinian peace agreement, saturated with clauses providing for economic cooperation.

After making peace with Eisav, Ya'akov proceeds to Shechem, where his association with the local population follows the same approach.

> *Ya'akov arrived whole in Shechem, and cared for the city....* (33:18)
>
> "*Whole in Shechem,*" – "*Whole*" in his money....
>
> "*Cared for the city*" – He set up monetary coinage for them....
>
> He developed markets for them....
>
> SHABBAT, 33b

> *Ḥamor and his son Shechem came to the city gate, and spoke to the townspeople, saying, "These people [Ya'akov and his sons] are peacefully inclined towards us, they will live here and do business here. There is a lot of room for growth in this country....*
>
> Much of the merchandise marketed around here remains unsold. (—Rashi[8])
>
> *"Their livestock, their possessions, and all their animals could be ours – just let us agree to their conditions and they will live with us...."* (34:21,23)

There is one serious inconsistency in Ya'akov's approach. If economics is the name of the game, there are plenty of sophisticated ways to provide profits without asking for a compromise on principles. Why then did Ya'akov put Eisav in the dangerously embarrassing position of needing to accept open payoff?

> *"I have plenty, my brother," said Eisav. "Let what is yours remain yours!*
> *"Please! No!" said Ya'akov. "If I have gained favor with you, please accept this gift from me...."*
>
> *He cajoled him, and he took it.* (33:9-11)

Eisav acted offended – but he kept his hand open!

BEREISHIT RABBA, 78:12

Here, I believe, we come to the deeper insight into Ya'akov's game plan. He wanted to achieve something much more important than material motivation. What the survival of Yisrael demands is *tolerance* – and tolerance means that Eisav must not stand on principle. Eisav must learn not to care too much.

Ya'akov needs to transform Eisav into a peace-loving liberal!

The name *Eisav* has the same numerical value (376) as *Shalom*, "Peace."

KALLA RABBATI, 3

Persecution was at least a sign of personal interest. Tolerance is composed of nine parts of apathy to one of brotherly love.
F.M. COLBY

This liberal Eisav is the secret of Yisrael's survival even during periods that might have allowed, logistically and politically, for the total extermination of the Jewish people.[9]

You [Eisav] detest blood.... (Yeḥezkel 35:6)

Eisav *detest* blood? But look at the righteous they have murdered, at the saints they have exterminated!

BAMIDBAR RABBA, 4:8

But this was the Eisav that Ya'akov had to *develop* – the Eisav who could not justify bloodshed, who found arbitrary beliefs too ephemeral to die or to kill for. This was Eisav the Tolerant.

The mass demonstrations viewed as modern surrogates of old-fashioned *shtadlanut* and bribery are no surrogates at all – they are a direct outgrowth of Eisav's acceptance of tolerance, a consequence of Ya'akov's gifts. Mass demonstrations are not even particularly 'modern'.

Once the Romans decreed that no Jew could study Torah, keep the Shabbat or circumcise a child.... The Jews organized a demonstration by night and shouted: *By God! Are we not children of one father? Are we not children of one mother? Why are we being singled out for ill-treatment?*

The Romans cancelled the decree.

ROSH HASHANA, 19a

America, the land founded on tolerance, has been a most fertile land for Yisrael. Europe, where people are enwrapped in historical and religious cares, was a nightmare.

Do not remove his bit.... (Tehillim, 140:9)

Said Ya'akov to the Holy One: Master of the Universe – do not allow Eisav his heart's desire – "*Do not remove his bit....*"

This prayer refers to Germany of Edom,[10] for if they were to be let loose, they would destroy the world!

MEGILLA, 6a-6b

Ya'akov's purchase of Eisav's birthright and his subsequent appropriation of the blessings was warranted by Eisav's disdain for meaning, his blatant fulfillment in consumerism and in the pleasures of transient life.

By being civilized we mean that there is a list of things about which we permit a man to have an opinion different from ours. Usually they are things which we have ceased to care about: for instance, the worship of God.

AUBREY MENEN

Pour me on some of that red red stuff, because I'm tired of it all.... (25:30)

Said Eisav, "You really believe in this *Olam Habah* business? You think the dead will come back to life?"

Said Ya'akov, "If that's your attitude, what do you need this *bechora* for anyway. "*Sell me today...*" (25:31)

MIDRASH HAGADOL, BEREISHIT 25:31

Yitzḥak's two sons bore the gifts of the family of Avraham. Together they were the future builders of Creation. But Yitzḥak's two sons were mirror images, living in mirror worlds:

The world was created only for the completely evil or the completely righteous....

[For one there was created] *Olam Habah*, the world to come;

[For the other there was created] *Olam Hazeh*, this world....

BERACHOT, 61b

There can be no developing a world without passion, without complete commitment to it. Ya'akov, in purchasing the blessings, made a commitment to *Olam Habah*. Eisav, in selling them, made a commitment to *Olam Hazeh*. Creation demands them both, and both demand fulfillment: there is no excuse for a half-done job at either.

Raba would tell his students, "I beg of you – don't inherit a double hell!"

> Do not toil in Torah in this world without putting your learning into practice, because then you lose the world to come and you did not even enjoy this world while you had the chance! (—Rashi[11])
>
> YOMA, 72b

Ya'akov had the right to those blessings – the right to be the exclusive Yisrael – only so long as Eisav had no otherworldly cares.[12] Yitzḥak had indeed promised Eisav that if ever he could find grounds to contest Ya'akov's expropriation of the *berachot*, Eisav could then repossess them.

> When you will have an opening to gripe over the blessings that Ya'akov took, then *you will free your neck from his yoke* (27:40). (—Rashi[13])

Anti-Semitism appears in its ultimate essence as a nomophobia, a revolt against the total moral law, or, religiously, a revolt against God...in the hatred of the Jew [lies] an unconscious hatred of Christ, a rebellion against the Christian yoke no longer found sweet (Matt. ii:30).

FATHER EDWARD FLANNERY

This is why it was so important for Ya'akov to gain Eisav's recognition and acknowledgment that the purchase was made in good faith. This is why Eisav must be the one to proclaim the name *Yisrael*.

> *He [Ya'akov] said, "I will not let you go until you bless me!"*
>
> *Said he [Eisav's guardian angel], "Your name will no longer be said to be Ya'akov, but Yisrael...."* (32:27,29)
>
> It will no longer be said that the blessings came to be yours through manipulation and deception, *akava/Ya'akov*, (עקבה–יעקב), but rather openly and through struggle, *sirara/Yisra'el* (שררה–ישראל). (—Rashi, 32:29[14])

The purchase *was* made in good faith, because the most destructive thing for Eisav would be his attempting to justify life in this world through *other*worldly religion. He would end up having neither, inheriting "a double Hell," his life made miserable through dogma and guilt. Life in *Olam Hazeh* can be completely fulfilling on its own terms, as long as it is lived in conformance with the seven Noachian Laws, but Eisav had to make that choice *himself* here.

Ya'akov knew that so long as Eisav viewed himself as his partner, neither of them could commit fully to his own world and destiny. It is here in *Vayishlaḥ* that Eisav recognizes – for himself – that Ya'akov was right. Eisav finally wants to live – fully in the present, fully accomplished, fulfilled with no need of justification.

"I have plenty, my brother," said Eisav. "Let what is yours remain yours!" (33:9)

Here Eisav relinquished the blessings. (—Rashi[15])

Until now the *berachot* were Ya'akov's only equivocally – at this moment they became unequivocally his: *"Let what is yours remain yours!"*

BEREISHIT RABBA, 78:11

Eisav hated the *bechora* in the first place, and would have [eventually] begged Ya'akov to take it off his hands – even if he would have had to pay him!

ZOHAR, 1:139a

Conscience—that Jewish invention.

ADOLF HITL

Ya'akov was willing to give up everything in order to bring Eisav to this recognition. For Ya'akov to live the way *he* wanted, he had no option but to offer Eisav the opportunity to live any way *he* wanted. In a verse that preserves what seems to be a world record for tactlessness and insensitivity, the Torah hints at Ya'akov's astounding sacrifice. After twenty years of worrying about Eisav's anger, of trying to make Eisav forget, of planning delicate ways to forestall Eisav's revenge, Ya'akov has the reckless audacity to refer to his gift to Eisav with the one word that he should have avoided at all costs:

קח נא את ברכתי

Please take my blessing as it has been brought to you.... (33:11)

It is precisely here that the midrash finds the clue to what Ya'akov was doing:

Said Ya'akov to him, "Take *both* blessings – yours and mine. *Take my blessing* – here, it's yours!"

Answered Eisav, "I want only the blessing that was originally meant for me by my father. The blessing that was meant to be yours should now go to you."

They wrote up a contract between them and signed on transferring the blessings back to the way they were meant to be.

When Eisav came triumphantly home, everyone objected: What you have done is ridiculous! You took blessings focused

> on *Olam Habah* and left him with this world – try to get him to accept them back again....
>
> Eisav came to Ya'akov and begged him to tear up the contract....
>
> YELAMDEINU, BATEI MIDRASHOT, 1:159

The most calamitous phenomenon in the culture of Eisav was the early Church whose progeny seek still the mantle of the name "*Yisrael*." In his religion, Eisav was deprived of this world and made to believe that he must sacrifice all to achieve salvation. Through it, he was cynically swindled out of the very possessions that should have made him joyful. For centuries he was misled, and deprived of education and culture. With all her might, the Church fought every enlightenment, every discovery, every new commitment to making the world a better place. Eisav grew cruel, and came to love blood. He came to hate Yisrael with a passion, to hate him most intensely for the dubious gift of religion that robbed Eisav of life. The more authoritative the religion, the more bloodthirsty the anti-Semitism.

History reveals the Church and the State as a pair of indispensable Molochs. They protect their worshipping subjects, only to enslave and destroy them.
ALDOUS HUXLEY

But the moment that "Eisav" was freed to love this world, he progressed towards understanding, towards tolerance, towards sacrifice. He began to make *this* world a better place to live. He came to appreciate all the fullness of this world, to know it thoroughly and so to love it all the better. In place of crusades for pillage, came crusades for peace and economic development. Never before in history was social welfare so developed; never before in history were armies dispatched on missions of peace and charity. The finest hours of Eisav are now his – through the care of Ya'akov.

Does this mean that Ya'akov himself is otherworldly, unable to feel love and care for all that is beautiful in *Olam Hazeh*? Quite the contrary.

> When Ya'akov and Eisav shared the womb, Ya'akov said to Eisav, "My brother Eisav! We are two sons, and there are two worlds before us, this world and the world to come...would you be interested in taking this world while I concentrate on the next?"
>
> ...Then, when Ya'akov returned from Lavan and Eisav saw that he had children and servants and maids, Eisav said to

> him, "Ya'akov, my brother! Did you not tell me that you were going to take *Olam Habah* – where in the world do you come by all this money. Why, you are taking as much from this world as I!"
>
> Said Ya'akov to him, "This is only property which I am *using* while in this world."
>
> TANNA D'VEI ELIAHU ZUTA, 19

I am not *taking* but *using,* says Ya'akov.[16]

No matter what degree of achievement and connection to this world Ya'akov attains, it offers him no fulfillment without a bridge to forever. Ya'akov's life is incomplete when limited to *Olam Hazeh,* and thus he takes nothing from it. But there is no sacrifice too great and no accomplishment too distant if through them Ya'akov and his world can evolve into eternity, and these uses drive his success.

Ya'akov was willing to take the long road, to suffer the pettiness and pain of poverty and exile, if that were the only way to reach the future. That choice of life put Eisav off for good:

> Said Eisav to Ya'akov, "Ya'akov, my brother! Let us make a partnership agreement, you and I. You take half of *Olam Habah* and *Olam Hazeh*, and I will take half of *Olam Hazeh* and *Olam Habah.*"
>
> Said Ya'akov to Eisav: *"My master knows that the children are tender and the flocks and herds giving suck are a care for me...I need to take it slow because of all the labor for which I have responsibility, and the children...."* (33:13,14)
>
> IBID.

> At that moment, Eisav, self-appointed "Guardian" of Ya'akov, decided it was time to leave, *so Eisav returned that day on his way to Se'ir....* (33:16)
>
> ZOHAR, II:100b

Ya'akov was ready to begin building a world that would be completed only with the completion of history itself. His children have followed after him, painstakingly placing brick upon brick, life upon life. They do so because of a clarity of vision which spans history and extends beyond all this world has to offer. In the fullness of that dedication and

אמרו כשהיו יעקב ועשו במעי אמן אמר יעקב לעשו, עשו אחי! שנים אנחנו לאבינו ושני עולמות יש לפנינו, העולם הזה והעולם הבא. העולם הזה יש בו אכילה ושתיה משא ומתן לשאת אשה ולהוליד בנים ובנות, אבל העוה"ב אינו כן בכל מדות הללו, רצונך טול אתה העוה"ז ואני אטול העוה"ב, מנין שכך הוא, שנאמר מכרה כיום את בכורתך לי, כשם שהיינו אומרים בבטן. מיד כפר עשו בתחיית במתים...באותה שעה נטל עשו בחלקו העוה"ז ונטל יעקב העוה"ב, וכשבא יעקב מבית לבן וראה עשו בנים ליעקב ועבדים ושפחות, אמר לו עשו ליעקב, אחי! לא כך אמרת לי שתטול אתה העוה"ב, ומניין לך כל הממון הזה? אתה משמש מהעולם הזה כמותי! אמר לו, הרכוש שנתן לי הקב"ה לשמשני בעולם הזה, שנאמר, הילדים אשר חנן אלהים את עבדך. באותה שעה האמיד עשו בדעתו, ואמר העוה"ז שאין חלקו כך נתן לו הקב"ה, העוה"ב שהוא חלקו על אחת כמה וכמה, אמר לו עשו ליעקב, יעקב אחי! בא ונעשה שותפות אני ואתה, טול אתה העוה"ז והעוה"ב חצי ואני אטול העוה"ז והעוה"ב חצי, שנאמר ויאמר עשו, אציגה נא עמך מן העם אשר אתי. אמר לו יעקב לעשו, אדני יודע כי הילדים רכים ואינם יכולין לעמוד בייסורין, שנאמר ודפקום יום אחד ומתו כל הצאן.

תנא דבי אליהו זוטא, יט

consecration, Ya'akov and his children were willing to make the ultimate sacrifice. They tossed over the keys to this world with all that it implied.

Pass ahead, please, my master, in front of his servant...

"If that is what it takes, brother Eisav, to make you trust and understand, then here – catch the keys to the world. We will build onwards from where you will finish...."

1 *Tanḥuma*, 8; Bereishit Rabba, 77:3; Cf. Ḥullin, 91a.

2 Bereishit Rabba, 75:5; *Tanḥuma*, 1; Zohar I:166b.

3 See *Mizraḥi*, 32:8, s.v. *Vayezer,* ד״ה ויצר לו.

4 Cf. Bereishit Rabba, 76:2, where the words are reversed. The Albeck edition Bereishit Rabba has Rashi's rendering.

5 Cf. Bereishit Rabba, 75:13.

6 For a fine treatment of the Jewish foundations of international banking, see Howard M. Sacher, *The Course of Modern Jewish History*, (New York: Vintage Books, 1990).

7 As a matter of historical curiosity, one of the most important of families to play a role in this economic history is the Rothschilds, who founded the first international brokerage house, as well as a number of nation banks. Their name (and emblem) means *Red* Shield— protectors of *Edom*, indeed.

8 34:21, s.v. *Veha'aretz*, ד״ה והארץ.

9 Pesaḥim, 87b; Avoda Zara, 10b.

10 Cf. Yoma 10a, glosses of the Vilna Ga'on. The printed version has "Germamia" in place of "Germania."

11 S.v. *Tartei*, ד״ה תרתי גיהנום.

12 There was only one time in Eisav's life when something mattered to him deeply—and it nearly cost the survival of the Jewish people.

> When Eisav heard his father's words, he screamed an exceedingly anguished and bitter cry... *"Bless me, too, my father!"* (27:34)
>
> Ya'akov was repaid for that *"exceedingly anguished and bitter cry"* [by Haman, Eisav's descendant] as it says, *Mordechai knew what was happening, and Mordechai tore his clothes... and cried* ***an exceedingly anguished and bitter cry***. *(Esther 4:1)*
>
> ESTHER RABBA, 8:1

For there is indeed one descendant of Eisav who cares very much indeed, who is actually *born* of care: Amalek.

> Menashe ben Ḥizkiya would mock the words of the Torah. He said, "Did Moshe have nothing better to write about than *Lotan's sister was Timna* (36:22) ...*Timna was a mistress to Eliphaz the son of Eisav....* (36:12)!"
>
> [Asks the Talmud:] Now that you mention it, what indeed *does* it teach us? That Timna was a princess, *Noble Lotan* (36:29) implies "Noble Timna." She wanted to join the Jewish people, and approached Avraham, Yitzḥak, and Ya'akov, but none of them would have her. So she went to become a mistress to Eisav's son, Eliphaz, saying, "I would rather be a maid among this nation than a princess among any other!" What came of her:
>
> *Timna was a mistress to Eliphaz the son of Eisav, and she bore him Amalek!* (36:12)
>
> SANHEDRIN, 99b

Amalek was a descendant of Eisav who allowed money to play no role—he was willing to *pay* to destroy Ya'akov, willing to risk his own survival if only he might take Yisrael along with him.

> *"If the king is willing, sign a decree to destroy them [the Jews], and I [Haman] will personally hand over ten thousand talents of silver to the ones who get the job done to be transferred to the king's treasury...."*
>
> *The king removed his signet ring from his hand, and turned it over to Haman... the archenemy of the Jews. "Keep the money," said the king, "and do what you want with the people!"* (Esther 3:9,11)

13 27:40 s.v. *Vehaya*, ד״ה והיה כאשר תריד.

14 S.v. *Lo Ya'akov*, ד״ה לא יעקב.

15 33:9, s.v. *Yehi lecha*, ד״ה יהי לך אשר לך.

16 Compare R. Yehuda haNassi, famous for his immense riches and high life style, who, on his death bed, "lifted his ten fingers towards heaven and said, 'Master of the Universe! It is open and known before You that...I did not take even as my smallest finger!" (Ketuvot, 104a). See also *Mishne Torah, Hilchot Teshuva*, 9:1.

IX Vayeshev

וישב

You Can't Go Home Again

In *Vayeshev* (literally, "he settled down"), the twenty-two year flight of Ya'akov comes to an end, at last. The threats from Lavan and Eisav are behind him, the long journey that brought the death of Rachel and the rape of Dina is over, and Ya'akov wants to start life again, as *he settled in the land where his father lived* (37:1). But the peace he seeks escapes him, and instead ensue the most difficult days of his life in which, for all intents and purposes, Ya'akov loses his family. Dissension tears apart the harmony of the primal Jewish home; Yosef barely escapes fratricide by his older brothers and is sold into slavery; Yehuda is rejected and leaves home and family for gentile partnerships; Ya'akov himself withdraws into interminable dolor, and the future appears bleak. The parasha ends as Yosef languishes in a dungeon, his hopes for release dashed by the ungrateful chief steward (40:23).

You Can't Go Home Again explores *Vayeshev's* motif of broken relationships—and it is hard to imagine a theme with more universal reverberation. The parasha teaches the centrality of human relationships—in all their pettiness—to life, and cautions against the "quest for peace."

YOU CAN'T GO HOME AGAIN

V*ayeshev* begins an era filled with the hope of new beginnings, and opens with the longings for serenity that accompany homesteading.

> *Ya'akov settled in the land where his father lived, in the Land of Cana'an.* (37:1)
>
> Ya'akov yearned to *settle* – to settle down in serenity.... (—Rashi[1])

Ya'akov dreamed of taking up the life he had left behind twenty-two years previously, to become again the *simple, scholarly man (Bereishit 25:27)*. This dream sustained him through the tough decades with Lavan and the showdown with Eisav.

> *You [Ya'akov] left because of your intense longing for your father's home....* (31:30)

Now, after suffering the rape of his daughter (34:1-31), the loss of his youthful wife (35:17-19), and the betrayal by his firstborn, Re'uven (35:22), he comes home at last to settle down, *in the land where his father lived.*

But it was not to be. Life shattered his dream.

> The righteous yearn to settle down in serenity. Says the Holy One, "What is prepared for the righteous in the World to Come is not enough for them? They crave peace in this world, too?!"
>
> RASHI[2]

That harsh pronouncement translated into the blackest decades of Ya'akov's life. His family was broken up, trust and belief were shattered, and the only son born and bred by his life's lost love was presumed dead for twenty-two years. Ya'akov was certain that his life was a failure, and that the nation he was to have founded had perished, stillborn.[3]

> *He refused solace, saying, "I will go to the grave mourning my son."* (37:35)

Ya'akov never fully recovered, and the toll these years of anguish took on him was evident later, in better times, as he stood before Pharaoh.

> *"My journey through life has lasted 130 years," replied Ya'akov. "Few and wretched have been the days of my life...." (47:9)*

Vayeshev's theme is of shattered hopes and shattered relationships. The very name of the parasha – "settling down" – intimates the yearning for serenity, the flaw in the dream that would become a nightmare.

But how is it possible that Ya'akov, who in the previous parasha was awarded the name of Yisrael, "The Fighter" (32:28), should suddenly withdraw totally? Why, the entire nature of the nation he dreams of building reflects struggle:

People wish to be settled: only as far as they are unsettled is there any hope for them.
EMERSON

> *Your name shall no longer be Ya'akov but Yisrael, for you have struggled with god and man – and you won! (32:28)*

We are speaking of a man who never rested, whose life was fashioned out of struggle and challenge, a man who ran one successful race after another.

> Ya'akov raced before Me like horses [race over quicksand – never able to let their feet rest].
>
> SANHEDRIN, 96a[4]

Is it reasonable to believe that, in complete reversal of his aspirations and his hard-won qualities, Ya'akov would turn his back on all his achievements and forget the object of the "journey through life" he speaks of so bitterly? Remember that Ya'akov is an archetype: the *Av* of Yisrael, whose personal name and nature embodied *Yisrael.* He is the one whose progeny have faced humanity's grimmest monstrosities and continue yet to thrive and grow, never resting on their laurels.

> Even in the World to Come they do not rest, as it says, *They go from strength to strength... (Tehillim 84:8).*
>
> MO'ED KATTAN, 29a

If such is the character Ya'akov bestows to posterity, how does he himself betray it? And if the righteous do not rest "even in the World to Come," how are we to accept their ostensible "yearning for serenity" in this world? The opening intimations of *Vayeshev* conflict with everything we know about Yisrael:

> *Vayeshev* – The righteous yearn to settle down in serenity. Says the Holy One, "What is prepared for the righteous in the World to Come is not enough for them? They crave peace in this world, too!?"

The trouble here lies, I believe, in the translation of the Hebrew word which describes the quest of Ya'akov and "the righteous." They search for "*shalva*" which is a very telling word. It means not "peace," not "serenity," and not "rest" or "relaxation." Observe its use:

> *Better is a dry morsel with shalva, than a house full of feasting strife. (Mishlei 17:1)*

טוב פת חרבה ושלוה בה
מבית מלא זבחי ריב
משלי יז:א

The opposite of *shalva*, then, is strife, dissension, disharmony. The English word, "tranquility," comes close to the idea (my dictionary has: "free from emotional disturbance or agitation"). *Shalva* connotes freedom from the petty hassling which can cheapen even the most glorious moments of life. It implies an environment conducive to work and achievement, far from the ravages of picayune politics and trivial argumentation. *Shalva* does not mean "peace" – it means peaceful relationships.

Any idiot can weather a crisis; it's day-to-day living that wears you out.

CHEKHOV

With the loss of *shalva*, the noble becomes crass and the sublime tawdry. Nothing is so effective at taking all the flavor out of life as the loss of *shalva* – and, paradoxically, the more trivial the issue, the more it can undermine life's elation and accomplishments.

> Here a person works to buy meat for the holiday, cooks it in his home, all for the sake of happiness – to honor the holiday. He manages to finish his preparations, proudly sets down the platter and proceeds to dish out the portions. What happens?
>
> "Hey, my brother's portion is bigger than mine!"
>
> So, he ends up miserable just as he was about to get happy!
>
> PESIKTA D'RAV KAHANA, (ADDENDUM) 2:8

אדם שמח בעולם הזה?
בא מועד, לוקח לו בשר ומבשל
בתוך ביתו לשמוח בשביל המועד.
לא עשה אלא בא לאכול ומתחיל
נותן לכל אחד ואחד מבניו חלקו,
של אחי גדול משלי! ונמצא מיצר
אפילו בתוך שמחתו. אבל לעתיד
לבא הקדירות מבשלות ואדם רואה
ונפשו שמח עליהם.
פסיקתא דרב כהנא

We are crushed by the devaluation such paltry relationships impose on our affairs. It is the *pettiness* of our own humanity that contradicts our dreams of significance and our deep concerns. The heroic battles, the epic struggles, are easier to face than the ugly ache of failure at home.

> Bad relationships in a person's home are harder to bear than the war of Gog and Magog.
>
> BERACHOT, 7b

Shalva is precisely what the creative genius and the real craftsman need the most *in order to produce*. No wonder the truly creative – the righteous – seek *shalva*! Ya'akov wants *shalva* to allow himself the very struggle he so desires, to fight the real battles, to defeat evil itself. A life spent on the petty demands brought by day-to-day interpersonal relationships, smoothing prickly egos and soothing trifling emotional outbursts, is a life imprisoned in trivia. After Lavan and Eisav and Shechem, Ya'akov *needs shalva*. And *shalva* is just what he does not get:

> *I had no tranquility, no quiet, no respite – and trouble came!* (*Iyov 3:25*)
>
> *No tranquility*... from Eisav;
> *No quiet*... from Lavan;
> *No respite*... from Dina;
> *And trouble came*... the troubles of Yosef began...
>
> BEREISHIT RABBA, 84:3

Ya'akov's life becomes enwrapped in pettiness – hairstyles and suit styles, charges of favoritism, dreams of grandeur, sibling rivalry, pent-up resentments, and at last an explosive breakdown of the most elementary relationships. The silliness of "Hey, his portion is bigger than mine!" ends up propelling the nation to Egypt and centuries of exile.

> For two *selahs* worth of extra material that Ya'akov gave to Yosef, his brothers became jealous, and one thing led to the next until our fathers went down to Egypt!
>
> SHABBAT, 10b

Great events make me quiet and calm; it is only trifles that irritate my nerves.
QUEEN VICTORIA[5]

The frustration, disappointment and defeat of Ya'akov here has the quality of broken-heartedness we taste when seeing whole regions of the world mired in blood, starvation and miserable suffering for no reason other than pettiness, when watching people sacrificing their own future and the lives of their children, losing everything valuable for trivialities that would be laughable if not so tragic. If only we had the chance – we dream – we could feed the world, defeat ignorance, house the homeless, cure the suffering – just a bit of tranquility to give us a chance, and the world could flower! What a waste....

Indeed, "*Few and wretched have been the days of my life....*" Instead of the great primal *tests* of the earlier *Avot*, Ya'akov's life is one that gives us a great Yiddish word that has made its way into everyday speech (and into the English dictionary): *tsores*,[6] "troubles."

> Ya'akov escapes Eisav – right away comes the *tsora* of Dinah.
>
> He finishes the *tsora* of Dinah, and along comes the *tsora* of Rachel.
>
> After all these *tsores*, he wants a little respite – along comes the *tsora* of Yosef...then the *tsora* of Shimon, then the *tsora* of Binyamin....
>
> TANḤUMA, MIKETZ, 10

יצא מעשו באה עליו צרת
דינה, יצא מצרת דינה
באה עליו צרת רחל,
אחר כל הצרות בקש לנוח
קמעא באה עליו צרת יוסף
והכתוב צווח לא שלותי
ולא שקטתי ולא נחתי...
אחר כך באה עליו צרת
שמעון. אח"כ צרת בנימין.

תנחומא - מקץ סימן י

The experiences of Yisrael-the-*Av* have become so much a part of the experience of Yisrael-the-nation, that *tsores* is a word that sums up much of a culture. How could it have come to be that Yisrael should live within – and be ruled by – the petty interplay of personal relationships and childish politicking that is so damaging to aspiration and meaning?

There is only one explanation: the responsibility assigned Yisrael here, the responsibility for interpersonal excellence, *is* itself the most meaningful of all tasks, the very stuff of human life. The word "*tsores*" preserves the résumé of a people in exile, and captures the way a culture has learned to deal with tragedy. "*Tsores*," for all its melancholy, is a word infused with self-deprecating humor and acceptance of the nature of the human condition.

There are great things to be accomplished in life, for humanity is entrusted with the completion of a flawed Creation, with making this a better world. And there is but a single concern labeled by God Himself as *the* accomplishment for there is only one flaw in Creation marked by God Himself as demanding our achievements. Where God is pleased with Creation, He certifies it as "Good" – and that leaves little room for improvement.

> *God saw that it was good.... (Bereishit 1:10)*
> *God saw that it was good.... (Bereishit 1:12)*

> *God saw that it was good....* (*Bereishit* 1:18)
> *God saw that it was good....* (*Bereishit* 1:21)
> *God saw that it was good....* (*Bereishit* 1:25)
> *God saw everything that He had made, and it was very good....* (*Bereishit* 1:31)

There is but one thing in all of Creation that is stamped "No Good!"

> *Said the Lord, God: It is no good that the adam should be alone....* (*Bereishit* 2:18)

That statement is not an opinion or editorial comment – it is one of the ten primal Utterances of Creation, no different than "*Let there be Light*." It is a statement that defines the nature of Being.[7]

אם היה יכול אדם לעלות השמימה
לראות בצבאות מעלה סדרם וישרם
לא היה מתענג בהשגתו עד שובו
הנה ויספר לחבריו את המראה
הגדול ההוא...זה דרך כל משכיל
להתאוה להודיע לזולתו כל מה
שישיג וישכיל מעוצם בינתו...

הקדמה לקונטרס הספקות

The entire spectrum of human relationship – to others, to God, to the cosmos – develops in the Creation narrative directly from that astonishing statement. Creation of woman is presented there as the paradigm for development of all forms of connectedness, and unfolds along with sexuality, naming, identity, and good and evil themselves. In the one area of human relationships lies the most fundamental constraint on Creation. That single area is *the* field for achievement and excellence. There is no avoiding it, nor is there anything petty about working on relationships. Supplying those "trivial" emotional needs is the most fundamental and significant service to Creation.

There *is* no way to *shalva*, no way for Ya'akov to simply go back home again *in the land where his father lived.* Creation itself proclaims that you *cannot* go home again.

> *Therefore, man must leave his father and mother and cleave to his wife....* (*Bereishit* 2:24)

There is no hope of joy except in human relations.
SAINT-EXUPÉRY

All human creativity and production are consequences of relationship, and failure at interpersonal excellence ultimately presages failure at life itself. *Vayeshev* brings that home to us by depicting a spectacular failure: that of Yehuda, leader of all the brothers.[8]

Yehuda disavows the petty concerns of human relationships, and is responsible for the sale of Yosef. As a result, he eventually leaves the family, joins a gentile business, marries a non-Jewess, and ends up burying his entire household.

It was at that time that Yehuda went down from his brothers, and turned away to an Adulamite friend whose name was Ḥira. (38:1)

This teaches that his brothers repudiated his leadership when they saw the pain their father was suffering.

"*You* told us to sell him," they said. (—Rashi[9])

Yehuda went down...

It was quite a *downfall* for Yehuda to marry a non-Jewish girl; quite a *downfall* that he buried his wife and children....

BEREISHIT RABBA, 85:2

Yehuda's marriage is only a matter of business expedience.

There Yehuda met the daughter of a merchant named Shua, and married her.... (38:2)

He married her for her father.

RAMBAN

His relationship with her is so problematic that she names her children after her disappointments. Yehuda does not even show up for the birth of his third son:

She gave birth again to a son, and she named him Shela – Yehuda was in Keziv when she gave birth to him. (38:5)

"Shela" means deception...for Yehuda was in Keziv, which means "disappointment." [The name] reflects her sense of rejection when she missed seeing her husband at the birth of her child....

SEFORNO

Which of us has known his brother?
Which of us has looked into his father's heart? Which of us has not remained forever prison-pent?
Which of us is not forever a stranger and alone?

THOMAS WOLFE

Yehuda's first two sons die because of their own rejection of relationship and its responsibilities. Instead of taking the wife of his deceased brother, Onan, Yehuda's second son, even lends his name until today to onanism, sexual satisfaction without relationship:

Onan knew that the child would not be his own, so when he came to his brother's wife he wasted [his semen] on the ground, so as not to give seed to his brother. What he did was evil in God's eyes, and He killed him, as well. (38:9,10)

> "*Killed him as well...*" as Onan died so did 'Er [the firstborn] die...for spilling his seed. (—Rashi[10])

It is only against his will that Yehuda is drawn into relationship. Tamar, his former daughter-in-law, waits in vain for Yehuda to offer her a husband. In her intense yearning[11] to build a future with him, she manages to draw him to her by posing as a prostitute. It was her commitment to the relationship that conquered him, at last.

> *She became pregnant to him.... (38:18)*
>
> "To him" implies heroes like him, righteous men like him.... (—Rashi[12])

This relationship, though effective only because it was non-involving, left Yehuda's most profound impact on history. Tamar's child from him, Peretz, is the founder of the line that culminates in King David and the Messiah to come.

In rejecting relationship, Yehuda became incapable of viable creativity. How sweet the irony that the only lasting yield of Yehuda's life came from the relationship he wanted to avoid; that it came from the force of Tamar's desire. In discovering Tamar and finally acknowledging her, Yehuda discovered himself: his name,[13] his kingdom,[14] his destiny,[15] and his true marriage.

> *He did not abstain again from knowing her.... (38:26)*
>
> Having known her once, he never abstained from her again.
>
> SOTAH, 10b

From that moment he begins his climb upward, until eventually it is he who takes responsibility for Binyamin,[16] he who stands up to the leader of Egypt.[17]

Indeed, "*The righteous yearn to settle down in* shalva...." The mistaken flight from the petty demands of relationship is a hallmark of the committed righteous who embark on impassioned quests for life's opportunities – only to find that opportunity stayed back at home. Ya'akov and Yehuda wanted passionately to escape the very "pettiness" that was to become their œuvre, the essence of their lives' achievements. This is precisely why the entire Torah is ultimately the study of relationship.

> Once a certain gentile came before Shammai and said, "I want to convert to Judaism, but on the condition that you teach me the entire Torah while I stand on one foot." Shammai drove him out with the rod he held in his hand.
>
> Then he came to Hillel, who converted him. Hillel taught him, "What you dislike, do not do to your friend. That is the whole Torah, the rest is commentary. Now go study it!"
>
> SHABBAT, 31a

It is not towards an abstracted Truth that we strive in Torah – it is towards existence itself, the *connection* that is our place in the cosmos. All of the mitzvot, all of the principles that we come to understand of the Torah and of life and nature, are important to us not as ideologies, but as passionate contact. In the end, it can only be the relationship that matters.

> *What you dislike, do not do to your friend.*
>
> Your "friend" refers to God, who is called *Your friend and the friend of your father – do not let Him down! (Mishlei 27:10)*
>
> RASHI, SHABBAT, 31a[18]

In *Parashat Vayeshev* Yisrael begins its move from the struggle of personal growth and national development, to the goal of *tikkun* – the repair of Creation. Here begins the only road that can take us home again, painfully and painstakingly stitching together the rents in life's fabric, the divisions, the jealousies, the loneliness – all the alienation that is creation's deepest contaminant. From this point on, to build Torah is to build relationship.

> ...all that leads to the objective of achieving the true good – that is, anything that leads to strengthening the Torah, and building the brotherhood of nations.
>
> MESILAT YESHARIM, INTRODUCTION

Throughout all the trauma and pain suffered by the players in *Vayeshev's* drama, there moved the presence of God, in search of *tikkun* for His creation. In this parasha, within a landscape peopled by men occupied in little worlds of *tsores*, were laid the foundations for a world made whole, a world free of tears at last.

שבטים היו עסוקין במכירתו של יוסף,
ויוסף היה עסוק בשקו ובתעניתו,
ראובן היה עסוק בשקו ובתעניתו,
ויעקב היה עסוק בשקו ובתעניתו,
ויהודה היה עסוק ליקח לו אשה,
והקב"ה היה עוסק-
בורא אורו של מלך המשיח.

בראשית רבה פרשה פה

The brothers were occupied selling Yosef,
Yosef was occupied in sackcloth and mourning,
Re'uven was occupied in sackcloth and mourning,
Ya'akov was occupied in sackcloth and mourning,
Yehuda was occupied in finding a wife...
The Holy One was busy, too – busy creating the light of *Mashiaḥ*.

BEREISHIT RABBA, 85:1

1 Second approach, printed along with 37:2 s.v. *Vayeshev*, ד״ה וישב. These words are not found in Rome edition, but do appear in Bereishit Rabba, 84:3.

2 Ibid.

3 Cf. *Tanḥuma*, *Vayeshev*, 9.

4 Cf. *Tanna devei Eliahu Zuta* 24:2.

5 Queen Victoria. From a letter to King Leopold of Belgium, April 4, 1848.

6 Another dictionary spells it "tsurus," reflecting an alternate Yiddish accent. The word, of course, is based on the Hebrew "tzarah."

7 Bereishit Rabba, 17:1.

8 Bereishit Rabba, 98:6; Zohar, I:186a, II:104a.

9 S.v. *Vayhi*, ד״ה ויהי בעת.

10 38:7, s.v. *Ra*, ד״ה רע.

11 Cf. Radak, 38:19.

12 S.v. *Vatahar*, ד״ה ותהר.

13 "*Yehuda*" actually translates as "admission," and cf. Bamidbar Rabba, 13:4.

14 Tosefta Berachot, 4:16.

15 Sotah, 7b.

16 Bereishit 43:9.

17 Bereishit 44:18.

18 S.v. *De'alach*, ד״ה דעלך.

IX Vayeshev

וישב

Kosher Lemehadrin
Ḥanukah I

In *Vayeshev,* Ya'akov's long journey comes to an end at last as *he settled* ("vayeshev") *in the land where his father lived* (37:1).
But the peace he seeks eludes him, and he faces instead the most difficult time of his life.
Dissension tears Ya'akov's family apart, as Yosef barely escapes fratricide by his older brothers led by Yehuda, and is sold into slavery.
The parasha traces Yosef's life as a slave in Egypt, dramatically contrasting it to Yehuda's life in Cana'an.
Kosher Lemehadrin considers the issues that underlie the dissension between Yosef and his brothers, and finds that *Vayeshev*'s theme shatters some cherished assumptions, while illuminating Ḥanukah with a new and disturbing light.
As Ḥanukah issues pervade the *parashot* this week and next (that these are the Ḥanukah-time *parashot* every year is too good to be coincidence), for the purposes of this essay I will treat the two portions as a single continuing saga: Ḥanukah I and II.

KOSHER LEMEHADRIN
ḤANUKAH I

Parashat Vayeshev provides crucial background for Ḥanukah, affording an opportunity to gain a more mature appreciation of the holiday that falls around the reading of this parasha. For the child's version of Ḥanukah – a simple story of 'Jew versus Greek' – hides a lot of painful truths from young ears. The real story is more about Hellenists than about Hellene; it is more about Jew against Jew than about Jew against Greek.

Ḥanukah is a story with much unfortunate relevance to our own times. Then as now Yisrael was tragically at battle with itself, exhibiting the nearly fatal flaw we as a People know so well: internal conflict. *Vayeshev* records the earliest manifestation of this battle – the struggle between Yosef and his brothers.

Vayeshev conceals the underlying dispute within a story that appears to be no more than a tale of sibling rivalry and deadly jealousies. In reality, the saga of Yosef and his brothers represents a House of Israel historically divided against itself. The ramifications of their conflict have been articulated emotionally, philosophically and politically over the course of millennia – today perhaps more than ever before.

What *Vayeshev* presents as a personal breakdown in the relationship between Yosef and the brothers led by Yehuda,[1] eventually became a historic political division of the nation into two kingdoms. Ultimately it led to a prolonged and tragic civil war,[2] a full six centuries before the Ḥanukah dissension.

> In Shechem they sold Yosef,
> And in Shechem the kingdom was divided (between Yosef and Yehuda[3]).
>
> SANHEDRIN, 102a

Long before Greece existed, the origins of schism found in *Vayeshev* and their later manifestations were prophetically and poetically linked by Zecharia to the victory of Ḥanukah.

> *I will draw back on Yehuda,*
> *As a bow filled with [Yosef's] Ephraim,*[4]
> *And incite your children, Tzion,*
> *Against your children, Yavan* (Greece[5])…. (*Zecharia 9:13*)

In light of both midrash and history, *Vayeshev* emerges as a chronicle of differing visions about the nature of *Klal Yisrael* and the competition for its leadership. These simmering contentions boiled over when exposed to Greece and Hellenization – and for good reason. The elements in Yosef that alarmed his brothers most were precisely those elements that make Greece and the West so attractive – and so dangerous – to Yisrael. To his brothers, Yosef was one of the "beautiful people," an ambitious dreamer in charismatic pursuit of individuality and universality. In their eyes, he typified the danger of the potential insinuation of subversive culture, philosophy, and sensuality into a nation still in sensitive formation.

Take joy, youth,
in your childhood;
let your heart gladden you in
the days of your youthfulness,
follow the paths of your heart….
KOHELET 11:9

Consider the accent of the Torah's introduction of Yosef:

> *Yosef was seventeen years old…and he was a youth….*[6] (37:2)

> Yosef would act the teenager: spiff up his eyes, pirouette on his heels, fashion his hair, so that he would look beautiful….
> BEREISHIT RABBA, 84:7 AND RASHI 37:2[7]

> The words of Kohelet and the words of the Torah parallel one another:
>
> *Take joy, youth, in your childhood….* (*Kohelet 11:9*), is a later equivalent of, *And he* [Yosef] *was a youth….* (*Bereishit 36:2*).
> ZOHAR, II:145a

The rest of the Yosef story centers around the same theme, and the Torah hints that Yosef's attractiveness is the secret ingredient of his great success:

> *He [Potiphar] left everything in the hands of Yosef, and concerned himself with nothing but the food he would eat – and Yosef was beautiful of form and beautiful of appearance.* (39:6)

Yosef continues to concern himself with personal magnetism, even during the captivity which brings such suffering to his father:

> Said the Holy One: Your father mourns you and you are busy curling your hair! I will sic your master's wife on you...[8]
>
> TANḤUMA, VAYESHEV, 8; RASHI 39:6

But Ya'akov himself recognized, appreciated, and even encouraged this aspect of Yosef. Why, just look at the role played by the gift of the beautiful coat which Ya'akov gave to Yosef. Ya'akov not only *acknowledged* this facet of Yosef, he sees it as Yosef's essence, his great contribution to the nation. Listen to the definitive blessing Ya'akov bequeaths to Yosef:

> *Yosef is a charming one,*
> *A graceful one to the eye,*
> *Daughters parade on the wall to see him.* (49:22[9])

Yosef the beautiful, young, charismatic Jewish leader of gentile Egypt stood in stark contrast to his more mature brothers. They made their opinion regarding intercultural contact very plain by exterminating the city of Shechem.[10] Yosef's brothers were mindful of his potential downside, the modern day accompaniments to Western culture: subtle twisting of individuality into egotism, warmth into lust, dreams into manipulation, and open-minded breadth into insipid emulation.

The brothers' suspicions about the potential dangers of a certain young dreamer are suggested by their caustic comment,

> *Behold – the Dream Master arrives!* (37:19)
>
> *Dream Master* (*ba'al ha'ḥalomot*): They said, "This one will lead them all to *Ba'al*[11] worship!"
>
> BEREISHIT RABBA, 84:14

They certainly were uncannily accurate in their assessment: Yosef's offspring *did* lead the nation toward worshiping the *Ba'al* and other idols. Seven hundred years after the events in *Vayeshev*, a great scion of Yosef, Yerov'am, founder of the breakaway Kingdom of Israel, renewed the worship of golden calves as an alternative to the Temple Service in Jerusalem, capitol of the Kingdom of Yehuda.

> Until Yerov'am, Klal Yisrael nursed from only one calf; from his time on they nursed from two or three.
>
> SANHEDRIN, 102a

When Yerov'am was young he was a tzaddik... The ministering angels said, "Allow him to live – the grandeur of Your Name comes through him..." God told them, "If you wish it, I will allow him to live..." and then he built the golden calves and caused all Yisrael to sin.

ZOHAR ḤADASH, AḤAREI, 40:8

Even that first calf appears to have been modeled on Yosef's persona. Calf worship expresses the golden-boy vision of eternal youth and the drives for license that Yehuda and the brothers had foreseen in Yosef. The midrash dramatically highlights this association:

> Aharon took the slate upon which Moshe had engraved the words "*Arise, Bull!*" to raise Yosef's coffin to the surface of the Nile. Aharon threw it into the furnace containing the molten gold earrings and the golden calf emerged, lowing....
>
> TANḤUMA, KI TISA, 19

This Yosef-associated deterioration opened a breach in Yisrael that left her vulnerable to Greece and the West:

Italia! O Italia! Thou who hast
The fatal gift of Beauty.
BYRON

> The very same day that Yerov'am introduced his calves in Beit El and Dan, a small shack was built that developed [over the centuries] into *Italia* of *Yavan* (Greece and her connection to Rome[12]).
>
> SHABBAT, 56b

For it is in the love of beauty and the openness of youth that Greece mounted the most insidious challenge to Yisrael, at the time of Ḥanukah and forevermore. Through such "infatuation with physical beauty"[13] and commitment to youth and art Greece achieved her grandeur.

> Greek science itself was a child of Greek philosophy – that youthful love of inquiry...the art of logic and the logic of art...cherish[ing] freedom, reason, and beauty.
>
> WILL DURANT, THE LIFE OF GREECE

Yehuda and his brothers were mistaken about one thing: The challenge derives not from the *differences* between Yisrael and Yavan, but from their *similarities*. In his description of the Vision of the Shechina's Chariot, Yeḥezkel alludes to Greece:

> *A shine surrounded it... (Yeḥezkel 1:4)*
>
> –This refers to the Kingdom of Greece. *A shine surrounding it* implies that it has aspects of *kedusha* of *emunah*. One is not allowed to treat it with contempt.
>
> ZOHAR ḤADASH, II:44b; ZOHAR, II: 203b

One would have thought, perhaps, that the Torah would locate Yavan's "aspects of *kedusha* of *emunah*," not in beauty, but in the pursuit of knowledge, ethics, and social justice that Greece shares with Yisrael.

But no – the very beauty that Yehuda and his brothers rejected as alien and a threat to their national identity, that very beauty is the premier and uniquely positive characteristic that Yavan and Yisrael share. This "*shine*" of Greece, the beauty of Greece, even shares in Yisrael's most precious and sacred possession:

> A Torah scroll may be written in no other language [besides Hebrew] but Greek, as is said: יפת אלוקים ליפת וישכון באהלי שם – *God shall expand (yaft–* יפת, also meaning "beauty") *Yefet* (יפת) *and dwell in the tents of Shem* (9:27).
>
> The *yaft*, meaning the beauty, of Yefet (i.e. the Greek language – Rashi[14]) shall dwell in the tents of Shem.
>
> MEGILLA, 8b,9b

But surely historical hindsight indicates that the brothers were correct in their assessments, at least, if not in their methodology? It is here that *Vayeshev* is at its most shocking. In a show-and-tell whose message is evident and which forms the primary theme of the parasha, *Vayeshev* points out the contrast between Yehuda and Yosef. For *Vayeshev* not only presents the point of contention between the brothers, it also furnishes a follow-up survey of the pragmatic ramifications of their views within the real world in a fabulous contrast of personal histories that the youthful, beautiful, and dangerous dreamer wins hands down.[15]

Yehuda failed in every single way that he suspected of Yosef, where Yosef himself triumphed! Let a few ironic examples suffice:

Did Yehuda believe that maturity and solidity are more essential for leadership than are dreams and charisma?

> *At that time, Yehuda went down from his brothers....* (38:1)
>
> He "descended" from his brothers, i.e. they divested him of his leadership.[16] (—Rashi[17])

Whereas Yosef was a natural leader, achieving positions of authority again and again[18] until at last

> *Pharaoh said to Yosef, "Behold – I appoint you over the entire country of Egypt!"* (41:41).

Did Yehuda claim that romantic dreamers threaten Yisrael with sensuality and license?

> *And Yehuda saw her and took her for a whore... and he said to her, "Here, now, let me lie with you...."* (38:15, 16)

Whereas Yosef proved impervious to the most explicit seductiveness:

> *She grabbed him by his coat saying, "Lie with me!" And he left his coat in her hands and escaped, bolting outside* (39:12).

Did Yehuda foresee a dangerous mingling with gentiles and foreign culture if Yosef were allowed his dreams?

> *And Yehuda went aside to a gentleman from Adulam by the name of Ḥira.* (38:1)
>
> He went into business with him. (—Rashi[19])

Whereas Yosef warned his brothers:

> *Tell him [Pharaoh], "Your servants have been shepherds from our youth until today, both we and our forefathers," so that you be allowed to live [apart] in the land of Goshen, for all shepherds are anathema to Egyptians* (46:34).

Did Yehuda believe that intermarriage and assimilation would be the lot of those who followed the path of Yosef?

> *And Yehuda saw there the daughter of a Canaanite man by the name of Shua and he took her* [as a wife[20]].... (38:2).

Whereas Yosef took *Osnat the daughter of Poti-Phera the priest of On for a wife* (41:45). Osnat was his own niece, the daughter of Dinah by Shechem, raised in the home of Poti-Phera after escaping with her life from Yosef's brothers.[21]

Did Yehuda believe that Torah and piety could not be reliably inculcated in a new generation conceived amidst alien ideas?

> *Yehuda's firstborn son 'Er was evil in God's eyes, and God killed him... and God considered what he* [Onan, Yehuda's second son] *did to be evil, and killed him as well.* (38:7,10)

Whereas Yosef's son – conceived and raised in a foreign land – grew to be the spiritual leader of his people:

> *He* [Yosef] *called [his son] Ephraim, for God has made me successful in the land of my distress....* (41:52)

> Before Ya'akov died he commanded that Ephraim was to be the head of the Tribes and the *Rosh Yeshiva*.
>
> VAYIKRA RABBA, 2:3

Yosef's antagonists believed that Yisrael could flourish only in isolation, forming the world while remaining unformed by it. But holiness is genuine only when grown from the earth, expressive of the inner beauty of Creation's potential. Piety without vitality is like a soul without a body and a color without a rose. The tzaddik remains always youthful, destined to regain the full bloom of childhood.

> Every single tzaddik...is destined to be restored to childhood... to have even a youthful body and renewed signs of pubescence, as it says, *They will flow freely once again in old age, virile and fresh shall they be....* (*Tehillim* 82:15).
>
> MIDRASH ALPHA BETA, 63

Beauty and charm were clearly victorious in this war of ideation, but the vicissitudes of exile have backed Yisrael time and again into retreat and isolation. Because of bitter experience we have taken Yehuda's fears as our own. We have begun to act as if Yosef's life could no longer have relevance to our own. Once again, individuals are torn by what they perceive as the only alternatives: spontaneity versus ritual, creativity versus replication, universalism versus parochialism, and fervent *avodah* versus analytic intellectualism.

Yet Ḥanukah proclaims that beauty remains the center of Yisrael. Ḥanukah insists that beauty be an integral part of the very definition of how a mitzvah must be performed.

> The mitzvah of Ḥanukah candle lighting is one candle for each home;
> For those who are *mehadrin*, a candle for each family member;
> For the *mehadrin* beyond mere *mehadrin*...add a candle with each passing night.
>
> SHABBAT, 21b

Now the word "*mehadrin*" means "those who make things beautiful."[22] This is the meaning of *hidur mitzvah*: "making mitzvot beautiful."

> זה אלי ואנוהו – *This is my God and I will make Him beautiful.* (*Shemot* 15:2)

> That is, make yourself beautiful in mitzvot: a beautiful *succah*, a beautiful *lulav*, a beautiful shofar, beautiful *tzizit*, a beautiful *sefer Torah*. . . .
>
> SHABBAT, 133b

Yet in a remarkable – and sadly telling – cultural inversion, "*mehadrin*" has come to mean "stringent," as in the expensive term "*Kosher Lemehadrin*." The truth is that *there is no such thing* – unless you are being served a specially beautiful kosher steak.

The parasha's lesson notwithstanding, the shine of the Ḥanukah lights, symbol of Yisrael's *yefeh to'ar* (39:6) victory over the beautiful "*shine*" of *Yefet*, has been ironically victimized by the longstanding and yet-unresolved conflict between Yosef and his brothers.

We dare not trivialize the Yosef/Yehuda conflict, just as we dare not oversimplify the conclusions forced upon us in this parasha. History bears unforgiving witness to the dangers we have faced and face now at these very crucial moments. Nonetheless, how different our lives would be if every *mehadrin* embodied a search for beauty and sweetness so beyond mere stringency and so consistent with the indelible message of *Vayeshev*.

Segue

There is more, of course. Neither Ḥanukah nor history is one-sided. Yehuda is the dominant element in the development of Yisrael, its kingdom and its future. He has a central role in Ḥanukah, as well. Indeed, as an expression of *Yehuda*, which means "to acknowledge," "to concede," and "to praise," Ḥanukah became the time for *hoda'ah*, a Jewish Thanksgiving:

וקבעו שמונת ימי חנוכה אלו להודות ולהלל לשמך הגדול

> They set aside these eight days of Ḥanukah to acknowledge (*l'hodot*) and to praise Your great Name.
>
> AL HANISSIM PRAYER

Yehuda secured his place through conceding his own missteps[23] and through acknowledging Yosef's achievement.[24] For though Yehuda plays the leading role on the stage of Jewish history, it is Yosef who creates the environment within which Yehuda can flourish, Yosef who provides for the viability and feasibility of Yehuda's approach.

How does Yosef overcome the dangers inherent in his approach? How does he succeed in restoring his own connection to Yehuda and *hoda'ah*? We will explore these questions in the next essay as our saga continues through the coming parasha. One thing is clear, though, and well worth remembering in these disturbing times of Jewish fragmentation: It takes Yehuda and Yosef together as one to build a nation, to build a future, and to turn back cultural and national disintegration. Ḥanukah helps bring that era of crowning synthesis a step closer.

1 Cf. Rashi 38:1.

2 See Melachim I,14:30 and 15:6,8,32.

3 Cf. Melachim I, chapter 12.

4 The reference is to the ten tribes lead by Ephraim from Yosef. See *Metzudot,* Zecharia 9:13.

5 The children of Yavan later founded the political entity, "Greece."

6 Actually, the literal translation is closer to "he youthed it up..." using נער as a verb. The only word in English that can be used for the noun "youth" and a related verb is "kid," which fascinatingly has much the same meaning involved in the context here. My thesaurus suggests "make eyes," "allure," and "charm."

7 S.v. *Vehu na'ar,* ד״ה והוא נער.

8 S.v. *Vayhi Yosef,* ד״ה ויהי יוסף.

9 As translated by Rashi.

10 In another ironical contrast, the vehicle of the brothers' Shechem treachery is *brit milah*, which to them symbolizes the untouchable uniqueness of the Jewish people. But Yosef gives that very *brit milah* to Egypt to prepare the way for Jewish life there (See Bereishit 41:55, Rashi, s.v. *Asher,* ד״ה אשר יאמר, Bereishit Rabba, 91:5).

11 See Shofetim, chapter 6; Melachim I, chapters 16,18; Melachim II, chapter 10.

12 Cf. Megilla, 6b

13 Will Durant, *The Life of Greece,* (New York: Simon and Schuster, 1966), 669

14 Rashi, Megilla, 9b.

15 It may not be an entirely fair contest for Yehuda, who is forced into compromising situations "not of his own free desire" (Bereishit Rabba, 85:8). But it certainly proves the point, and comes to teach us—otherwise we would be out of bounds even in discussing it publicly (cf. Megilla, 25b).

16 Fascinatingly, this divestiture shows up historically as well. When the kingdom split into two, [*Shevet*] Yehuda was abandoned by nearly all the brothers, who went along with [*Shevet*] Yosef led by Yerov'am ben Nevat.

17 Cf. Bereishit Rabba, 85:2 and *Tanḥuma, Ki Tisa,* 22:1.

18 Cf. 39:4 and 39:22.

19 S.v. *Ad ish,* ד״ה עד איש.

20 *Radak*, op. cit.

21 *Ḥizkuni,* 41:46, *Yalkut Shimoni, Vayishlaḥ,* 134.

22 Cf. Rabbeinu Ḥannanel, op. cit. Though Rashi uses the words "*after* the mitzvot" taking *mehadrim* in the sense of "seekers," in Alfasi the language of Rashi is "the mitzvot" alone, implying "beautifying the mitzvot." In every other reference I know of, *hidur* is justified on the basis of *This is my God and I shall make Him beautiful.*

23 Bereishit 38:26; Bava Kama, 92a; Bereishit Rabba 89:8; Targum Yonatan, Bereishit 49:8. For a full treatment, see my *Patterns in Time* (Jerusalem and New York: Feldheim, 1988), volume 8.

24 Bereishit Rabba, 95:1; Zohar, I:206b.

X Miketz

מִקֵּץ

Requiem for a Spy
Ḥanukah II

Miketz ("At the Conclusion") heralds the dramatic end of Yosef's prison term, two years after his own plans for an early release backfire. Here Yosef is hauled from a dungeon to begin a brilliant career as leader of Egypt and pacesetter of world civilization. The parasha opens with the dreams of Pharaoh and the impending world drought for which Yosef must prepare. But *Miketz* also speaks on another plane, for Pharaoh's dreams have a personal interpretation for Yosef, furnishing the strategy he must take in drawing his brothers to him and towards his vision. Yosef must prove the value and power of relationship, healing a rift festering for twenty-two years.

In the previous essay, we explored the Kulturkampf between Hellenists and traditional Jews driving the events of Ḥanukah, and discovered its historical and philosophical roots within the fundamental schism between Yosef and his brothers depicted in *Vayeshev*.

Miketz continues to develop the covert Ḥanukah theme, and formulates a resolution to conflict in Yisrael against the backdrop of Yosef's spectacular success—a triumph that ultimately leads out of exile and into the Land of Israel.

In *Miketz*, within the unconventional performance of Yosef, are to be found suggestive allusions to the victory of Ḥanukah and elusive suggestions for a resolution of our contemporary disharmony.

Requiem for a Spy analyzes the parasha's intrigue and dreams; considers the substance of ends and means; and proposes safeguarding charisma, exposure, and love from spies and their schemes.

REQUIEM FOR A SPY
ḤANUKAH II

In a story with a fairy-tale surface reminiscent of Cinderella, Yosef the despised slave-brother rises to the top of the kingdom after being taken under the wing of Pharaoh himself. It would seem that Yosef rightly denies credit for his success: "*Not I! – God will respond to Pharaoh's welfare* (41:16) – I am nothing more than the right man in the right place at the right moment." Pharaoh wholeheartedly disagrees.

"*There is no one as discerning and wise as you* (41:39)," is Pharaoh's rationale for the astonishing snap decision that places the administration and future of the world's leading civilization tightly in Yosef's hands. If the truth be told, however, Yosef appears to flourish in his new position not through brilliant insight but primarily through the force of personality. It is his personal charisma that propels him to superstar status in Egypt. Pharaoh does his level best to encourage this popular image of Yosef, and the Torah describes the Kennedy-like aura surrounding Yosef in Camelot.

> *[Pharaoh] dressed him in linen clothing and put a golden chain upon his neck, and had him driven around in his personal associate chariot, and announced before him: Av-rech,* אברך. (41:42,43)
>
> *Av Rech* means a "master" (*Av*-אב) in learning who is "tender" (*rach*-רך) *in years. . . .*
>
> SIFREI, DEVARIM 1

> *Yosef was thirty years old as he stood before Pharaoh, king of Egypt, and Yosef emerged from the meeting with Pharaoh and toured the breadth of the land of Egypt.* (41:46)
>
> Princesses would peek through the cracks to see him, tossing their necklaces, rings, bracelets and earrings just trying to get his attention. . . .
>
> BEREISHIT RABBA, 98:18

Pharaoh dreamed that he was standing by the Channel, when out of the Channel there came seven cows, beautiful to look at and full-fleshed, and they grazed in the marsh. But presently, seven other cows came up from the Channel close behind them, ugly and gaunt, and stood beside the other cows on the river bank. And the seven gaunt cows ate up the seven beautiful, full fleshed cows. And Pharaoh awoke. He fell asleep and dreamed a second time: Seven ears of grain, healthy and full fleshed, grew on a single stalk. But close behind them sprouted seven ears, thin and scorched by the east wind. And the thin ears swallowed up the seven solid and full ears. Then Pharaoh awoke – and it was a dream. Next morning, his spirit was agitated, and he sent for all the magicians of Egypt, and all its wise men; and Pharaoh told them his dreams, but none could interpret them for Pharaoh.

...Thereupon Pharaoh sent for Yosef, and he was rushed from the dungeon. He had his hair cut and changed his clothes, and he appeared before Pharaoh. And Pharaoh said to Yosef, "I have had a dream but no one can interpret it. Now I have heard it said of you that you hear a dream so as to tell its meaning." Yosef answered Pharaoh, saying, "Not I! God will respond to Pharaoh's welfare."

Look more closely, though, and you will find that Yosef's superstar stance was neither a colorful byproduct of his personality nor an accident of bureaucratic stature. Compare and analyze the two dreams of Pharaoh, and you will find that they demand precisely what Yosef delivered. Consider:

Why dual dream images – cows and ears of grain? Would not the urgency of the repetition be just as powerful if the *same* dream were repeated twice?

> *As for the dream occurring twice to Pharaoh – the matter is determined by God, and God hurries to carry it out.* (41:32)

Why are the cows given location and setting, while the ears are given neither?

> *Out of the Channel came seven cows, beautiful to look at and full fleshed, and they grazed in the marsh.* (41:2)
> *Seven ears of grain, healthy and full-fleshed, grew on a single stalk.* (41:5)

Why is the *appearance* of the cows important, but when it comes to the ears, only their *condition* is mentioned?

> [*The cows were*] *beautiful to look at....*
> [*The ears were*] *healthy and full-fleshed ....*

The emaciated cows first *stood by the other cows on the river bank* (41:3) before devouring them – why? And why does this detail have no counterpart in the second dream?

Another contrast: In the first dream, the emaciated cows not only devour the fattened cows – implying that the years of plenty will pass – but also,

> *after they had ingested them you could never know that they had ingested them – they remained as emaciated as they were at first.* (41:21)

Now, Yosef interprets this last point as a significant issue quite distinct from the first:

> *All the plenty of the land of Egypt will be forgotten.* (41:30)
> This is the interpretation of the ingestion itself. (—Rashi[1])

No trace of the abundance will remain in the land. (41:31)

This is the interpretation of *you could never know that they had ingested them.* (—Rashi[2])

But this entire issue has no counterpart in the second dream where

the thin ears swallowed up the seven solid and full ears. Then Pharaoh awoke.... (41:7)

It would appear that the two dreams are not simple projections of the same message, a point the Torah highlights in stressing that Pharaoh awoke between the dreams:

And Pharaoh awoke. He fell asleep and dreamed a second time.... (41:4,5)

Pharaoh stresses the same point to Yosef:

[Pharaoh said to Yosef]...and I awoke. And then I saw in my dream... (41:21,22).

Why does Yosef not interpret the differences between the dreams?

He does, of course. Consider: just who asked Yosef for his opinion and advice, anyway?[3] He was ordered to interpret Pharaoh's dreams, yet with astounding temerity, he went on to hint of the need for none other than himself.[4]

Not to mention that he is awfully vague about the job description – other than his indelicate suggestion that Pharaoh shall *appoint him over the entire country of Egypt* (41:33). We tend to take for granted that he is referring to something like a National Director of Emergency Nutritional Resources, but clearly he meant much more than that as Pharaoh was well aware.

Pharaoh said to Yosef, "I am Pharaoh! Without your say-so, no one may do so much as lift his hand or foot in the entire country of Egypt!" (41:44)

What would justify the creation of such a unique position, and what could justify the suggestion coming from Yosef himself? Only the unequivocal import of Pharaoh's own dreams.

Though the two dreams refer to the same general scenario, they do so in very different ways. The first dream could be seen as suggesting that

Then Pharaoh said to Yosef, "In my dream, I was standing on the bank of the Channel, when out of the Channel came up seven cows, full fleshed and beautiful to look at, and grazed in the marsh. Presently there followed them seven other cows, gaunt and ugly and emaciated – never had I seen their likes for ugliness in all the land of Egypt! And the seven lean and gaunt cows ate up the first seven cows, the healthy ones. After they had ingested them you could never know that they had ingested them, they looked just as bad as before – and I awoke. And then I saw in my dream, seven ears of grain growing on a single stalk, full and excellent. Right behind them sprouted seven ears, shriveled, thin, and scorched by the east wind. And the thin ears swallowed the seven quality ears. I have told my magicians, but none has an explanation for me."

problems lurking beneath the surface of Egypt's prosperity had the potential for disaster. But the additional dream framed the vision as an actual prophecy, and provided Yosef a specific blueprint for interpretation and a specific timetable: *As for the dream occurring twice to Pharaoh – the matter is determined by God* – i.e. something *specific* is going to happen, *and God hurries to carry it out* (41:32) – it is going to happen *now*.

It is only *the seven empty ears* of the second dream that are interpreted as *seven years of famine* (41:27), not *the seven cows* of the first dream. For the first dream spoke more of *why* than of specifically *what*. It pinpoints the nature of the national failing that endangered the future existence of Egypt. This is why it opened with a scene at "*the Channel*" – the symbol of Egyptian national identity and mythos[5] – rather than opening at "*the River*:"

> No other river is referred to as "channel" except the Nile, because all of Egypt is crisscrossed by man-made channels which are filled by the annual Nile flooding, as there is no reliable rainfall in Egypt.
>
> RASHI 41:1[6]

Despite total dependence on the Nile river system (*the Channel*), despite the fact that failures are anticipated (*the emaciated cows stood next to the other cows at the bank* before devouring them), the years of prosperity are to be *forgotten* and therefore can *make no impression* on the tough times to come (this is the critical significance of the two stages: *And the seven lean and gaunt cows ate up the first seven cows* followed by, *After they had ingested them you could never know that they had ingested them*). The dream thus declared that there would be no planning for the future, no banking[7] for the future, because Egypt was a land without functional *memory*, without an ability to store information – or grain – for future restoration. A land without memory is a land without meaningful past or viable future. Egypt was a land without identity.

A society can make difficult decisions – can suffer immediate deprivation for the sake of the future, can plan in peacetime for war, in prosperity for poverty, in youth for old age – only if it has an integrated identity. Over the long haul, running a country takes more than bureaucracy or secret police – it requires the commitment of its citizenry to a

And Yosef said to Pharaoh, "Pharaoh's dream is one and the same: God has told Pharaoh what He is about to do. The seven excellent cows are seven years, and the seven healthy ears are seven years; it is the same dream. The seven emaciated and ugly cows that followed are seven years, and the seven empty ears scorched by the east wind are seven years of famine. This is just as I have told Pharaoh: what God is about to do He has revealed to Pharaoh. Immediately ahead are seven years of great bounty throughout the land of Egypt. Coming after them are seven years of famine, and all the plenty in the land of Egypt will be forgotten – the famine will ravage the land. No trace of the abundance will remain in the land because of that following famine, for it will be exceedingly severe. As for the dream occurring twice to Pharaoh – the matter is determined by God, and God hurries to carry it out. Now, let Pharaoh find a man of discernment and wisdom, and set him over the land of Egypt....

vision, a belief in national significance and destiny. Without that vision, Egypt was a disaster waiting to happen. The proximate failure of the earliest links in the food chain (*ears of grain*) would lead to the rapid destruction of their only stockpile (*the cows*) and the collapse of society.

Yosef made no suggestions of his own. He discovered *in the dream itself* that Egypt needed a vision, not a National Director of Emergency Nutritional Resources. Money and officialdom are impotent in the face of disintegrated vision. Not long ago, Somalia suffered the same fate that here threatened her neighbor Egypt, and all the financial resources in the world proved insufficient to prevent starvation in that non-nation.[8] Pharaoh's dreams projected a seven year window of opportunity to achieve an Egyptian national vision capable of responding to the challenge of survival. The key to that opportunity was beauty.

The vision thing...
GEORGE BUSH

Those *cows, beautiful to look at,* symbolized the years of prosperity not because they were *full fleshed*, but because they were *beautiful.*

> *Beautiful to look at...*
>
> This symbolizes the years of prosperity, when people look beautiful to one another, for no one is jealous of the other. (—Rashi[9])

Memory feeds a culture....
ELIE WIESEL

What Egypt needed was someone who could reflect the beauty, the vigor, the vision, and the youthful potential of the country. Egypt needed to become a vital and viable whole. It needed a leader who could provide a personal face and identity to nationhood.

Where there is no vision, the people perish...[10]
MISHLEI 29:18

Yosef was able to brilliantly and sensitively *interpret* the information and pinpoint the problem – and, not coincidentally, Egypt found in Yosef exactly what the dream required. Here was a man who made feeding the population of the planet a *personal* matter, not a bureaucratic one.

> All the nationalities came to purchase food and would bring taxes to Egypt and a gift for Yosef. And he would speak to each individual in his own language....
>
> PIRKEI RABI ELIEZER, 39

> Yosef nurtured the world during famine the way a shepherd cares for his flock.
>
> BEREISHIT RABBA, 91:5

Yosef transformed Egypt from a nation of residents demanding entitlement programs,[11] endlessly asking "What can my country do for me," into a nation of citizens asking, "What can I do for my country?"[12] Only *ḥen* (חן[13]), the charisma[14] which was the hallmark of Yosef throughout his life,[15] could have elicited that kind of personal response and care. Only Yosef could have accomplished this national metamorphosis.

What is stunning in this story is that Pharaoh's dreams and Yosef's achievements are precise analogs of everything that Yosef had insisted upon all along to his brothers. The entire story is a living example of the triumphant success *of everything his brothers had rejected*!

Yosef had claimed that personal vision, beauty, youth and charisma were essential to national survival, while Yehuda and his brothers argued that nothing could be more dangerous to national survival. To build morality, national vision, and business success on personal dreams, they thought, was a virtual guarantee of ultimate personal, national, and religious corruption.

> *Behold – the Dream Master arrives!* (37:19)
>
> *"Dream Master"* (*ba'al ha'ḥalomot*): They said, "This one will lead them all to *Ba'al* worship!"
>
> BEREISHIT RABBA, 84:14

Yosef needed to provide the same vision for Yisrael as he did for Egypt. To do so, he needed to demonstrate to his brothers that his approach was critical to the future of Yisrael. At the story's climax in the next parasha, *Vayigash*, Yosef is able to contrast his own success with his brothers' failure. It was "Selfish" Yosef who cared for Ya'akov; it was the brothers who nearly destroyed him. It was "Vain" Yosef who escaped seduction; it was Yehuda who had to admit indiscretion. It was "Dangerous" Yosef who showed care to his brothers when they fell into his hands; it was his brothers who attempted to murder him. "Dreamer" Yosef was the success story of the globe; his brothers could not even feed themselves.

Here in *Miketz*, Yosef proves that the charisma, beauty, dreams and personal relationships his brothers disdain are actually the secret of his success in Egypt. He demonstrates that the suspicions his brothers harbored of him were pure projection – the implications of *their* approach, not his. Yosef compels his brothers to confront the power of relationship instead of the relationship of power.

Although Yosef's strategy was endlessly subtle, we have room here to trace some of the more obvious twists of irony that ended in Yehuda's recognition of the truth (not to mention the opportunity to shed light on some of the mysterious twists of plot in the parasha).

Notice, for instance, how Yosef mysteriously returns their money twice, never referring to it again. Now, the brothers are convinced that this was done as a power play, a ploy to accuse them.

> *The men [the brothers] were afraid when they were brought to Yosef's house and said, "It is because of the money returned in our sacks from the beginning that we are being brought here to terrorize us and intimidate us, to take us as slaves!"* (43:18)

They entreat the "*Master of the house*" (actually Yosef's son, Menashe[16]), hoping to convince him of their innocence:

> *"Please sir...when we came to the hotel we opened our sacks, and behold every man's money was in the mouth of his sack...and we have brought it back in our hands and brought other money to purchase more food. We have no idea who put the money into our sacks...."* (43:20-22)

The man listens bemusedly to this long explanation, and waves them off amiably,

> *"Everything's fine...nothing to worry about...I received the money."* (43:23)

But it was not a ploy at all – and the only one who caught Yosef's meaning was Ya'akov himself. He says to his sons,

> *"If that is the case, do this: take the man a gift – a little balm and a bit of honey...peanuts and almonds. And take along double your money just in case it was a mistake."* (43:11,12)

But if it was *not* a mistake, how in the world could Ya'akov think that bringing some peanuts would somehow derail the orchestrated frame-up that they suspected? It must have been clear to Ya'akov that the man wanted a *personal* response to *personal* overtures, and was insisting that money was not the object. Only after the brothers found themselves in Yosef's waiting room – quite unaccused but hopelessly confused – did they recognize that their father must have been right on the mark. It was then that they took up his suggestion:

> *They prepared the gift for when Yosef would come at noon…and when Yosef returned home they presented him with the gift.* (43:25,26)

Yosef catches them completely off guard with his sincere concern for their family, with his tears at meeting Binyamin, and with his gentle treatment of the imprisoned Shimon. Even when he accuses them of stealing his cup, what matters is not the mad temerity of stealing a fabulously valuable chalice from the private collection of Egypt's ruler, but the violation of a relationship:

> *Why did you repay good with evil? Is this not the cup from which my master drinks?* (44:4,5)

The brothers learned that it was through charisma and relationship that Yosef triumphed in Egypt. This is not the whole story, however. We know from our own national experience how right the brothers were, as well. Charisma is dangerous and beauty is nothing to rely on, and Yosef and his descendants did lead Yisrael to idolatry and destruction.

> שקר החן והבל היופי...
> *Charm is false and beauty is trivial….* (Mishlei 31:30)

It is true that by withstanding the most aggressive blandishments of power, money and sex,[17] Yosef himself became the prototype of utter integrity. But those who followed him have failed. History is full of illusions of Camelot, cluttered by the broken dreams of corrupted charisma.

Does Yosef offer a solution to the brothers' objections? Does he present a feasible and judicious approach to a life of beauty? Or is

Yosef's success an accident, a once-in-history aberration that should be given its rightful place and then promptly forgotten as a model?

Anyone who gives the traditional Shabbat-eve blessing to his sons will have no trouble answering that last question:

> Just as Ya'akov blessed Yisrael with the three *Avot*, so did he bless them with the name of Yosef and made them all dependent on Yosef, as it says, *With you [Yosef] will Israel bless, saying "May God make you as Ephraim and Menashe...."* (*Bereishit* 48:20).
>
> BAMIDBAR RABBA, 14:5

Yosef is clearly a model, the dream for the future of our own children. As *Mashiaḥ ben Yosef*, he is the harbinger of the final redemption and the name by which all of Yisrael is known.

> All of Yisrael is called by the name of Yosef, as it says, *Perhaps God will grace the remnant of Yosef* (*Amos* 5:15).
>
> MIDRASH TEHILLIM, 3:3

If Yosef is indeed to be our model, then he must offer here an approach that mitigates the danger of his vision. He has had a lot of time to think about it, for over twenty years have passed since he last saw his brothers. The very first thing he says to them sums up his vision and approach, identifies the source of the downturn they have experienced, and warns them of the trials that are to come.

> *You are spies – you have come to see the nakedness of the land!* (42:9)

Yosef passionately believed the essence of this accusation. All of *Parashat Miketz* is the story of his dedicated battle to prove that he was right. To Yosef, all of the differences between himself and his brothers throughout history – the philosophical schism, the political divisions,[18] the civil wars,[19] even the different approaches to learning and understanding Torah[20] – are traceable to a fundamental difference in primal choice: to spy or not to spy.

The choices that lead down the paths of good and evil are those that define each individual's response to the undeniable existence of a reality separate and independent from himself. This is primal challenge, the ultimate sibling rivalry: infants kick and cry, others may lay down and die, but functionality demands an accommodation of sorts between the world of our self-awareness and the self-aware world. Most people struggle with existence, maintaining a separate peace. They search for advantages, tools for molding the world in their own image, for "making things happen." They gauge success by such achievement, whether in business, culture, spirituality, or in building Torah, utopia and the World to Come. But if such is the criterion of success, if the ends are what matters most, then corruption is only a step away. The ends eventually justify the means, any means.

To a seeker of such success, relationship itself serves as means to an end and becomes manipulative, menacing. The manipulator becomes a spy, snooping on life to find a vulnerable opening to achieve his ends – *it is the nakedness of the land you have come to espy! (42:12)*. His life becomes the life of a voyeur, who has lost passion for life itself and can live only through others, measuring his moments by his chances. The spy's goal is often the most excellent and holy of purposes, of course – but he remains a spy nonetheless. No wonder that power corrupts and charisma perverts him no matter the cause to which he couples them.

When one isn't dominated by feelings of separateness from what he's working on, then one can be said to "care" about what he's doing.

ROBERT PIRSIG, ZEN AND THE ART OF MOTORCYCLE MAINTENANCE[21]

To Yosef, the struggles of the spy and his existential separation are the harbingers of tragedy. The only ultimately moral accommodation between personal ego and reality must redefine relationship with the world: The question must become not how the world can be used – neither what can be done to it nor about it nor even for it – but what can be done together with it. To Yosef, sharing was his self, not an expression of his self. His goal was the relationship itself, not its payoff. The achievements of the disciple of Yosef are entirely his own. He has no interest or pleasure in anything extraneous – and that is what makes him so thoroughly reliable.

> Everything given to Yosef was entirely of his own making.
>
> BEREISHIT RABBA, 90:3

The resolution of the schism between the brothers and Yosef – a schism which engenders not only Ḥanukah, but much of the historical dissension from which we suffer both nationally and personally – lies in the resolution of the conflict between self and non-self. What Yehuda and his brothers had proposed as a model for Yisrael – isolation and domination – was nothing more than a national projection of the "spy" persona. And though the national and personal dangers associated with charisma and relationship are undeniably real, Yosef recognized them as the pitiful consequence of spying on life rather than living it. With his own life, within the dangers of beauty and vitality, Yosef discovered the essence of righteousness, the path to the restoration of Eden.

There was only one occasion in Yosef's life when he made the mistake of acting the spy. In a moment of weakness, Yosef tried to take advantage of a prisoner's dream and future – he attempted to get ahead by using something that was not his own. The two words he used cost him two years in prison.

> *Words of the lips just diminish things.* (*Mishlei* 14:23)
>
> Because Yosef said to the Chief Butler the two words זכרתני – *remember me* – and הזכרתני – *mention me* [to Pharaoh] – he needed to spend two years in prison, as it says:
>
> ויהי מקץ שנתיים ימים...
>
> *And it was at the end [Miketz] of two years....*
>
> BEREISHIT RABBA, 89:2

Miketz is named for the expensive lesson that is its theme, a lesson that formed Yosef's world view and made possible his rapprochement with his brothers.

Yosef had come to understand that the ends never justify the means – but that the means always justify the ends. As long as the definition of success depends not on what happens externally but on how one has striven and cared, there can be no failure but personal failure. As long as success is not measured by how well one asserts himself over the world, but only by the faithfulness, courage and integrity one has invested in it, there is no danger of the corruption that comes of needing specific pre-defined results. Ḥanukah enshrines this resolution of schism: embracing life passionately and defending a beloved world by living for the means instead of the ends.

Charisma knows only inner determination and inner restraint...The charismatic leader gains and maintains authority solely by proving his strength in life.

MAX WEBER

There was scant chance of victory against the Greeks at the time of Ḥanukah. But to fight and care for all that was precious meant more to the Maccabim than victory over Greece. The means to them were more valuable than the end – whatever that end would be – as they are to all who fully relate to life. This is why the true battles are always intensely personal, no matter how much "for the sake of heaven." So it was that Yosef's achievements became the source of Ḥanukah's glory.

רבת את ריבם,
דנת את דינם,
נקמת את נקמתם....

תפילת על-הניסים

We could be free as a people of all the baseless hatred that destroys us if only we could come to recognize that achievement is always personal, that faithfulness is always personal, and that care must always be personal. Such is the deepest "Sake of Heaven," for we share most deeply with God in showing our care for what He cares.[22] And our reward is the appearance of His presence in the light of Ḥanukah – His show of care for what we care.

You battled their battles,
You struggled their struggles,
You avenged their vengeance....

AL HANISSIM, ḤANUKAH PRAYER

Incredible! Jews gave up their lives to make the world safe for *God's* commandments, and that is *our* battle? Jews fight the entire Greek empire so that *His* home, the *Beit Mikdash*, can survive, and that is *our* struggle? Jews risk the lives of their children to destroy enemies of *His* Torah, and that is *our* vengeance? But that is precisely the lesson of *Miketz*, and of Ḥanukah as well. If only we would recognize that it is always *our* battles that we fight, we would become strangers to hate, to conflict, and to jealousy. We would no longer view life as a zero-sum game. And at last we would experience the other allusion of *Miketz:*

[It says], ויהי מקץ, *At the* end *of two years....*

So too it says, קץ שם לחושך, *He set an* end *to darkness (Iyov 28:3).*

There will come an end to the years which the world must spend in darkness....

BEREISHIT RABBA, 89:1

1 S.v. *Venishcaḥ*, ד״ה ונשכח .

2 S.v. *Velo*, ד״ה ולא יודע.

3 Daniel was punished for giving advice under similar circumstances to Nebuchadnezzar. Cf. Bava Bathra, 4a.

4 Cf. Ramban, 41:33 and Seforno, 41:34.

5 Shemot Rabba, 9:8. Egypt was represented as the center of the universe, and the creative process of *Nun* was renewed annually with the rise and fall of the Nile.

6 S.v. *Al*, ד״ה על היאור.

7 What a lovely coincidence that the word in English for the edge of the Channel is the same as the word signifying depositing for the future.

8 A fascinating book by Michael Maren, *The Best Intentions: How International Charity and Food Aid Ravaged the Third World* (Free Press, 1996), details the destruction of Somalia by Western food.

9 S.v. *Yefot*, ד״ה יפות מראה.

10 The literal translation is, incredibly enough, "Visionless, people are *pharaohed*," פר״ע, meaning "exposed," "ruined," "broken down."

11 Bereishit 47:15.

12 Bereishit 47:19.

13 The Greek word used in the Septuagint for חן is χαρτσμα, which is the root of "charisma."

14 "Charisma" has a venerable history related to *grace, charm, divine favor,* that still means (in my dictionary, at least) "a special quality conferring extraordinary powers of leadership and the ability to inspire veneration; a personal magnetism that enables an individual to attract or influence people; a divinely conferred gift or power." Some of the word's negative and more recent connotations are addressed infra.

15 Bereishit 21:23; 39:4; 49:22, (Rashi).

16 Bereishit Rabba, 91:8.

17 Yoma, 35b; Bereishit Rabba, 87:5,10; Radak on Bereishit 39:7; *Yalkut Shimoni*, Vayeshev 145; *Al Yithalel*, Greenhut.

18 Melachim I, 12.

19 Melachim I, 14:30, 15:6,8,32.

20 Eiruvin, 53a; Sanhedrin, 42a, Tosafot s.v. *V'rav*; ד״ה ורב, Horayot 14a.

21 Robert M. Pirsig, *Zen and the Art of Motorcycle Maintenance* (New York: William Morrow and Co., 1984), 297.

22 Avot, 2:4.

X Miketz

מִקֵּץ

The Interpretation of Dreams

Miketz opens with the riddles of Pharoah's dreams and the spectacular fallout of Yosef's successful interpretations. But it continues with a more elaborate and enigmatic riddle, one posed by Yosef to his brothers: In an allusive series of maddening cues and clues, Yosef challenges them to interpret his message and his identity.

The Interpretation of Dreams finds that dreams, the pivotal precipitators throughout the saga of Yosef and his brothers, are paradoxically the crucial component for successfully perceiving a painful reality and triumphantly facing it.

THE INTERPRETATION OF DREAMS

Sigmund Freud once said that "the interpretation of dreams is the royal road to knowledge...."[1] It is a royal road that the king of Egypt traveled most attentively, and *Miketz* opens with a royal dream crying out for interpretation:

> *It was at the end of two years, and Pharaoh was dreaming.... In the morning, he was distraught. He summoned all the magicians and sages of Egypt, and Pharaoh told them his dream – but no one could provide Pharaoh a satisfactory interpretation.* (41:1,8)

Dreams are thematic in the saga of Yosef. The "two years" which end here are themselves counted from another dream – that of the Chief Steward who "forgot Yosef" in the concluding verse of the previous parasha. In the Torah scroll a gap separates the end of that parasha, *Vayeshev*, and the beginning of *Miketz*, a gap representing a two year hiatus between dreams – now, Pharaoh was dreaming....

Dreams seem to play a definitive role throughout Yosef's life. The sale of Yosef is triggered by his brothers' resentment of his repetitive dreams. Yosef's success in Egypt is a result of dreams as well: he is brought before Pharaoh because of a cellmate's dreams, and reaches the pinnacle of success through his successful interpretation of the dreams of Pharaoh.

> Yosef was sold [into captivity] only because of dreams, as it says, *Look! – the dream master himself is coming!* (37:19).
>
> And he was liberated only through dreams, as it says, *It was at the end of two years, and Pharaoh was dreaming....*
>
> AGGADAT BEREISHIT, 1:67

It is not only in Yosef as an individual that dreams play such a pivotal role. Beginning with Ya'akov's departure to build the family that was later to be so rocked by dreams, the subject of dreams and their interpretation is set squarely at center stage of this crucial period in Israel's history.[2]

> Ya'akov came into his own through a dream: *He dreamed, and he saw a ladder....(28:12)*;
>
> Yosef came into his own through a dream: *Pharaoh was dreaming....*
>
> TANḤUMA, MIKETZ, 3

Contemporary research and events have brought much disrepute to the practitioners who travel Freud's "royal road," and there are many who consider them no more effective than Pharaoh's magicians. But there is no denying the essential difference of approach between the earlier and later wizards (if so they be). Freud's road is fundamentally rational, and is meant to lead to an understanding of the effects of an individual's *past*; Pharaoh's approach appears primitive – he sought a dream interpretation that would magically unveil the *future*.

Not mine own fears,
nor the prophetic soul
Of the wide world
dreaming on things to come.
SHAKESPEARE, SONNETS, 107

The two roads, then, exhibit only a most superficial resemblance. Freud saw dreams as a communication of the unconscious mind, a crucial component of "the scientific method by which the unconscious can be studied."[3] To him, dreams are creations of the human mind, and speak to us not of external reality, but of an individual's ambiguous and confused perception. The Torah, on the other hand, seems here to regard dreams as prophecies, unambiguous visions of an objective reality coming from Beyond – visions that *use* the individual as a mere tool of communication.

A case could even be made that the animosity between Yosef and his brothers developed primarily out of their differing viewpoints regarding dreams. Yosef experienced his dreams as truth, undeniable messages of an inevitable future in which he would be an honest pawn. Just as he could be a psychic *dreamer* himself, so too would he be psychically able to interpret the dreams of others. To his brothers, however, Yosef's dreams spoke *of Yosef* himself and exposed nothing but his own subconscious. In their eyes, the more Yosef told them, the more he exposed sociopathic narcissism and dangerous egomania. The thought of Yosef attempting to *interpret* the dreams of others was nonsensical to them, like putting the patient in the doctor's seat. They spoke of "*the dream master*" with a sneer. If the underlying issue is indeed the nature of dreams, we would have to read *Miketz* as a warning to take dreams and dreamers more seriously.

However, the situation is not quite so simple. The Torah sees dreams as anything but unambiguous visions of the future. Ya'akov himself, upon awakening from the very dream which has come to symbolize him – the ladder stretching from earth to heaven – was not convinced that it had objective meaning.

> *Ya'akov took an oath, saying: If God will be with me and watch me along this path....* (28:20)
>
> Why did he not believe God's promise [in his dream]? He said to himself, "Look, it's only a dream...if it really happens, *then* I will know that it is true!"
>
> ZOHAR, 1:150b

When Yosef presented his dreams to his father, Ya'akov's response was less than enthusiastic:

> *"What sort of dream did you have? Do you really expect that I, your mother, and your brothers are to come and prostrate themselves on the ground to you!?"* (37:10)
>
> – Your mother is already dead, is she not!?" (—Rashi[4])

The dream is obviously misleading, said Ya'akov, but nonetheless – *his father* [Ya'akov] *waited to see* (37:11).

Dreams themselves are confusing enough, but the Torah's relationship to them is even more confusing.

> When Shmu'el [the sage] would have a disturbing dream, he would say, *Dreams tell fabrications....* (*Zecharia* 10:2).
> But when he would have a good dream, he would say, "Could it be that dreams speak fabrications? Does it not say, *I speak to him in dreams* (*Bamidbar* 12:6)!"
>
> BERACHOT, 55b

The rule of thumb in the Talmud is that dreams are self-fulfilling prophecies, products of their own self-generated interpretations, and anything but objective.

עשרים וארבעה פותרי חלומות היו בירושלים, ופעם אחת חלמתי חלום והלכתי אצל כולם, ומה שפתר לי זה לא פתר לי זה וכולם נתקיימו בי, לקיים מה שנאמר כל החלומות הולכים אחר הפה.

ברכות נה:

> There were twenty-four dream interpreters in Jerusalem. I once dreamed a dream and went to all of them – and every single one gave me a different interpretation. And they all came true! As they say, *All dreams follow the mouth* [that interprets them].
>
> IBID.

And, in an astounding twist, the Talmud bases its conclusion on nothing other than *Miketz*. The very parasha that seems to proclaim the success of dreams and their grand master Yosef, is presented as proof that dream interpretation is personal and *not* objective.

> How do we know that "*All the dreams follow the mouth [that interprets them]*"?
>
> From what it says, *The way that he [Yosef] interpreted it was exactly the way it worked out.... (41:12)*!
>
> IBID.

The Talmud takes it yet a step further, making it clear that not only are the interpretation and the self-fulfilling response personal, but the very dream itself is a product of the dreamer's subconscious.

> A person sees only from his own subconscious, as it says, *You king, your own thoughts emerged in your sleep.... (Daniel 2:29)*.
>
> IBID.

A suitable warning to the dream interpreter...would be, "Do anything you would like, only don't try to understand!"
CARL JUNG

And then, the Talmud's final extreme: manipulating the subconscious – tapping anxieties through powerful imagery – to create dreams to order!

> Caesar once challenged R. Yehoshua b. Ḥanania: "You Jews claim to be very wise – tell me what I will see in my dreams!"
>
> He answered, "You will see yourself captured by the Persians who will set you to grinding date stones and shepherding rodents with a golden staff."
>
> He thought about it all day and sure enough – at night he dreamed it!
>
> BERACHOT, 56a

In a sense, what Yosef does in *Miketz* is create a preposterous dream – actually, a nightmare – for his brothers, and then challenges them to find the interpretation. It is remarkable that though he constantly reveals more and more, hinting ever more openly at his identity, they never even begin to suspect what is the only reasonable explanation of the bizarre events that continue to hound them. The entire world was aware that a Hebrew captive had risen to prominence in Egypt,[5] yet despite all Yosef's hints, they never suspect a thing!

All their precautions notwithstanding, Yosef has his brothers identified, apprehended and brought to him.

> When Ya'akov's sons entered Egypt, each one entered at a different border crossing, and registered his name. That evening when the records were checked, Yosef closed all the granaries but one, and left orders that they [his brothers] were to be arrested as they showed their passports.
>
> BEREISHIT RABBA, 91:6

Yosef peppers them with personal questions about their father and about their brother; he displays a magical awareness of their personal lives – yet they suspect nothing.

> *Yisrael said, "Why did you do such an awful thing to me, telling the man that you had another brother!?"*
>
> *They replied, "The man kept asking about us and our family. He asked, 'Is your father still alive? Do you have another brother?' We simply answered his questions...."* (43:6,7)
>
> He even knew secrets from our nursery!
>
> BEREISHIT RABBA, 91:10

היה מנשה בן יוסף יושב לפניהם
א"ל אביו קום אתה, מיד קם מנשה
והכהו מכה אחת הכניסו בבית
האסורים ונתן עליו כבל,
אמר שמעון לאחיו, אתם
אומרים מכה של מצרים
הוא זה? אינה אלא של בית אבא!
תנחומא, ד

The brothers are imprisoned for three days, on trumped-up charges of spying. Though they recognize that this is a reflection of how they treated Yosef, they attribute it only to divine retribution.

> *They said to one another, "We deserve to be punished because of what we did to our brother. We saw him suffering when he pleaded with us, but we paid him no attention. That's why this disaster is happening to us!"* (42:21)

Neither does it occur to them for a moment that they may have been *wrong* about Yosef – only that they should have shown him more mercy.

Then, apparently arbitrarily, Yosef singles out Shimon and imprisons him. Now Shimon just happens to be the brother who threw Yosef into the pit.[6] This mysterious leader seems to *know* everything.

> Yosef said, "I see in my [magic] chalice that two of you murdered the entire city of Shechem!"
>
> TANḤUMA, MIKETZ, 8; VAYIGASH, 4

The brothers return to find that Shimon had been treated like family during his putative incarceration – yet they suspect nothing. Their payment for the food was secretly – and graciously! – returned in their packs. Yet again they suspect nothing.

> *He said, "Peace to you! Have no fear – your God and the God of your father gave you a treasure in your packs. I did receive your money." He brought them out Shimon....* (43:23)
>
> As soon as they had left, Yosef took Shimon out of jail and had him washed and wined and dined.
>
> TANḤUMA, MIKETZ, 8

The eye of man hath not heard,
the ear of man hath not seen,
man's hand is not able to taste,
his tongue to conceive,
nor his heart to report,
what my dream was.
A MIDSUMMER-NIGHT'S DREM, IV, i

In a dreamlike flight of absurdity, the former "spies" are then invited to a royal banquet in honor of their return. There the enigmatic and erratic leader, strangely overwhelmed, tearfully greets their youngest brother, Binyamin. And once again, he knows all.

> He took the chalice, tapped it, and said, "I thought that Yehuda was the firstborn, because he always speaks first. But now I see that Re'uven is the firstborn and Yehuda is just a big talker!"
>
> He set Re'uven first at the table.
>
> He tapped the chalice again and announced, "Shimon, you are next in line – sit next to him."
>
> He continued this way in order of their births.
>
> TANḤUMA, VAYIGASH, 8

The brothers are amazed, but suspect...nothing.

> *The brothers stared at each other in amazement.* (43:33)

Yosef then reveals his special love for Binyamin, making it clear that the two of them fit together – like a last missing piece of a jigsaw puzzle.

> At last, Binyamin alone was left.
> Yosef said, "I can perceive that this one had a brother who was torn from him, and he has no mother. I, too, had a brother who was separated from me and I have no mother – sit him down next to me!"

> Then each one was served a portion, and Yosef turned and gave his own portion to Binyamin. Osnat [Yosef's wife] gave Binyamin her portion, too, as did Ephraim and Menashe, so that Binyamin had five portions, as it says, *Binyamin's portion was five times larger....* (43:34).
>
> TANḤUMA, IBID.

Even as they watch this perfect piece fit into the puzzle, the brothers see nothing but a marvelous coincidence.

The brothers begin their return journey to Cana'an, but Yosef has more theatrics planned. He orders his "magic chalice" placed in Binyamin's bag in a frame-up that is an obviously orchestrated recreation of the scene where Rachel – Yosef and Binyamin's mother who was so resented by the other brothers – stole her father's magical devices. Instead of picking up on the message, the brothers choose to believe that indeed Binyamin *is* just like his mother!

> *The chalice was found in Binyamin's pack....* (44:12)
>
> They said to him, "You thief the son of a thieving woman!"
>
> Answered Binyamin, "Is Yosef around? Are there any goats around [for you to dye my shirt with their blood]? You brothers who sold your own brother [have the nerve to accuse me!]....
>
> At that point, *they tore their clothing....*
>
> BEREISHIT RABBA, 92:8

> [Dreams are] *no more prophetic than a medical diagnosis or a weather forecast.*
>
> CARL JUNG

With nearly lunatic oblivion, they even respond with the same disastrous words which Ya'akov inadvertently spoke of Binyamin's mother[7] when accused by Lavan of stealing the magic,

> *Whoever is found to have it shall die....*(44:9)

And, in the height of irony, they return to hear Yosef join Binyamin in accusing *them*:

> "I know why the boy stole the cup – he probably wanted to discover where his brother is!"
>
> TANḤUMA (BUBER), MIKETZ, 14

Yehuda responds viciously, as Yosef, knowing full well that Binyamin is the one person without whom they cannot possibly return home, makes a grand gesture: all are free to *go in* peace *to your father* (44:17) – except, of course, Binyamin. Some "*peace*"!

> Yehuda said to Yosef, "What will we say to my father!?"
>
> Said Yosef, "Tell him, 'The rope just fell in along with the bucket' (i.e. Binyamin went the way of Yosef)."
>
> Said Yehuda, "This is a kangaroo court!"
>
> Said Yosef, "Nowhere near as bad as the one that sold your brother!"
>
> Said Yehuda, "I can feel the fire of Shechem burning in my heart!"
>
> Answered Yosef, "The fire of your daughter-in-law Tamar can quench that problem."
>
> Yehuda shouted, "I will dye the streets of every market in Egypt with blood!"
>
> Said Yosef, "You *have* had a lot of experience dyeing – you dyed the coat of your brother with blood, too!"
>
> TANḤUMA, VAYIGASH, 5

None of this makes any difference. They are blind, completely blind. Every last detail of Yosef's staging is calculated to make them realize each mistake that they had made, but they see nothing. Not even when it was in front of their very eyes.

והיה קורא, יוסף בן יעקב בוא אצלי!
יוסף בן יעקב בוא אצלי!
והיו מסתכלין בארבע פינות הבית,
אמר להם מה אתם רואים!
אני יוסף אחיכם!
מיד פרחה נשמתן,
שנאמר ולא יכלו אחיו...

בראשית רבה צג

So, Yosef rubs their noses in it.

> Yosef said to them, "Did you not claim that this one's brother is dead? I *purchased* him, and I will call him now to come here!"
>
> He began to shout, "Yosef, Ya'akov's son, come to me! Yosef, Ya'akov's son, come to me and speak with the brothers who sold you!"
>
> Their eyes darted to every hidden corner of the house.
>
> Said Yosef, "Why are you looking from side to side – you are looking at him!"
>
> *I am Yosef!* (45:3)
>
> At that moment they collapsed in shock.
>
> IBID.

But how could the brothers have been so impossibly, so insanely, oblivious to the obvious? The midrash offers a wretched explanation:

> [Yosef was unrecognizable because] he had left without a beard, and stood now before them as a bearded king.
>
> IBID.

This explanation is even more maddening than the rest of the story.

Unless that is the whole point. The blindness of the brothers was a creation of a lifetime of postulates and assumptions, a creation of twenty-two years of misjudgment, miscalculations, dishonesty, and rationalizations. So much had been invested by the brothers into seeing things their own way, that the new context was simply inconceivable to them. The midrash underscores how the most slender of disguises – the beard that is masquerading's cliche – was sufficient to hide Yosef from his brothers, simply because they were convinced *that he could not possibly be there*!

In dreams begins responsibility.

YEATS

This is the fabulous denouement of the drama of dreams played out in *Miketz*. The brothers had announced the coming of *the master of dreams*:

> *We shall see what will come of his dreams!* (37:20)
>
> [Said God] "Indeed we shall – let us see who wins in the end: you or I!" (—Rashi[8])

Here is where we see at last what does come of his dreams. Surely nothing that Yosef ever imagined in his worst nightmares – but nonetheless his dreams came true, and ever so crushingly to his brothers. The more convinced they were that his dreams were lies, the more overwhelming was the shock of the truth.

There is no doubt that we can enhance [dreams'] effect considerably by understanding, and this is often necessary because the voice of the unconscious so easily goes unheard.

CARL JUNG

Dreams are indeed ambiguous, and can mean almost anything at all. But, curiously, even dreams that are projections of one's own subconscious are filled with an immensity of new information. In dreams, the mind may be released, and the limits of suppositions and presumptions breached. These are the dreams of discovery, the famous dreams in which months of fruitless work suddenly burst into bloom, the dreams so familiar to creative individuals that many keep pen and paper at bedside for noting dream insights.

Descartes' vision of knowledge as a series of interconnected truths came to him in a series of dreams on a November night in 1619. Through symbolic dream images containing melons, thunder, books, and spirits, he came to see the universe as united throughout by cause and effect. These dreams laid the groundwork for Enlightenment thought that came to fruition in the eighteenth century.

One of the most well known dream stories concerns the discovery of the benzene ring. In the mid-nineteenth century, Friedrich Kekule was immersed in one of the most perplexing problems of his day: to find the structural basis of organic chemistry. Kekule had dwelt intensely on the behavior of organic compounds, but found no solution. It was in a dream – a dream projected by his own subconscious, [and, incidentally, full of Freudian allusions, which changes nothing at all] – that he discovered the solution. In his dream, chains of carbon atoms seemed to come alive and dance before his eyes, and then suddenly one coiled and twisted on itself like a snake seizing its own tail. He had the solution: the benzene molecule is a ring of carbon atoms joined to themselves, surrounded by bonded hydrogen.

The atoms were gamboling before my eyes. I saw how, frequently, two smaller atoms united to form a pair; how a larger one embraced two smaller ones; how still larger ones kept hold of three or even four of the smaller; whilst the whole kept whirling in a giddy dance. I saw how the large ones formed a chain...all twining and twisting in snakelike motion. But look! What was that? One of the snakes had seized hold of its own tail and the form whirled mockingly before my eyes.

FRIEDRICH KEKULE

Dreams are limited by the limits of wishful thinking. Only someone free enough to grasp a dream's gift of discovery can be rewarded by his dreams. But twist a dream to show what we *need* to believe, and the dream will imprison us. It will *blind* us. Yosef spent his years in Egypt doing only one thing: losing all personal agenda. His life was a study of performing flawlessly *whatever needed to be done*. The incident with his master's wife was the test of his ability to avoid personal desire and wishes when they were out of place. The only time he failed was when he tried to *make* a dream work.

> *Yosef said to him, "This is the interpretation: The three branches are three days. In three days, Pharaoh will lift your head and restore your position. You will place the cup in the hand of Pharaoh, just as you did before, when you were his steward.*
>
> *"When things go well for you, just remember me with you. Do me a favor, and say something about me to Pharaoh – maybe you will be able to get me out of this place!"* (40:12-14)

The "*miketz*," the end, of the two years mentioned in the opening verse of this parasha, refers to the two years of incarceration that Yosef suffered for that single sentence.

> *The chief steward did not remember Yosef – he forgot all about him* (40:23).
>
> Because Yosef relied on this intervention, he needed to suffer another two years in prison. (—Rashi[9])

Yosef gained not only freedom, but mastery, through learning to accept surprises and respond to new situations. The more faithful he was to reality, the more strongly his dreams opened new possibilities. The moment he attempted manipulation for his own needs, his dreams imprisoned him.

Ironically, in *Miketz* those who rejected dreams altogether – those who sought a controlled and well-planned objectivity – ended up unable to perceive anything other than their own projections. So real is this phenomenon, that results of clinical studies are considered significant only if conducted "double-blind," so that neither the patient nor the researcher knows which compound is being administered. Otherwise, the introduction of some subtle bias will inevitably distort the results.

אמר עולא, מחשבה מועלת אפילו
לדברי תורה שנאמר [איוב ה]
מפר מחשבות ערומים
ולא תעשינה ידיהם תושיה

סנהדרין כו:

Reality's ambiguity is itself a dream of sorts, constantly tantalizing with alternative futures and making equivalent demands on our interpretive abilities. The wishful thinking, the self-fulfilling oracles, the tunnel vision, the rationalizations – all the blinders that restrict the interpretation of dreams – are a very real threat in a very real world. Even planning with due deliberation is paralyzing if it comes at the cost of responsiveness.

> Planning is effective [at ruining] even Torah, as it says, *He frustrates the planning of the cunning, and their hands cannot perform their goal (Iyov 5:12).*[10]
>
> SANHEDRIN, 26b

שמעו נא החלום אשר חלמתי-
דבעא מנייהו דישמעון ליה.
ואיהו אודע להו ההוא חלמא
דאלמלא אינון דאהפכו ליה
לגוונא אחרא הכי אתקיים
ואינון אתיבו ואמרו המלוך תמלוך
עלינו אם משול תמשול בנו
מיד אמרו ליה פשרא דחלמא
וגזרו גזרה ובגין כך ויוסיפו
עוד שנא אותו.

זוהר ח"א דף קפג:

It is the non-dreamers who here lose all contact with reality. If not for Yosef and the new solutions opened by his dreams, there would have been no future for Yisrael in Egypt, no preparation for the great day of the Exodus, no creation of a viable nation-in-exile. Those who would twist dreams end as putty in the hands of dream-interpreters who mold the future through perceptions. The ultimate irony is that it was actually the brothers' fears that provided both the interpretation and the eventual actualization of Yosef's dreams.

> *Said his brothers to him, "Are you then to be king over us! Are you to rule over us!?"* (37:8)
>
> At that moment *they themselves* gave the dream its definition and its destination!
>
> ZOHAR, 1:183b

Only their anxieties, their fears of being crushed by Yosef, transformed what should have been a liberating development (as ultimately it most literally was!) into a crushing experience.

אוי לנו מיום הדין
אוי לנו מיום התוכחה!
ומה יוסף הצדיק שהוא בשר ודם
כשהוכיח את אחיו לא יכלו לעמוד
בתוכחתו, הקב"ה שהוא דיין ובעל
דין ויושב על כסא דין ודן כל
אחד ואחד על אחת כמה וכמה
שאין כל בשר ודם יכולים
לעמוד לפניו!

בראשית רבה צג

Through the multifaceted interpretation of dreams, *Miketz* presents a model for interpretation of reality – and a typology of the dark dangers of self-inflicted blindness. In a single instant, Yosef's brothers were forced to see straight through the intricate web of self-deception that had nearly obliterated their future. The horror they experienced, the trauma they felt, at seeing their elaborately built house-of-cards collapse is a metaphor for each of us. Every human being must eventually face his individual revelation and the dissolution of his own web.

> Woe to us from the day of Judgment! Woe to us from the day of reproof!
>
> When Yosef – who is mere flesh and blood – showed his brothers the truth, they collapsed before him.
>
> When God Himself judges every human being, just imagine how no flesh and blood will be able to stand before *Him*!
>
> BEREISHIT RABBA, 93:11

Had you been there tonight you might also have known how your world may be changed in just one burst of light,
and what was right seems wrong,
and what was wrong seems right.
LES MISÉRABLES

Every human being must eventually face himself in that full light. If only it be sooner, in his own discovery of truth, rather than later.

Miketz bears its literal meaning "at the end" as it brings an end to darkness: the darkness of the two-year penalty imposed on a dreamer out-of-bounds and the darkness of twenty-two years of pain and gloom that had enveloped Ya'akov and his family. But more to the point, *Miketz* also introduces the elements of a path that leads toward a universal end to confusion and darkness.[11]

Miketz [מקץ] – *It was at the end of two years....*

So too does it say, *He set an end* [קץ] *to darkness....(Iyov 28:3).*

There will come an end to the years that the world must spend in darkness....

BEREISHIT RABBA, 89:1

It is not a coincidence that every year *Miketz* is the parasha of Ḥanukah.[12] The end of darkness is a fitting message for the holiday of Light, which itself brought an end to a period of dark confusion.

Darkness on the face of the deeps... (Bereishit 1:2)

"Darkness" refers to the Greek exile....

BEREISHIT RABBA, 2:4

Everything we shut our eyes to, everything we run away from, everything we deny, denigrate, or despise, serves to defeat us in the end.

HENRY MILLER

Yet we live once again in a period of deep divisiveness and confusion. We live, as Yosef's brothers did before us, a dream that beggars our power of interpretation. It sometimes seems as if we are constantly moving further from *Miketz*; further from the denouement of an interminable exile that has us entrapped in a series of reruns, an endless cycle of ancient errors. But *Miketz* teaches that this investment of thousands of years and millions of lives may reach fruition in a sudden and traumatic rush, as truth stares us in the face as it did Yosef's brothers. The more elaborate the distortions embedded in our beliefs, the more dramatic and powerful the confrontation with truth. The more comfortable we are with our answers, the more devastating the critique of our temerity. Nothing was or will be wasted, for history awaits each contribution.

There will surely be no end to the surprises that accompany the dawning of the light as the time for authentic interpretation of reality draws nigh. Only the removal of the blinders of comfortable presuppositions, emotional prejudice, and artificial props can make truth survivable, if not palatable. This is the uncomfortable but joyous light *Miketz* and Ḥanukah offer us: the ability to live faithfully, dependably – and in scrupulous peace with our dreams.

A song of ascent: When God restored the prisoners of Zion we were as dreamers.... (Tehillim 126:1)

1 *The Interpretation of Dreams*, chapter 7.

2 28:12; 31:10; 31:24; 37:5; 37:9-11; 37:19,20; 40:8-20.

3 Quoted by Lionel Trilling, *The Liberal Imagination*, 1957.

4 S.v. *Havo navo,* ד״ה הבוא נבוא.

5 Cf. 43:32.

6 *Tanḥuma, Vayigash*, 4.

7 Bereishit 31:32.

8 S.v. *Venireh*, ד״ה ונראה.

9 Cf. Bereishit Rabba, 92:9.

10 Rashi, s.v. *Mefer,* ד״ה מפר: Plans that people work out, establishing goals for themselves, are effective in impeding those goals, even for Torah study, e.g. "I will complete X by date Y."

11 The actual end to the entire Egyptian galut, the Exodus, is introduced with the same word: "*Miketz*"—*It was at the end of four hundred and thirty years – on that very day – that all the legions of the Lord left the land of Egypt. (Shemot 12:43).*

12 Cf. *Shelah, Derasha Tzon Yosef*, and my *Patterns in Time*, (Jerusalem and New York: Feldheim, 1988), vol. 8.

XI Vayigash
ויגש

Jealous Love

Vayigash opens with the dramatic denouement of twenty-two years of alienation, changes, and hopes. Yehuda is moved to confront Yosef, and in doing so is brought to confront himself and his own mistakes. The broken relationships of a lifetime are restored, bringing together at last the entire family of Ya'akov. The parasha concludes with the successful settlement of Goshen, and the productive cultivation of a nation destined to be born in exile.

What Yosef accomplished in the manipulation of his brothers is clear. But what is not clear is just *how* he managed to reestablish the relationships that were shattered so many years before. After all, the special love Ya'akov felt for Yosef remained unchanged, and is expressed once again (48:5) in the gift of the birthright to Yosef. Yet somehow the jealousies and ideological arguments dissipated as Yosef deftly drew his brothers towards the truth. *Jealous Love* finds in *Vayigash* a primal model for achieving the unity that continues to elude the progeny of the parasha's protagonists.

JEALOUS LOVE

Vayigash is a parasha of reconciliation. Though the title denotes a 'face-down' – the confrontation of Yehuda and Yosef – it also intimates the rapprochement that follows, introduced with the identical root – for *vayigash* means literally "he came close."

> *"Come close to me (gashu,* גשו*), please," said Yosef to his brothers,*
> *and they came close....* (45:4)

Here in *Vayigash*, the long-estranged children of Ya'akov join together again, to settle in a land named for reconciliation: the land of *Goshen* (גשן–same root again).

Powerful historical currents are generated both by the jealousies between the brothers and by the new understanding achieved here. The significance of the rapprochement is reflected in the parasha's *haftara*:

> *Take a piece of wood and write on it "For Yehuda..."*
> *Take another piece of wood and write on it "For Yosef..."*
> *Draw them close one to the other...and they will become one in your hand....*
> *For I shall make them one nation in their land....*
> *They and their children and their grandchildren will dwell there forever....* (*Yeḥezkel* 37:16-25)

But the nature of this reconciliation is extraordinary. Consider that Yosef finds his family shattered and himself in Egypt only because of jealousy – his brother's undying resentment of Ya'akov's favoritism in his special love for Rachel and her son Yosef. To pull the family together now, twenty-two years later, Yehuda and his siblings must overcome their bitterness and painfully learn to adjust, to accept their father's undeniable partialities. But this is not what happens at all. We find no hint of hurtful acceptance. Instead, in a fabulous reversal of roles, we are treated to the spectacle of Yehuda castigating Yosef (-in-disguise) over his appalling insensitivity to the importance of Ya'akov's special loves.

My father said to us, "You know that my wife bore me only two children...." (44:27)

"Rachel is my only real wife, and her children are my only children – the rest are all like children of maidservants to me."

RAMBAN[1]

The resentment of Yehuda was transformed here into its antithesis – he was prepared to defend with his very life the love that he himself once nearly destroyed.

You are no different than Pharaoh himself. (44:18)

If I have to pull my sword, I will start with you and finish with Pharaoh, your master!

BEREISHIT RABBA, 93:6

Now if I come back to my father and the boy is not with me – and his soul is tied to his! (44:30)

How can I come back to my father without the boy! What if I witness the horror that will befall my father?!... (44:34)

Yosef listens as Yehuda attacks him for the very same things that Yehuda was guilty of himself, nearly killing his father. Yosef's counter thrust is paralyzing and deadly:

I am Yosef – is my father still alive!?
His brothers could not say anything, they were so stunned. (45:3)

Here, then, is a saga that began with a jealous resentment of a relationship, but ended with a jealous protectiveness for the same relationship. It is fascinating that "jealous" can connote both envy of another and deep personal concern for one's own. In Hebrew (קנאה, *kin'ah*) as well as in English,[2] a single word embodies seemingly contrary emotions.[3]

Jealousy is always born together with love...
LA ROCHEFOUCAULD

Then God was jealous for His land, and had compassion for His people. (Yo'el 2:18)

"Jealous" implies that He took the land's pain to heart, and fought for her needs. (—Rashi)

When "jealous" is followed by "for" it always means "for the *care* of that object." (—Malbim)

But the *protective* sense of jealousy is intensely *personal* – and no matter how Yehuda had changed, how could he possibly have felt personally protective of a love which he viewed with some detachment (to put it delicately)? Yosef seems aware of a subtle emotional interplay involved in the two faces of jealousy, and has managed here to magically effect the transformation of one into the other.

In their jealousy of Ya'akov's relationship with Yosef, the brothers were motivated by love. They had wanted to be close to their father, and felt deprived precisely *because* they cared so much. But the resentment came of envy, which implies desire to *possess* their father, to make him over so that he would be as they wished. The transformation of their jealousy into care grew out of a subtle but exceedingly critical maturation: the recognition that sharing is devastated through possession.

Love does not cause suffering: what causes it is the sense of ownership, which is love's opposite.

SAINT-EXUPÉRY

The brothers' very need to have their father nearly destroyed him. Their attempt to wean him of his special commitments led not to closer relationship, but to estrangement from him and his values. Each of them followed his own vision of Ya'akov, so none of them found Ya'akov himself.

For twenty-two years, Ya'akov's children watched as he sank into an abyss of hopelessness. They came to understand that in destroying his relationship with Yosef, they had destroyed Ya'akov's dreams, his ideals, and his future. All that was precious to him was linked to the unique moments and hopes he had shared with Rachel and Yosef. More than anything else, that preciousness *was* their father. In the calamity that they had inflicted on Ya'akov, the brothers came to appreciate that what they cared for was their father, Yisrael, himself, and that they had nearly destroyed what they thought to love. They no longer wanted to have their father – they just wanted their father.

In threatening the remaining concern of Ya'akov's life, Yosef forced his brothers to confront how deeply their father was identified with what he held precious. Their care for Ya'akov then moved them to protect jealously everything he held dear – and in that moment they became fully his children and achieved the relationship that had eluded them for so long. They came to cherish what he cherished and value what he valued *because* it was so uniquely and specially his.

Ya'akov's sons discovered at last that the deepest relationship is achieved not through possessiveness, but through sharing a vision of what is precious and unique. In a life that has no unique care, cheap variations on a theme are all that can be shared – which is to share nothing. For it is not the other's being that we can share, but life that we can share together. The sharing of care creates a little world, a veritable sanctuary for the precious, within which we live uniquely together, unshaken by the "important," but singularly non-precious, events outside. Outside, things can be owned, but cannot be our own. So it is that even God Himself relates to Ya'akov only through the joy of shared preciousness:

Jealousy: that dragon which slays love under the pretense of keeping it alive.
HAVELOCK ELLIS

> Said the Holy One to Ya'akov: You are so precious in My eyes that your image is fixed on My Throne...as it says, *Of your preciousness in My eyes you were honored, and I have loved you....* *(Isaiah 43:4).*
>
> BAMIDBAR RABBA, 4:1

This encounter with the two faces of jealousy and love was Yosef's *announced* intent all along. If his brothers had only listened carefully to what he was saying they would have saved themselves much fear and anguish. For as soon as the brothers came to Egypt, Yosef maneuvered them into confronting their own motivations:

> – You are spies, and have come here to find where this land is vulnerable! Why else would you have attempted to enter at separate border crossings?
>
> – *Your servants are twelve brothers, the son of one man in the land of Cana'an. The youngest is with our father and one is missing.* We scattered only to recover him!
>
> – And suppose you would have found him, and they would have demanded a fortune in ransom?
>
> – We would have paid anything.
>
> – And suppose that they would have refused any offer, then what?
>
> – We came here to kill or be killed, if necessary.

> Said Yosef to them, "*That is just what I said to you – you are spies!* You see, you did come to murder our citizens!"
>
> *This shall be your test…bring your youngest brother here…for if not – by Pharaoh's life! – you are indeed spies!* (42:9-16)
>
> BEREISHIT RABBA, 91:6[4]

What sense are we to make of this exchange? The brothers were accused of being spies and they responded saying, "*No, we are not spies – we are brothers!*" as if the two were somehow mutually exclusive. And Yosef seems to accept this inane argument – he just wants them to prove that they are, indeed, brothers.

In fact, Yosef has maneuvered his brothers here to precisely where he wants them. They claim that their mission is personal and precious: No one could possibly object to a family taking extreme measures to rescue a brother from whoredom[5] and slavery: *We are twelve brothers…* because everyone respects what is held precious.

> *Love, fierce as death,*
> *Jealousy, cruel as hell…*
>
> SHIR HASHIRIM 8:6

But Yosef questions their motivations in the rescue: do you truly act out of a jealous protectiveness which anyone would admire? Might this not be just another way for you to achieve your own agenda, possess what you have lost, and espy your own advantage in Egypt's vulnerability – just as you did to your father?

So Yosef proposes a test – bring Binyamin and we shall see. But "see" what? Yosef, after all, had maintained that they were spies even as he *accepted* that they were searching for a brother: "*That is just what I said to you – you are spies!* You see, you did come to murder our citizens!" What he needed to do, then, was to test their *motivation*. The only possible way he could accomplish that would be through forcing the brothers to protect Binyamin, to see if they would defend him even while believing him guilty of stealing the chalice. It is here in *Vayigash* that the brothers pass the test that Yosef had spelled out right at the beginning – if only they had been listening. It is here that they finally achieve the bonding after which the parasha is named.

In maturing beyond the need to own, and learning instead to value one's own, the children of Ya'akov achieved a new perception of their father – and of love itself. In growing from possessiveness to protectiveness, the children of Ya'akov came to cherish that which he cherished and to reach for that which he reached. These children blossomed in *Vayigash* into the carriers of all Ya'akov's latent potential. Though *he* may still be Ya'akov, *they* have triumphantly become the Children of *Yisrael.*

> *Ya'akov set out from Be'er Sheva and the Children of Yisrael carried their father Ya'akov along with their children and wives on the wagons that Pharaoh had sent to carry them.* (46:5)

There are as many different ways to love Yisrael the father as there are children who love him, but all share one love, nonetheless. The yearnings and aspirations of each individual are a part of what is cherished by Yisrael the nation. No matter how different our own approach may be, if there be a deadly threat we leap to jealously defend any who value our own aspirations – even though we may bitterly disagree about how to achieve them. It is the very uniqueness and dedication of the other's commitment that is so precious to us, and we all share that appreciation – we care that others care. We would be devastated by the loss of some of the very factions we may love to detest, because preciousness itself would be the poorer. It is jealousy that ultimately divides us – the desire to have Yisrael all to ourselves – and it is jealousy therefore that ultimately unites us to all who so desire Yisrael.

They are not ever jealous for the cause,
But jealous for they are jealous.
OTHELLO III, IV

> *How precious to me are Your loves, God!* (*Tehillim* 139:17)

The intense jealousies that divided Yosef and his brothers are embedded in the fabric of the nation into which they grew. Throughout its history, the Jewish people has struggled with those same resentments clad in various disguises. For centuries, these jealousies were the roots of the bitter division between the rival monarchies of Yehuda and Yosef and of the open civil wars that followed. But for the most part the estrangement has smoldered, sublimated into those profound philosophical differences which today divide us more deeply than ever before. Once again, for the first time in millennia, those same issues have brought Yisrael face to face with political differences that threaten[6] genuine violence.

In such times, it is important to remember *Vayigash*. Incredible as it may appear, this primal model for surmounting our differences and achieving a transcendent national identity proclaims that something as elusive as the nature of love, jealousy and uniqueness underlies our ideological and political crises. And it points to a subtle – albeit difficult – change in world-view as the solution to what appears intractable.

Here in *Vayigash*, Ya'akov's children retained their fundamental psychological, philosophical and ideological distinctions – and they have maintained these differences throughout history. None of that changed. What *did* change in *Vayigash* was *perception*. The brothers learned what moved them so deeply to *care* about their differences – and discovered therein what they shared most profoundly. *Vayigash* teaches that the "possession" of truth corrupts it just as surely as the "possession" of relationship corrupts love and the "possession" of vision corrupts the future.

The prophecy of a Messianic era is predicated entirely on achieving this subtle reconciliation between competing convictions:

> *Take a piece of wood and write on it, "For Yehuda...."*
> *Take another piece of wood and write on it, "For Yosef...."*
> *Draw them close one to the other ... and they will become one in your hand....*
> *For I shall make them one nation in their land....*
> *My servant David will be their leader, forever.* (*Yeḥezkel* 37:16-25)

Yisrael's long historical journey is essentially the process of discovering true love and care.

We, too, will be moved either to protect all that is precious to Yisrael and come thereby to care and to share, or we will be moved to control all that is precious to Yisrael, and come thereby to destroy it, ourselves, and each other. In preciousness alone lies the secret of Yisrael's survival and eventual triumph. In caring for it we become, ourselves, precious.

> Yisrael is called precious, as it says: *Ephraim is a precious child to Me....* (*Yermiah* 31:19)
>
> VAYIKRA RABBA, 2:1

ואתה בן אדם קח לך עץ אחד
וכתב עליו ליהודה ולבני ישראל
חבריו ולקח עץ אחד וכתוב עליו
ליוסף עץ אפרים וכל בית
ישראל חבריו. וקרב אתם
אחד אל אחד לך לעץ אחד והיו
לאחדים בידך. כאשר יאמרו
אליך בני עמך לאמר הלוא תגיד
לנו מה אלה לך. דבר אלהם כה
אמר ה, א, הנה אני לוקח את עץ
יוסף אשר ביד אפרים ושבטי
ישראל חבריו ונתתי אותם עליו
את עץ יהודה ועשיתם לעץ אחד
והיו אחד בידי....ועשיתי אתם
לגוי אחד בארץ בהרי ישראל
ומלך אחד יהיה לכלם למלך
ולא יהיו עוד לשני גוים ולא יחצו
עוד לשתי ממלכות עוד....והיו לי
לעם ואני אהיה להם לאלקים
ועבדי דוד מלך עליהם ורועה
אחד יהיה לכלם ובמשפטי ילכו
וחקתי ישמרו ועשו אותו וישבו
על הארץ אשר נתתי לעבדי ליעקב
אשר ישבו בה אבותיכם וישבו עליה
המה ובניהם ובני בניהם עד עולם
ודוד עבדי נשיא להם לעולם.

יחזקאל לז:טו-כה

1 S.v. *Atem*, ד״ה אתם.

2 My dictionary gives the *primary* definition of jealous as "watchful or solicitous in guarding or keeping."

3 See my *Patterns in Time* (Jerusalem and New York: Feldheim, 1988), volume 8, chapter 19, for a more extensive analysis.

4 S.v. *Hu asher*, ד״ה הוא אשר דברתי.

5 Bereishit Rabba, 91:6.

6 These words, originally published in 1993, proved painfully prophetic.

XI Vayigash
ויגש

The Merits of Assimilation

Ya'akov and his children leave the Land of Cana'an to join Yosef in Egypt, beginning the first of the exiles prophesied to Avraham: *Your children will be strangers in a foreign land* (15:13), prototype of exiles to come. *Vayigash* describes Yosef's dramatic exposure to his brothers, traces the diplomatic efforts and negotiations involved in settling the family of Ya'akov in the Land of Goshen, and fills in the missing details of Yosef's reign during the years of famine.

The Merits of Assimilation examines the substantial and substantive differences in approach between Yosef, his brothers, and their father Ya'akov toward this benign phase of the Egyptian Exile. Each of those outlooks has certainly played its part in molding the Jewish national response to exile in all its variety, but the fundamental role of exile in the national identity of Yisrael is expressed primarily through the historic achievements of Yosef in our parasha. No one since Yosef has more fully or more successfully embodied the identity of a host culture, achieving all that is right about assimilation.

THE MERITS OF ASSIMILATION

The variety of Jewish responses to the Diaspora is as diverse as the variety of Jewish experiences in the Diaspora. There have been golden ages of tolerance and reigns of horror, and there have been blue-blooded Jews and Jews of the ghetto, often side by side. The spectrum of contemporary responses to *galut* is just as broad, though the extremes may be more strongly manifest than the middle. *Yeridat Mitzrayim*, the descent into Egypt presented in *Parashat Vayigash*, not only inaugurates the prototype of *galut*, it also introduces the exemplar of Jewish creativity and growth within *galut:*

> *He went down to Egypt with a small number of people and lived there as an immigrant, yet there he became a great, powerful, and populous nation.* (Devarim 26:5)

The philosophical and psychological attitudes that contributed to this success were by no means uniform, and the parasha describes the different approaches of Yosef and his brothers to living as *strangers in a foreign land* (15:13). Look carefully at the verses describing the machinations of Yosef and his brothers in obtaining Pharaoh's sanction of their settlement in Egypt, in the land of Goshen:

> *To his brothers and his father's family Yosef said, "I will go and inform Pharaoh, and this is what I am going to tell him: 'My brothers and my father's family from Cana'an have come to me. These men are shepherds because they have always been livestock dealers, and they have brought along their sheep, their cattle, and all their possessions.'*
>
> *"Now, when Pharaoh summons you and inquires as to your occupation, you must say: 'Your servants have been ranchers all our lives, we and our fathers.' You will then be able to settle in the Goshen district, because all shepherds are taboo in Egypt."* (46:31-34)

The conspiratorial tone of this conversation comes through loud and clear. Yosef has a plan for dealing with Pharaoh's reservations about creating a Jewish enclave in Egypt. Delicate diplomacy will be involved here, and that means that the precise wording of every statement is crucial. Not only does Yosef tell his brothers exactly what he would say to Pharaoh, he told them precisely what they must say.

Yosef stresses several points here:

1. Let Pharaoh know that you came not to escape Cana'an, but to be with me. This insures that he will not deal with you separately from me, that he will not look at you as indigent refugees from famine, but as landed immigrants who plan long term settlement.

2. I will let Pharaoh know that you are shepherds and therefore taboo in Egypt – I do not want him fearing mercantile competition[1] or insisting that you settle near him and accept government positions.[2]

3. You must not mention "shepherding" directly. Instead you must use the word "ranchers," (*anshei mikneh*, "livestock dealers"). Give him the sense that you are substantial businessmen, and that you are here for a long term investment of your livestock and property, just as I will already have mentioned in my own conversation with him.[3]

4. Do not mention Goshen directly – it is important that it just "happen."[4] Before you speak to Pharaoh, I will have insinuated to him that he is dealing with people the country needs but who are a social embarrassment. The Goshen option will almost suggest itself.[5]

Notice how careful Yosef is not to come right out and *ask* for Goshen directly. About as far as he will go is to say, "*My father and brothers have come from Cana'an...and they are currently staying in Goshen.*" (47:1)

You would imagine that Yosef's twenty-two years of experience in Egyptian politics would count for something to his brothers and that they would trust him sufficiently to be careful not to wreck his efforts – but no. They go out of their way to say exactly the opposite of everything that Yosef has directed.

> *They [the brothers] said to Pharaoh: We your servants are shepherds.*
> *And they said to Pharaoh: We only came to sojourn in your land temporarily because we have no grazing left for our flocks – so severe is the famine back in Cana'an.*
> *Let us stay for now in Goshen, please.* (47:3,4)

Astounding! We are *not* businessmen, just *shepherds.* We *are* indigent refugees, make no mistake about it. We never came to see *Yosef,* only to find some grazing land. Moreover, "*we only came to sojourn in your land temporarily,*" we will be *leaving* just as fast as the famine ends. In the *meanwhile,* we want you to know that it has to be *Goshen.*

There was nothing careless about these comments – they were a purposeful attempt to undermine Yosef's design. Note the repetition of the words "*They said to Pharaoh.*" The brothers went out of their way to make sure they got their message across even though Pharaoh had given them no opening – their comments were an unwarranted and inappropriate interjection! It boggles the imagination to think of the havoc this might have played with Yosef's plans. But it turns out that Pharaoh had his own agenda, in any case.

Yosef was sure that they would be summoned to the palace: *When Pharaoh summons you...* (46:33). But Pharaoh does nothing of the sort, so that Yosef is forced to introduce them to Pharaoh of his own accord: *Yosef selected five men from among his brothers and presented them to Pharaoh* (47:2). Pharaoh then pretends the brothers do not exist – except as extensions of Yosef. He disdainfully ignores them and their *faux pas,* an undiplomatic interjection, and, turning to Yosef, discusses the brothers as if they are objects in Yosef's care:

> *Pharaoh said to Yosef: Your father and brothers have come to you – the land of Egypt is at your disposal. You shall ensconce them in a choice location – let them be settled in the Goshen district. And if in your opinion there be capable men among them, appoint them officers over my own livestock holdings....* (47:5,6)

In effect Pharaoh was saying, "Yosef, whatever they say it is clear to me that they came only because of you, and you will determine what is to be done with them. Only, 'let them be settled in the Goshen district', i.e. make sure that they settle-in permanently. I leave to you the decision regarding any offer of government appointments."

We need not inquire here into the detailed motives and plans of the various parties. But we can certainly see one thing quite clearly: the brothers wanted no part in any plan to settle down and invest in Egypt.

They wanted no misreading of their intention that the stay be strictly temporary. They understood the dangers of possible assimilation and loss of national identity involved in any hint of permanence – they wanted to establish the Egyptian experience as forever foreign, so as to assure Yisrael's eventual exodus.

The importance to the Exodus of the brothers' words to Pharaoh is enshrined in the Haggada of Passover. We repeat and stress the implication of their message annually at the Seder:

> Ya'akov never went down to Egypt to become ensconced there, for it says: *And they [the brothers] said to Pharaoh: We have come only to sojourn in your land temporarily because we have no grazing left for our flocks – so severe is the famine back in Cana'an. Let us stay for now in Goshen, please.*[6] (47:3,4).

Yosef had the opposite idea, it would seem. He insisted on a future in Egypt. He wanted Yisrael to live there, to become established and entrenched in security and comfort:

> Yosef did not want his brothers to be as immigrants in the country. He purchased homes for them, and provided them with plantations and vineyards. This he did with the complicity of Pharaoh, for they [the brothers] had said, "*We have come only to sojourn in your land, temporarily, not to dwell here,*" implying, "when the famine passes we will return to our own land." But Pharaoh said to Yosef, "*settle your father,*" implying "settle them in permanently to live like everyone else, as full citizens of Goshen."
>
> RAMBAN, 47:12

Yosef's own prominence in Egypt was purchased at the cost of immersion in the concerns of his adopted country. There could be no way for him to captivate the nation as he did other than through capturing its quintessence within himself. Even his children's names reflected his preoccupation with his new life:

> *Yosef named the firstborn Menashe,* מנשה, *because "God has made me forget* (נשני) *the house of my father."*
>
> *He named his second son Ephraim,* אפרים, *because "God has made me fruitful* (הפרני) *in the land of my destitution."* (41:51,52)

> Yosef said: Thank God that I have been able to forget the home of my father.
>
> TANHUMA, VAYESHEV, 8:1

Yosef's approach here was as important for the Jewish environment *in* Egypt as his brothers' approach was for the Jewish exodus *out* of Egypt.

> *Yisrael dwelt in the land...of Goshen and made it their own – and they grew and proliferated exceedingly* (47:27).
>
> Goshen became an eternal inheritance...there was no heartache in Goshen and they lived there in the lap of all the world's luxuries.
>
> ZOHAR, 1:211b

The nature of the Jewish experience in Egypt became the template for the later exile in Bavel (Babylon), as the prophet enjoins Yisrael:

> *[A proclamation] To all those whom I have exiled from Yerushalayim to Bavel: Build homes and dwell in them, plant gardens and eat of their fruit, take wives and bear sons and daughters...Seek the welfare of the city to where I have exiled you and pray to God for it, for in its peace will you have peace. (Yermiah 29:4-7)*

Success in *galut* is a function of a Yosef-like commitment to the land of exile.

It seems impossible to find common ground between these alternative approaches. The brothers' uneasy, unsettled, and uninvolved sojourn appears hopelessly opposed to Yosef's assimilation into Egyptian society and opulence. Yet both were essential to the historical process of nurturing a nation in an Egyptian womb destined to become a crucible.[7] Indeed, certain "inconsistencies" in Yosef's approach intimate that the polarization was never quite as extreme as it seemed.

In engineering the agreement to settle in Goshen, Yosef created an enclave that would always advertise the Jewish difference. Despite his own Egyptian preeminence, Yosef had created the ghetto![8] So it has remained through the centuries – *I will set apart the land of Goshen, which My people inhabit.... (Shemot 8:18).*[9]

Even at the height of his power, Yosef sustained the taboo against Hebrews, such that the most lowly Egyptian could not eat with him.[10]

And he bequeathed the words and oath that provided the belief and key[11] to eventual redemption:

> *Yosef bound the children of Yisrael by oath: God will remember and send for you....* (50:25)

It was Yosef's descendants who attempted a return to the homeland eighty years before anyone else[12] was moved to even thoughts of redemption:

> The children of Ephraim attempted to defect from Egypt before the appointed time, and lost 300,000 people in the struggle.
>
> SHEMOT RABBA, 20:11

So committed was Yosef to his own origins that, in a contrast to Moshe, he becomes the prototype of Hebrew identity:

> Moshe said: Why should *I* not be buried in the Land – after all, Yosef's remains are being brought into the Land?
>
> Answered the Holy One: One who acknowledges his land is buried in it; one who does not acknowledge his land is not buried in it.
>
> Yosef said, "*I was kidnapped from the land of the Hebrews.*" (*Bereishit 40:15*).
>
> But when *you* were identified by the daughters of Yithro as "*An Egyptian man rescued us*" (*Shemot 2:19*), you heard it and acquiesced!
>
> DEVARIM RABBA, 2:8

א"ר לוי אמר לפניו רבש"ע עצמותיו של יוסף נכנסו לארץ ואני איני נכנס לארץ. אמר לו הקב"ה: מי שהודה בארצו נקבר בארצו ומי שלא הודה בארצו אינו נקבר בארצו? יוסף הודה בארצו מנין גבירתו אומרת, ראו הביא לנו איש עברי, ולא כפר אלא,
גנב גנבתי מארץ העברים, נקבר בארצו מנין שנאמר, ואת עצמות יוסף אשר העלו מארץ מצרים קברו בשכם.
את שלא הודית בארצך אין אתה נקבר בארצך. כיצד? בנות יתרו אומרות איש מצרי הצילנו מיד הרועים והוא שומע ושותק? לפיכך לא נקבר בארצו.

דברים רבה ב:ח

Besides, Yosef's efforts were dedicated not towards making Yisrael more suitable for Egypt, but towards making Egypt more suitable for Yisrael. He circumcised the Egyptians,[13] shifted populations so that his brothers would not be stigmatized,[14] and he supported a priestly caste with state funding[15] to create the infrastructure for the special status later conferred in Egypt to the tribe of Levi.[16]

The key to appreciating Yosef's efforts lies in a striking anomaly in the parasha's structure: the curious regression (see 47:13-26) to the original story of the years of famine without any literary or graphic transition. The disproportionate space allotted to these details of Yosef's financial achievements on behalf of the Egyptian treasury seems especially inappropriate for *Vayigash*. After all, our parasha has as its theme the settlement of Yisrael, not the development of Egypt, and, in any event, there is no reason to separate this part of the story from the original description of Yosef's emergency policies as found in *Miketz* (see 41:48-57). This is especially true if the reference is chronologically misplaced here, as Rashi assumes.[17]

Even more inexplicable is the non-sequitur which follows immediately after this section, again without the slightest transition – a single verse, closing *Vayigash*:

> *Yisrael dwelt in the Land of Egypt, in the territory of Goshen, and made it their own – and they grew and proliferated exceedingly.* (47:27)

The Torah seems to insist here that Yosef's endeavors for Egypt and Yosef's endeavors for his family converge. It points to Yosef's underlying mission:

> All the money and gold of the entire world was collected by Yosef and brought to Egypt, as it says *Yosef collected all the wealth in existence...and brought the money to the house of Pharaoh....* (47:14)
>
> When Yisrael left Egypt they took it all with them.
>
> PESAHIM, 119a

אמר רב יהודה אמר שמואל כל כסף וזהב שבעולם יוסף לקטו והביאו למצרים, שנאמר, וילקט יוסף את כל הכסף הנמצא. אין לי אלא שבארץ מצרים ושבארץ כנען, בשאר ארצות מנין? תלמוד לומר וכל הארץ באו מצרימה. וכשעלו ישראל ממצרים העלוהו עמהן, שנאמר וינצלו את מצרים. רב אסי אמר, עשאוה כמצודה זו שאין בה דגן. רבי שמעון אמר, כמצולה שאין בה דגים.

פסחים קיט.

Yosef was indeed an assimilationist, and wanted all Yisrael to assimilate along with him. But "assimilate" has two quite contrary meanings. In its primary sense, as a transitive verb, assimilate means "to take in and appropriate: absorb into the system."[18] Only in its tertiary definition,[19] as an intransitive verb, does it mean "to *become* assimilated." [20]

Yosef viewed *galut* not as a "time-out" from the fundamental direction of Yisrael, but as a time of carefully nurtured growth through such *primary* assimilation and challenge – a time to take in and appropriate what Egypt had to offer. The Egyptian experience would provide not only the test of Yisrael's identity, but the answer to the nature of that identity.

> [Avraham asked:] *How can I know that I will inherit it?*
>
> [God answered:] *You will certainly know, because your children will be strangers in a foreign land....* (15:8,13)

Yosef achieved the breathtaking breadth of such assimilating identity in his own life, and this became the pattern for all the hues and tones of the varied exiles of Yisrael. The quintessence of many cultures, some long vanished from the earth, shines forth – transformed, purified, and beautiful – in the characteristics, speech, poetry, and song of Jews with the fabulously varied backgrounds of their own respective wanderings. In becoming the purified expression of the *galut* culture, Yisrael becomes the conqueror instead of the conquered.

> Why was Yisrael subjugated to all the nations? So that within Yisrael they would live on, for Yisrael must incorporate the world.
>
> ZOHAR, II:16b

So it was that Yosef, in providing the path for *galut*, provided the path to *ge'ula* as well.

It is no coincidence that the names of all the seventy children of Yisrael are given for the first time here in *Vayigash*:

> *These are the names of the children of Yisrael coming into Egypt....* (46:8)
> *...all the individuals in the house of Ya'akov coming to Egypt – seventy.* (46:27)

I will insist that the Hebrews have done more to civilize men than any other nation. If I were an atheist and believed in blind eternal fate, I should still believe that fate had ordained the Jews to be the most essential instrument for civilizing the nations.
JOHN ADAMS

For these are the seventy members of Yisrael who parallel the seventy nations of humankind.

בהנחל עליון גוים – בהפרידו בני אדם
יצב גבולות עמים – למספר בני ישראל

When the Most High gave nations their heritage,
As He split up the sons of Man,
He set the boundaries of nations,
To parallel the number of Yisrael's descendants. (Devarim 32:8)

> According to the number of *B'nei Yisrael* who went down to Egypt – seventy nations for the seventy individuals. (—Rashi[21])

Yet to suggest that Yosef was connivingly Machiavellian, or even that he was subject to "dual loyalties," would contradict the Torah's entire characterization of Yosef as the height of integrity and faithfulness. Could he have masqueraded all his life as *the* patriotic Egyptian while planning all along the plunder and expropriation of everything he achieved? Could he have fooled all of the people all of the time? Could he have been lying when he named his children? No – Yosef could only assimilate through intimacy, through care, through complete awareness, attention, and affinity. Therein lies the incredible challenge of *galut*, a challenge to which Yisrael as a nation has been equal, time and time again.

Perhaps the synthesis of the two approaches to exile is to be found in Ya'akov, for he tells Pharaoh something that differs from the messages of both Yosef and his brothers:

> *The days of my sojourning through life have been one hundred and thirty years…and did not attain my forefathers' days of sojourning.* (47:9)

It was not specifically with respect to Egypt that Ya'akov was a sojourner – it was with respect to life itself. He would never mistake the transient for the eternal or the part for the whole. For Ya'akov was a true Wandering Jew, unceasingly conscious of life as a journey towards the wholeness and fulfillment that only living within the details can achieve.

One completely overcomes only what one assimilates.
ANDRÉ GIDE

But the Wanderer is the *most* sensitive admirer of the moments of life around him. To him, all transient things are exquisite in their instant, purified in their poignancy, yet formidable and vital in their linkage to the eternal reality of Yisrael, for now and forever – for now *because* of forever. Only the Wanderer can savor and treasure the details as they are lived by the seventy nations, lived as if they are full and sufficient within themselves. This is why Ya'akov is nearly a God to Egypt,[22] why Ya'akov's death precipitated months of national mourning in Egypt.[23] This is why the life of Ya'akov is characterized by the verse,

> *Ya'akov lived within the land of Egypt….* (47:28)
>
> That is, Ya'akov lived not only for himself, not only for his city, not only for the land of Goshen – Ya'akov lived for the entire nation of Egypt.
>
> MESHECH HOCHMA[24]

It is Yisrael's mission to be completely committed to the world and to totally assimilate it – through love and consciousness and incorporation of the details that are the substance of the symphony called Creation. Only the Wandering Jew sees no contradiction in saying both,

> *"I am a stranger and a countryman to you all. . . ."*
> *(Bereishit 23:4).*

1 Josephus, *Antiquities* 2:7.

2 Radak, 46:34 and cf. also Rashi, 47:2, s.v. *U'mekzei,* ומקצה אחיו. This seems to be a serious consideration, in light of Pharaoh's reluctance to pass up any opportunity to introduce high quality management— see 47:6.

3 *"They have brought along their sheep, their cattle, and all their possessions."*

4 *You will then be able to settle in Goshen...*

5 Rashbam, 46:34.

6 Cf. also *Sifrei, Tavo* 5:5, שלא ירד להשתקע.

7 Melachim I, 8:51.

8 *Pirkei Rabi Eliezer,* 26:1 explains that Goshen was actually Jewish territory, having been ceded to Sarah by an earlier Pharaoh.

9 Also Shemot 9:26.

10 Bereishit 43:32.

11 Bereishit 50:25; *Targum Yonatan,* Shemot 3:16; Bereishit Rabba, 5:13.

12 *Pesikta d'Rav Kahana,* 11:11.

13 Bereishit Rabba, 91:5; Cf. Rashi, Bereishit 41:55, s.v. *Asher,* ד"ה אשר יאמר.

14 Ḥulin, 60b; Cf. Bereishit 47:21 and Rashi, s.v. *Ve'et,* ד"ה ואת העם.

15 Bereishit 47:22,26; Shemot Rabba, 5:16.

16 Rashi, Shemot 5:4, s.v. *Lechu,* ד"ה לכו.

17 Bereishit 47:13. His source is Bereishit Rabba, 89:11. But see Radak, 47:14, who understands the reference here as to the remaining years. Ramban, based on *Sifrei, Ekev* 38, and *Tosefta,* Sotah, understands these as the years following the death of Ya'akov, which supports my case, as well.

18 *Webster's New Collegiate Dictionary,* 1977.

19 Ibid.

20 Ibid.

21 S.v. *Lemispar,* ד"ה למספר.

22 Bereishit Rabba, 96:5; *Tanḥuma, Vayḥi,* 3:1; Rashi, Bereishit 47:29, s.v. *Al na,* ד"ה אל נא תקברני.

23 Bereishit 50:3. See also Bereishit 50:11.

24 Rav Meir Simḥa Cohen, *Meshekh Ḥochma,* opening to *Vayḥi.*

XII Vayḥi

ויחי

Manifest Destiny

Vayḥi is the final portion of the *Book of Bereishit*. Here, the formative era of the *Avot* ends, and the book closes on the lives of Ya'akov, Yosef and the founding generations. It is understandable, then, that much of *Vayḥi* should consist of that venerable carrier of vision bequeathed: *berachot*, blessings for the future. Ya'akov, the repository of national vision, bestows in his final words individual blessings upon his children, leaving each with a particular direction and conception of the future handed down by Avraham and Yizḥak. But above and beyond this, he gives his son Yosef *"your father's blessings that overwhelm the blessings of my own ancestors. . . . (49:26),"* an additional *beracha* that is Ya'akov's alone, directly granted by God. Yosef is bequeathed here a unique mission along with the double portion in the Land of Israel originally meant for the firstborn.

Manifest Destiny makes sense of that additional blessing and unique mission, tracing it back to its source, finding in it a deeper understanding of the "wandering Jew" and an exile that seems to stretch interminably.

MANIFEST DESTINY

The passing of Ya'akov in *Vayḥi* marks the end of the Patriarchal era and the conclusion of the first book of the Torah, *Sefer Bereishit.* But *Vayḥi* actually means "He *lived,*" and depicts the surprising vitality of Ya'akov's twilight years, far from home.

> *Vayḥi – Ya'akov lived in the land of Egypt for seventeen years....* (47:28)
>
> He really *lived* those seventeen years...[1] in the lap of luxury and joy. This is the first time in Ya'akov's life that he truly *lived,* for all his other days were filled with suffering....
>
> During those seventeen years, the Shechina was with Ya'akov, and because of this they are called "*living.*"
>
> ZOHAR, I:116b

All his life, Ya'akov had dreamed of settling in the land of Cana'an in peace and fulfillment. It is both poignant and ironic that he found contentment only in the land of Egypt, in an exile he had once dreaded.[2]

Ya'akov, however, never did relinquish his dream of returning home. In *Vayḥi,* he makes arrangements with Yosef for one final journey to Cana'an. After his death, Ya'akov was brought home at last.

> *Yosef went north to bury his father...His sons carried him to the land of Cana'an, and buried him in the cave of the field of Machpela, the field near Mamre, which Avraham had bought for a burial site from Efron the Hittite.* (50:7,13)

Yet it is not as if Ya'akov was fully returned to Cana'an, leaving the years in Egypt behind him. Even in death, Ya'akov could not escape his newfound identification with life in a foreign land, and his funeral was a state occasion.

> *With him [Yosef] went all of Pharaoh's courtiers who were his palace elders, as well as all the sages of Egypt, all of Yosef's household, his*

brothers, and his father's family...a chariot brigade and horsemen also went with them, a very large assembly.... (50:7-9)

More than a state occasion – it was an event that left its mark on the history and even the place names of its time.

When they came to Goren haAtad, which is beyond the Jordan, they held there a very great and solemn lamentation...and when the Canaanite inhabitants of the land saw the mourning at Goren haAtad, they said, "This is a solemn mourning for the Egyptians." That is why it was named Avel-Mitzrayim ["Egyptian-Mourning"] which is beyond the Jordan. (50:10,11)

It is almost as if late in his life Ya'akov attained a new identity, becoming a father figure not only to "the sons of Yisrael" but to the Egyptians as well. Yet with all the fresh happiness of his life in Egypt, Ya'akov's personal thoughts and dreams were of the land he left behind. Before he died, he shared with his children some of his vision for their future – a future in the Land of Yisrael.

He tethers his ass to a vine, his ass's foal to a choice vine;
He washes his garment in wine, his robe in blood of grapes. (49:11)

He [Ya'akov] prophesied that the land of Yehuda would flow with wine as a fresh stream. (—Rashi[3])

His eyes are darker than wine, his teeth are whiter than milk. (49:12)

From the great quantities of milk that will be in his land, from abundant pasture for flocks of sheep. (—Rashi[4])

Shimon and Levi are a pair, their weapons are tools of violence....
I will divide them in Ya'akov, scatter them in Yisrael. (49:5,7)

He spread them out in Israel...and so it was, for the inheritance of Shimon was scattered within the children of Yehuda, as it says, *And their inheritance lay inside the portion of the children of Yehuda* (*Yehoshua* 19:1). Their cities were separate from each other throughout the portion of Judah. The inheritance of Levi, cities of refuge, were scattered throughout Israel. (—Ramban[5])

Zevulun shall dwell by the sea shore; he shall be a haven for ships, and his flank shall rest on Sidon. (49:13)

> He will have coastal land...and his borders will reach near Sidon. (—Rashi[6])
>
> A haven for ships, as he will travel across the sea with exports such as *tarith* fish, *ḥilazon* (for royal purple), and clear glass. (—Seforno[7])

He [Yissachar] saw that security was good, and the land pleasant.... (49:15)

> He saw that his land was blessed, and good for producing fruit. (—Rashi[8])
>
> His land will give food effortlessly and sustenance without pain. (—Seforno[9])

Asher's bread shall be rich, and he shall yield royal dainties. (49:20)

> He will have many olive groves in his portion, and they will flow with oil like a wellspring. (—Rashi[10])

Naphtali is a hind let loose, which yields lovely fawns. (49:21)

> This is the valley of Ginosar, which ripens its fruit quickly and easily, like the hind which runs swiftly and lightly. (—Rashi[11])

התחיל אוכל ושותה מסלסל בשערו ואומר, ברוך המקום שהשכיחני בית אבי.

תנחומא, וישב ח

And to his beloved son Yosef, he gives a special gift: a *double* portion in the Land of Yisrael.

Now, the two sons who were born to you in Egypt before I came here shall be considered as mine. Ephraim and Menashe shall be just like Re'uven and Shimon to me. (48:5)

> *Considered as mine* – Just like my own children, they will each take a separate portion in the Land. (—Rashi[12])

But this, too, is ironic. At the very moment that Ya'akov plans the apportionment of *Eretz Yisrael*, the only progeny he selects as special are the two children of Yosef who grew up in *Egypt*! Not merely in Egypt, mind you, but specifically *"before I came here"* – the only two grandchildren who were raised in complete isolation on foreign soil. These children were even *named* in honor of Yosef's new life in an adopted land.

Yosef named his firstborn Menashe (מנשה) because "God has made me forget (nashani/ נשני)... the house of my father."

He named the second Ephraim (אפרים) *because "God has made me fruitful (hif'rani/*הפרני*) in the land of my deprivation."* (41:51,52)

Yosef said, "Thank God that I have been able to forget the home of my father!"

TANHUMA, VAYESHEV, 8

What is more, these were children well-integrated in Egyptian society.

Yosef's children were…men of arms and men of war in Egypt.

MIDRASH TEHILLIM, 91:7

Something else is curious about Ya'akov's blessing to Ephraim and Menashe. He gives them a completely generic blessing – "Have lots of children!" – with no reference to their uniqueness:

May He bless the lads, and let them be called by my name, along with the names of my fathers, Avraham and Yitzhak, and may they increase in the land like fish. (48:16)

This is in striking contrast to the blessings Ya'akov gives to his own sons in this parasha. Each of them was given what he merited, only what his own character could support – and was even left out if undeserving.[13] Whereas not only was the *beracha* to Ephraim and Menashe indifferent to their *specific* traits, it was given to them despite Ya'akov's sense that they were thoroughly unsuitable.

Ya'akov saw Yosef's sons and said, "Who are these!?" (48:8)

From where did these children come to be so undeserving of blessing? (—Rashi[14])

It is not only that the *beracha* grants something so universal as having children – it is that reproductive prowess was the basis of the very choice of these two children, and the sole arbiter of which son is placed first! In his blessing, Ya'akov gives priority to Ephraim, the younger brother, whose name literally *means* productive, and responds to Yosef's objection,

I know, my son, I know. He [Menashe] *too shall become a people and he too shall be great. Yet his younger brother shall be greater than he, and his offspring shall fill the nations….* (48:19)

The population of Ephraim was greater than that of Menashe…and will *"fill the nations."* That is, when Ephraim is

> exiled among them, his children will swell the population of the various nations. (—Radak)

Since when is quantity and not quality the basis of *beracha*? And what is so wonderful about swelling the immigration quotas of the various nations?

Look more closely at Ya'akov's blessing and you find this enigma dramatically highlighted: The blessing Ya'akov gave to Yosef's children had a long history, and at every single stage of that history it was *reproduction* that was important. Ya'akov himself introduces the blessing with some of that history.

> *Ya'akov said to Yosef, "God Almighty appeared to me in Luz, in the land of Cana'an. He blessed me and said to me, 'I will make you productive and numerous, and have you give rise to an assembly of nations....'"*
>
> *"Now, the two sons who were born to you in Egypt before I came here shall be considered as mine...."* (48:3-5)

A glance at the words of "God Almighty" Himself as He gave this blessing provides another snippet of its history and attests to Ya'akov's precision:

> *God said to him, "I am 'God Almighty': Be productive and grow. A nation and an assembly of nations will come from you...."* (35:11)

But the history of this blessing from "God Almighty" goes back even farther. As Ya'akov left Cana'an to escape Eisav, Yitzḥak gave him some final words of encouragement that, again, precisely mirror the blessing here.

> *"God Almighty will bless you, and make you productive and numerous, and you will become an assembly of nations."* (28:3)

Ya'akov bestowed this thrice-blessed productivity and prolificacy upon Yosef. But the blessing also hints on all three occasions to another, closely related gift, that here Ya'akov adds to Yosef.

> *"He blessed me and said to me, 'I will make you productive and numerous, and have you give rise to an assembly of nations'...."*

He told me that I was yet to expand into another "assembly" and "nation." From this I understood that one of my children would be doubled:

"Now the two sons who were born to you in Egypt before I came here shall be considered as mine...." (48:3-5)

Now, I give this gift to you: *the two sons who were born to you in Egypt before I came here shall be considered as mine.* (—Rashi[15])

The mystery deepens: another parallel is evident throughout the three versions of the blessing. This *beracha*, though it seems universal and unassociated with the Land of Israel *per se*, is thrice presented as the source of Ya'akov's ultimate possession of the land. In Yitzḥak's version of the blessing to Ya'akov:

"God Almighty will bless you...to have you and your children with you inherit the land of your wanderings that God granted Avraham." (28:3-4)

In God's own wording of the blessing to Ya'akov:

"I am God Almighty...The land I granted to Avraham and Yitzḥak, I grant to you and to your children after you...." (35:11,12)

And in Ya'akov's version of the blessing to Yosef:

"God Almighty appeared to me [saying]...I will give this land to your children after you for an everlasting inheritance." (48:3,4)

This aspect, too, was stressed by Ya'akov in his gift to Yosef:

Now, the two sons who were born to you in Egypt before I came here shall be considered as mine. (48:5)

Considered as mine – Just like my own children, they will each take a separate portion in the Land. (—Rashi[16])

Which brings us back to where we began. Clearly, this *beracha* is both unique and uniquely fundamental. It is the definitive basis of the gift of land and future to Yosef with which, even today, we bless our own children every Friday night in a custom based on Ya'akov's instructions:

On that day [Ya'akov] blessed them, and said: Yisrael will use you as a blessing. They will say, 'May God make you like Ephraim and Menashe!' (48:20)

Why then indeed was such a special beracha given specifically to those who grew outside of the Land of Yisrael, and specifically to those separated even from the influence of Father Yisrael? Why does it take a form that is so universal, a form that involves "the fill of the nations"? Why is generic productivity the basis of inheritance? And why would such be the blessing we choose for our own children?

I suspect that the key to this *beracha* is to be found in another mystery: the inexplicable inclusion of the subject of Rachel's burial in this discussion with Yosef.

> *When I was on my way back home from Padan Aram, Rachel died on me in the land of Cana'an on the road, a short distance before we came to Efrat, and I buried her there along the road to Efrat....* (48:7)

The generally accepted[17] explanation of this verse is Rashi's suggestion[18] that Ya'akov felt he owed Yosef an explanation. After all, he was asking Yosef to bury him in the Machpela Cave even though he had not done the same for Yosef's mother:

> Although I am burdening you to travel far and bury me in the land of Cana'an and I did not do the same for your mother... indeed, I did not even carry her into Beit Leḥem, and I know that you have resented me for that! But I want you to know that I acted so on the basis of a prophecy.... (—Rashi[19])

There are, however, two serious problems with Rashi's approach. First, if the explanation is tied to Ya'akov's request for burial then that is when it should have been mentioned. Why wait until Yosef's later visit, to bring it up right in the middle of a blessing to his children, when no further mention was being made of Ya'akov's burial? Second, the explanation ignores a striking pattern, another triple parallel in this *beracha*. Ya'akov's mention of Rachel cannot be tied here just to his immediate needs, because every other occasion of this blessing is also unfailingly linked to Rachel and her burial!

Only mothers can think of the future – because they give birth to it in their children.
GORKY

When Ya'akov left for Padan Aram,

> *Yitzḥak called Ya'akov and he blessed him...Get up and go to Padan Aram...and take a wife from the daughters of Lavan, your mother's brother.* (28:1,2)

And then:

> *When Ya'akov saw Rachel...he kissed Rachel, and began to cry aloud.* (29:10,11)
>
> He cried because he foresaw that she would not be *buried next to him.* (—Rashi[20])

When Ya'akov returned from Padan Aram,

> *God appeared to Ya'akov again when he was coming back from Padan Aram and blessed him....* (35:9)

And then:

> *Rachel died and was buried there on the road to Efrat, Beit Leḥem. Ya'akov raised a marker on her grave, the marker of Rachel's tomb to this very day.* (35:19)

When Ya'akov gave the *beracha* to Yosef,

> *God Almighty appeared to me...and blessed me.* (48:3)

And then:

> *And Rachel died on me in the land of Cana'an on the road, a short distance before we came to Efrat, and I buried her there along the road to Efrat, which is Beit Leḥem.* (48:7)

Take the long way home,
Take the long way home...
SUPERTRAMP

When seen in this context, it is evident that Ya'akov was telling Yosef something that related directly to the blessing that he had just bequeathed. Ya'akov recreated for Yosef not only the precise words of his *beracha*, but its precise setting! He handed over to Yosef not only the blessing itself, but its aftermath: the burial of Rachel along the road to Efrat, which is Beit Leḥem, the burial whose relevance the Torah extends to "this very day."

What is so important about this "marker of Rachel's tomb to this very day," and how does it relate to the *beracha*?

> I buried her there so that she would be a comfort to her children when they would go into exile....
>
> RASHI[21]

> Why did Ya'akov bury Rachel on the road to Efrat? He saw that the children exiled from the land of Israel would one day walk that road and pass by her and she would pray for them, as it says, *A voice is heard in Rama, lament and bitter weeping – Rachel*

> *cries over her children, refuses to be comforted over her children for they are lost....*
> [The Holy One answers her,[22]] *"Stop crying, stop your tears...there is hope for your future," says the Lord, "and the children will come home again." (Yermiah 31:14-16).*
>
> BEREISHIT RABBA, 82:10

Rachel's burial along the road expresses all that is special about this *beracha*. She would never surrender, never bend to the "inevitable." To her, *Eretz Yisrael* was the Manifest Destiny of her children. They would return no matter how long it would take. Rachel was the mother of total commitment, of everlasting belief. She can find no fulfillment until that destiny is complete.

Thus Ya'akov gave the *beracha* just as it was given to him – both in loss and in hope. It is a blessing that can transform farewell into the first step of a triumphant return. This is the blessing given to one who embarks on the road, to one leaving the "Land of Life" towards exile in *Ḥutz la'Aretz* ("Outside the Land"). It is the blessing given to one who starts out towards an uncertain future.

"The Land of Life" (Tehillim 142:7) refers to Eretz Yisrael...

ZOHAR, I:115A

This is the blessing that draws the eyes to "*the hope for your future*," and to the painful recognition that such future will be constructed not *in* the land – but specifically "*on the road*." The "road to Efrat" – and to the House of David in Beit Leḥem – did not even exist when Rachel died in Rama. She was buried there as a marker to, and for, the future.

> Where does the verse intimate that Rachel's burial was a message to her children in the future? It says here "*Rachel died on me along the road...and I buried her there on the road.*"
>
> But, in fact, she died in Rama, a city in Binyamin and she was buried there. This intimates, therefore, that *she died along a road of the future!*
>
> RAMBAN, 48:7

Real generosity toward the future lies in giving all to the present.

CAMUS

Yitzḥak gave Ya'akov the map of the long way home. This unique *beracha* endows the present with some of its future fulfillment, and establishes the road to "Outside the Land" as the only way home. In the midst of aching emotional turmoil, as Ya'akov prepared to leave behind all he loved and cherished, Yitzḥak gave him a blessing of hope, a blessing to create and ensure the future that could be crafted only of the fabric of Ya'akov's journey.

Ya'akov came to recognize that the years "away" were not unfortunate interludes, but were an essential and indispensable part of the road to *Eretz Yisrael*. The only way to a manifest destiny in *Eretz Yisrael* is along the road of *galut* – and this fact itself is the premise of the primary covenant for the land:

> *As the sun was setting, slumber fell over Avram, and behold, a dread – dark and deep – fell upon him. He [God] said to Avram, "Know clearly that your seed shall be strangers in a land not their own, and they will enslave and oppress them for 400 years... and they will leave with great wealth."* (15:12-14)[23]
>
> This "dread" was an intimation of the suffering and pain of *galut*. (—Rashi[24])

Those 400 years included nearly two centuries of life in Cana'an, as yet *strangers in a land not their own*. For the land is not 'Home' until the journey is done, and it is a journey replete with kaleidoscopic images of an exotic history of cultures and countries far away. The road goes on and on....

> *And behold, a dread – dark and deep – fell upon him.*
>
> *"Fell upon him"*– refers to Babylon,
> *"Deep"*– refers to Media,
> *"Dark"*– refers to Greece,
> *"Dread"*– refers to Edom.
>
> BEREISHIT RABBA, 44:17

The nearly inconceivable distances that would need to be traveled along the extravagant route of Yisrael's history were brought home to Ya'akov in his relationship with the woman he loved, a relationship set always in the future. The years Ya'akov invested to earn her hand only to suffer her death in the prime of life are reflected in the millennia invested by his children, through unutterable loss, towards a world in which love lives forever. From the very first moment Ya'akov laid his eyes upon Rachel, she was to him a magical embodiment of belief and vision and utter commitment to the future they loved. That was how he knew – in that same instant – that she could never rest until it was all over. He knew at once that to her, the road was everything.

> *"Peace! Here is his daughter Rachel coming with the sheep!"* (29:6)
>
> Ya'akov was speaking here of the *galut* to come:
> There will one day indeed be *"Peace"* to those exiled from the Land, [for *"here is Rachel,"* i.e.] *in merit of Rachel, just as it says, "Stop crying, stop your tears . . . there is hope for your future," says the Lord, "and the children will come home again."*
>
> BEREISHIT RABBA, 70:10

The magic of Rachel's belief imbued every step of Ya'akov's present with the land[25] and the woman of his dreams, though he was so far away from them both.

> *The years seemed to him but a few days, in his love for her.* (29:20)

That same unrelenting belief is the comfort to Rachel's children in their own estrangement, and imbues life Outside with some of the connection and fulfillment of the Land – and even with prophecy:

> Why did God speak to prophets *Outside* the Land? Only in merit of the progenitors, as it says, *A voice is heard in Rama, lament and bitter weeping – Rachel cries over her children, refuses to be comforted over her children for they are lost...the children will come home again (Yermiah 31:14-16).*
>
> TANḤUMA, BO, 5

The productivity of the years in darkness Outside becomes part of the building of *Eretz Yisrael*, becomes a living link to *Eretz Yisrael* – because of this vision and *beracha*. The children *will* come home again, home along this road of Rachel's.

> *"There is hope for your future," says the Lord, "and the children will come home again....*
> *"Erect markers (tzionim,*[26] ציונים*)! Set up signposts! Keep in mind the highway, the road that you traveled...."* (*Yermiah* 31:17,21)

This, then, is the *beracha* for the road: to implement every new society, every new situation, every new culture, every new world and, through building them unstintingly, build one's own future. This was the blessing that Yitzḥak gave Ya'akov as he started on the road Outside. It was a blessing that God Himself had bestowed on a Creation that needed to begin growing towards its own future:

Be productive and grow.... (*Bereishit 1:28*)

It was a blessing that God Himself would bestow once again, this time on the singular individual who embodied that future: Ya'akov, Yisrael-to-be.

Be productive and grow.... (*Bereishit 35:11*)

That productivity and growth, almost entirely a return on some "futures" in Egypt, would eventually build the Land of Israel.[27]

This *beracha* of explosive, but directed,[28] growth toward future-and-return was also the blessing bestowed by Ya'akov on Yosef. No gift from Ya'akov could have been more appropriate. Yosef was a traveler on the same road of exile along which his mother was buried. Only Yosef would make it possible for the exploding population of Yisrael to successfully convert the Egyptian experience into nationhood, wealth, and the first phase in settling the land of Israel. Yosef's characteristic was production. All his investments were in futures, and even his name was symbolic of children yet-to-come: *She called him Yosef* ("Increase") *saying, "May God add me another son."* (*Bereishit 30:24*).

Productivity itself is a function of belief in the future. Yosef's vision sustained his productivity and his productivity fueled his vision. It was only in Egypt that we *became a great and vigorous nation* (*Devarim 26:5*). There was no question of "dual loyalties" for Yosef. The more profound his investment in Egypt, the more productive his future. The one who did the most for Egypt became the greatest builder of Israel in his success. Yosef came to embody in his life the vision carried by his mother, until he became himself identified with the dream called Zion.[29]

All that happened to Yosef, happened to *Tzion*....

TANḤUMA, VAYIGASH, 10

בא וראה, כל צרות שאירע ליוסף אירע לציון: ביוסף כתיב, וישראל אהב את יוסף, בציון כתיב, אוהב השם שערי ציון; ביוסף כתיב, וישנאו אותו, בציון, נתנה עלי בקולה על כן שנאתיה; ביוסף, והנה אנחנו מאלמים אלומים, בציון, בא יבא ברנה נושא אלמותיו; ביוסף, המלוך תמלוך עלינו, בציון, אומר לציון מלך אלהיך; ביוסף, ויחלום יוסף חלום, בציון, בשוב השם את שיבת ציון היינו כחולמים; ביוסף, הבא נבא אני ואמך, בציון, אפיס ארץ ישתחוו לך; ביוסף, ויקנאו בו אחיו, בציון, קנאתי לציון קנאה גדולה; ביוסף, לך ראה נא את שלום אחיך, בציון, ודרשו את שלום העיר; ביוסף, ויראו אותו מרחוק, בציון, זכרו מרחוק את השם; ביוסף, ויתנכלו אותו, בציון, על עמך יערימו סוד; ביוסף, ויפשיטו את כתונת הפסים, בציון, והפשיטוך את בגדיך; ביוסף, וישליכו אותו הבורה, בציון, צמתו בבור חיי; ביוסף, והבור רק אין בו מים, בציון, ובבור אין מים כי אם טיט ; ביוסף, וישבו לאכול לחם, בציון, אשור לשבוע לחם; ביוסף, וימשכו ויעלו את יוסף, בציון, וימשכו את ירמיהו בחבלים ויעלו אותו מן הבור; ביוסף, ויקרע יעקב שמלותיו, בציון, לבכי ומספד; ביוסף, וימאן להתנחם, ובציון, אל תאיצו לנחמני; ביוסף, והמדנים מכרו אותו אל מצרים, ובציון, ובני יהודה ובני ישראל מכרתם לבני היונים.

ומה שאירע ליוסף טובות אירע לציון טובות, ביוסף ויהי יוסף יפה תואר ויפה מראה, וציון יפה נוף משוש כל הארץ; ביוסף, איננו גדול בבית הזה ממני, בציון, גדול יהיה כבוד הבית הזה; ביוסף, ויהי השם את יוסף; בציון, והיו עיני ולבי שם; ביוסף, ויט אליו חסד, ובציון, זכרתי לך חסד; ביוסף, ויגלח ויחלף שמלותיו, ובציון, אם רחץ השם את צואת בנות ציון; ביוסף, רק הכסא אגדל ממך, ובציון, בעת ההיא יקראו לירושלים כסא השם; ביוסף כתיב, וילבש אותו בגדי שש, ובציון, עורי עורי לבשי עזך ציון לבשי בגדי תפארתך; ביוסף כתיב, ואת יהודה שלח לפניו, ובציון, הנני שולח מלאכי.

תנחומא, ויגש י

Yosef, as Ya'akov, indeed had his best years in a foreign land. But his investment and success in Egypt were the key to the first stage in settling the Land of Israel, just as investment and success in Babylon were to be the key to a later stage of settlement:

> *So says the Lord...to all the Golah that I have exiled from Yerushalayim to Babylon: Build house and dwell in them, and plant gardens and eat their fruit...grow there – do not become diminished! And seek the fulfillment of the city to which I sent you into captivity...in its fulfillment lies your own.* (*Yermiah* 29:4-7)

It is no coincidence that the normative historical modality for Yisrael is not reflected as much in the privileged periods inside Eretz Yisrael as it is in the much longer periods of life in *galut*, in exile. Though Creation itself proclaims the Manifest Destiny of Yisrael in *Eretz Yisrael*,[30] Creation itself also proclaims elements of history – the history of *galut*:

> *The earth was desolate and void, and darkness upon the face of the deep....*(*Bereishit* 1:2)
>
> *"Desolate"*– refers to the *galut* in Babylon....
> *"Void"*– refers to the *galut* in Media....
> *"Darkness"*– refers to the *galut* of Greece....
> *"The deep"*– refers to the *galut* of Edom....
>
> BEREISHIT RABBA, 2:5

The two themes are intertwined – exile and redemption, *Outside* and *Eretz Yisrael*. The potential grows Outside, to be realized and actualized in the Land.

> *Of Tzion it shall be said: This man, that man, was born within her – the Highest Himself will establish her!* (*Tehillim* 87:5)
>
> [The repetition of "*This man – that man*"] implies that both one who was actually born in *Tzion* and one who longs for her [are equally her children]....
>
> One of us [in *Eretz Yisrael*] is as good as two of them [Outside]....
>
> But one of them who arrives here [from Outside] is as good as two of us!
>
> KETUVOT, 75a

Tzion's children will return to her, grown from their work in the world and their journey through history, swelled with offspring and ideas and new potential, able to build a new land and a new nation nearly overnight.

> *Can a land truly be built in a day!? Can a nation be born instantaneously!? (Isaiah 66:8)*

But the land and nation will be built only of the vision of centuries and the toil of millions who lived far away, nearly forgotten:

> *[Tzion,] you will say to yourself, "Who gave birth to these!? I lost my children – a recluse, an exile, a wanderer – who raised these? For sure, I was left alone – so where do these come from!?" (Isaiah 49:21)*

This is the *beracha* and dream of Yosef, the man who provides the key to both the exile and the redemption. It is not an easy road, for it is the long way home. But it is the only way, the way of Ya'akov and Rachel, the way of the children who in the battle for the future may lose their lives, but never their dreams.

> *Rachel died on me....* Surely, Yosef was well aware of how Rachel had died!...This refers rather to those who died Outside of the Land in sanctification of the Name....
>
> There will be great battles on the "*road to Efrat*," and many will lose their lives. But they are destined to live again, to achieve more – *along that road* – than any who had lived in Yerushalayim!
>
> ZOHAR, 1:215a

With the death of Ya'akov, Yosef, and the brothers at the close of *Vayḥi*, Yisrael entered a period of dormancy. Destiny would wait. But inside the Egyptian chrysalis[31] a metamorphosis was slowly taking place.

1 This period serves as a model for life fulfillment, and R. Yehuda haNassi viewed the last seventeen years of his own life in Zippori as a parallel to these special years of Ya'akov. See Bereishit Rabba, 96:5 and *Tanḥuma, Vayḥi*, 3.

2 Cf. Bereishit 46:3.

3 S.v. *Oseri*, ד״ה אוסרי.

4 S.v. *Meiḥalav*, ד״ה מחלב.

5 49:5 s.v. *Klei*, ד״ה כלי חמס.

6 S.v. *Zevulun*, ד״ה זבולון and s.v. *Veyarkato*, ד״ה וירכתו.

7 S.v. *Vehu*, ד״ה והוא .

8 S.v. *Vayare*, ד״ה וירא .

9 S.v. *Ve'et*, ד״ה ואת הארץ.

10 S.v. *MeAsher*, ד״ה מאשר.

11 S.v. *Ayala*, ד״ה אילה.

12 S.v. *Li*, ד״ה לי .

13 Cf 49:4-7; Bereishit Rabba, 99:6; *Midrash Tehillim*, 90; Rashi, Devarim 33:7; Ramban, Devarim 33:6.

14 S.v. *Vayomer*, ד״ה ויאמר.

15 S.v. *Untaticha*, ד״ה ונתתיך.

16 S.v. *Li*, ד״ה לי .

17 Cf. Ibn Ezra, Ramban, Ḥizkuni, and Radak, all on 48:7. However, see Seforno, op. cit. for a radically different explanation.

18 Based on Pesikta Rabbati, 3.

19 48:7.

20 As per Bereishit Rabba, 70:12.

21 Bereishit 48:7, s.v. *Va'ekbe'reha*, ד״ה ואקברה שם.

22 Added by Rashi.

23 The exiles also appear in a far more primal setting, in the Creation narrative. Cf. Bereishit Rabba, 2:5.

24 S.v. *Vehinei*, ד״ה והנה אימה.

25 Cf. Rashi, Bereishit 29:18.

26 Beautiful! The word *tzion* literally *means* a "road marker."

27 This is why the very same Ya'akov whose most fulfilling years were spent in Goshen bequeathed his children a map for the long desert-journey back to the Land of Israel:

> *I stretch my wisdom to the distance. . . .(Iyov 36:3)*
> —The encampment and banners in the desert were the creation of their father Ya'akov . . . in the same layout that they carried his coffin

> back to Cana'an, that is how they traveled through the desert back to Cana'an.
>
> BAMIDBAR RABBA, 2:8

28 The literal translation of *El Shaddai*, the name of God that speaks here, is "Delimiting Power."

> What is the meaning of *I am "El Shaddai": Be productive and grow. . . .* (35:*11*)? It means, "I am He Who said to My world: *Dai!* ("Enough!").
>
> ḤAGIGA, 12A

29 Cf. note 26.

30 Cf. Rashi, Bereishit 1:1 and *FrameWorks,* Bamidbar, 1.

31 This relationship of *vision* to the stages of national metamorphosis is expressed linguistically in the words for biological metamorphosis:

> imago n. pl. an adult insect.
> [1790-1800; < NL, L imago IMAGE (the adult being perceived as the true exemplar of the species, as opposed to the larva "ghost" and pupa "doll")]

XII Vayḥi
ויחי

Apocalypse Now

We have come to the end of the beginning. *Vayḥi* closes the *Book of Genesis*, for with the death of the last of the *Avot*, Ya'akov, comes the conclusion of the first stage in Yisrael's development. Much of our parasha is concerned with the transition from the era of Ya'akov to that of his children, and we read here of the *berachot*, the blessings through which Ya'akov conveys his vision and direction for the future, first to Yosef and later, on his deathbed, to all his children.

But Ya'akov had intended to reveal a great deal more: he wanted to succor his children with a messianic vision, a conception of "The End of Days." God stopped him. The attempt and its frustration are both important enough to appear at this critical moment: in prophecy and revelation lie dangers. *Apocalypse Now* argues that the very nature of Yisrael is linked to a careful balance between the significance of the messianic vision and its perils.

APOCALYPSE NOW

Projecting, predicting, and prophesying are all big business nowadays. Of course economic, technological, social, and political forecasting may be legitimate, if not essential, features of modern intercourse. But even the augurs do a brisk and surprisingly respectable business: an incredible ten percent of French businesses subscribe to *Divini*Tel via Minitel, France's teletext system. FFr350 (about $60) is all it takes for an astrological analysis of takeover timings – the ultimate competitive edge.[1] Dr. Iben Browning publishes *The Browning Newsletter* for American businessmen who cannot resist the revelations of a man who predicted the Mount St. Helens eruption (though presumably they are unaware that the prediction was made after the USGS had already evacuated the area).[2]

Apparently futurology in all its forms strikes a deep chord. The "British Israelites" believe that the lost tribes of Israel ended up in the United Kingdom and that the secrets of tomorrow were hidden in the Great Pyramid. Of course, they debunk the foolish belief that you can figure out the future just by looking at the Great Pyramid. "Ridiculous!" insisted a member some time ago. "Why, with the sort of precise measurement involved, such calculations can take up to a week."[3] Yet, the real Israelites in Egypt apparently *were* sustained by visions of things to come.

A vista of the future accompanies the end of this *Sefer Bereishit*, in the form of the last words of the *Av*, Ya'akov.

> *Ya'akov called his sons and said, "Gather round, and I will tell you what will happen to you in the end of days. . . ."* (49:1)

He was not allowed, however, to reveal all:

> Ya'akov planned to reveal to his children The End, the *Kets*, but the Shechina withdrew from him.
>
> PESAḤIM, 56a

Nonetheless, there was much that he *was* able to reveal. His final blessings encompass allusions to such events as the war of Gog and Magog,[4] the building of the Temple,[5] Ḥanukah,[6] and future exiles.[7] Men and women of the then distant future inhabit these blessings: Devorah and Sisra;[8] Sha'ul and David,[9] Mordechai and Esther,[10] Gideon[11] and Shimshon,[12] Koraḥ and Zimri,[13] and even future leaders in Bavel (Babylon).[14]

There must be something dreadful and exclusive in the uncensored vision of "The End" if Ya'akov was permitted to reveal just about everything else. Indeed, "Apocalypse" is the dramatic English word for the *Kets* ("End"), in its sense of foretelling the ultimate destiny of the world. (Though "apocalypse" comes innocently enough from the Greek for "uncover" and primarily means nothing more dreadful than "prophetic revelation," it has become associated with cosmic cataclysm because of early Christian writings – not to mention a more recent production.)

עוד ביקש (יונתן בן עוזיאל)
לגלות תרגום של כתובים,
יצתה בת קול ואמרה לו דייך!
מאי טעמא! משום דאית ביה
קץ משיח.

מגילה, ג.

The withdrawal of the Shechina leaves Ya'akov blinded to the apocalypse, though just a moment before it was something he knew. Was it that he suddenly lost recall of the date of the coming of the Messiah? What of the visions he did divulge? They seem to expose plenty "secrets of the Shechina"[15] themselves.

More remarkable is the Zohar's contention that Ya'akov *did* reveal the *Kets*, revealed it right here in front of our eyes in these words of blessings to his children:

> If you think that Ya'akov did not expose precisely what he set out to expose, how do you explain the fact that the Torah follows Ya'akov's introduction with those words – with nary an interruption – if in fact they were unfinished and fragmentary? Clearly, he completed everything he wished to divulge, only he revealed it while yet concealing it, without leaving out even a single letter....
>
> ZOHAR, I:234b

The message is here perhaps, but its meaning is well hidden until after the *Kets*.

> [Only] in the days of the *Mashiaḥ* will the significance and implications of the messianic metaphors used by the prophets become common knowledge.
>
> MISHNE TORAH, HILCHOT MELACHIM, 12:1

But if that is the case, what is the point of the dramatic deathbed setting here in *Vayḥi*? What meaning can there be to 'prophecy' that addresses the future only when such future is already the past? The identical question can be directed at the entire body of messianic prophecies, for none of them is meant to be unambiguously understood in advance.

> But *no one* really knows anything about all these things until *after* they take place, for they are exceedingly concealed in the words of the prophets, and the sages have no received traditions about these matters....
>
> IBID., 12:2

Yet the author of those words is the very one who deems thirteen principles as unequivocally essential to any possible Judaic belief system – and one of those principles is the belief in the advent of a phenomenal leader who will be anointed (Hebrew: "*mashuaḥ*") as king:

> The twelfth principle of the Jewish belief system is the confidence in the coming of the days of the *Mashiaḥ*...to believe that he will be superior to and more worthy and honored than any leader in history; to support and love him....
>
> RAMBAM, COMMENTARY ON MISHNA[16]

The centrality of the *Mashiaḥ* concept is immortalized in the *Ani Ma'amin,* a veritable catechism of Jewish faith based on Rambam's principles.

There must be something dramatically meaningful about the belief in a *Mashiaḥ* if without it Judaism as a belief system is inconsistent and inconceivable. Yet the selfsame Rambam not only debunks any prospect of obtaining explicit information about *Mashiaḥ*, he insists that spending any time studying or thinking about the issue is futile and even counter-productive.

> A person should never invest effort in the *aggadot* or spend time on the *midrashim* which deal with this messianic matter or related ideas, nor should he consider them as pivotal, for they

> do not lead a person to either awe or love of God. One must not work out "The End," as the Sages said: May the apocalypse analysts all drop dead!
>
> MISHNE TORAH, HILCHOT MELACHIM, 12:2

Rambam takes this pragmatic approach a step further in asserting that the Jewish desire for sharing the "Epoch of the Messiah" is neither mystical nor cosmic, but simply expedient.

> The reason that all of Yisrael...have hungered for the days of the *Mashiah* is in order to be left alone by the governments... to find the peace of mind necessary to grow and progress in understanding....
>
> MISHNE TORAH, HILCHOT TESHUVA, 9:2

Vision is the art of seeing things invisible.
JONATHAN SWIFT

You can see the pattern of ambivalence here. The *fact* of the *Kets* is crucial and climacteric, but understanding of its specifics is not only unimportant – it is downright damaging to spiritual wholesomeness. Ya'akov must not speak here *apocalyptically,* though he does speak *prophetically,* and certainly refers to *Mashiah* in his blessings.

> *The scepter will not depart from Yehuda, nor the power of the law from his descendants, until the coming of Shilo....*(49:10)
>
> *Until the coming of the Mashiah.*
>
> TARGUM; BEREISHIT RABBA, 99:8; RASHI[17]

What could be the relevance of a purely academic position, not to be pursued or fully understood? Why would such a general, theoretical belief form one of the few truly fundamental elements of Judaism?

I think a closer look at Ya'akov's *berachot* may give us the key. After all, Ya'akov was blessing his children here,[18] not granting final oracles:

> *These are the words which Ya'akov spoke as he blessed them, giving each his unique blessing.* (49:28)

Why then did he think that messianic disclosures would be the path to blessing? What role did the prophetic revelations play in the context of benediction – especially if some of what was voiced was unfavorable and even hurtful?[19] These seem like mighty peculiar *berachot.*

What is more remarkable is that Ya'akov was not telling his sons what he *already knew* – he was discovering, and reacting, even as he spoke:

Let Dan be a snake on the road, a viper on the path, who bites the horse's heel so that the rider falls backwards. God, I hope for Your deliverance! (49:17,18)

Ya'akov first thought that Shimshon of Dan was *Mashiaḥ*. But then he watched him die, and he exclaimed, "He too dies! *God – I hope for Your deliverance!*"

BEREISHIT RABBA, 98:14

Ya'akov's visions were clearly projections and extrapolations of the character and personalities of each of his children into the future. Each individual was blessed here with self-awareness of his context in the direction of history and with the drives and reserves to meet the challenges ahead. And that is the essential meaning of *beracha*– 'addition'.[20] The word relates to *beraicha*, 'pool', for the increment innate in "blessing" (ברכה) must overflow from a "pool" (בריכה) already extant.

What is meant by '*beracha*'? Imagine a king who plants trees in a garden. Although it may rain and the ground may absorb much moisture, it must ultimately be irrigated from its own pool.[21]

SEFER HABAHIR

So while we might convey our own best *wishes* for someone, these wishes would not constitute a true *beracha*. The only efficacious *blessing* consists of grasping and amplifying an individual's innate gifts.[22]

The future enters into us, in order to transform itself in us, long before it happens.
RILKE, LETTERS TO A YOUNG POET

If such is the definition of *beracha*, what are we to make of the non-specific *beracha* given by Ya'akov earlier in our parasha to Yosef's offspring?

May He bless the lads, and let them be called by my name, along with the names of my fathers, Avraham and Yitzḥak, and may they increase in the land like fish. (48:16)

Now, this is a purely generic blessing, meant to be applied to every Jewish child throughout history, regardless of individual personality:

Israel will use you as a blessing, saying: May God make you like Ephraim and Menashe. (48:20)

Such a formula makes a striking contrast to the blessings Ya'akov gave to his sons. In those blessings each child was given only what he deserved. Each was given only what his own character could support – he was even left out if undeserving.[23] But in the blessing to Ephraim and

Menashe, the focus of the *beracha* is universal to the point of complete indifference to the boys' traits. What is more, Ya'akov blessed Ephraim and Menashe even though he perceived that the *beracha* was inappropriate. These two were indeed undeserving.

> *Ya'akov saw Yosef's sons and said, "Who are these?!"* (48:8)
>
> From where came these to be so undeserving of blessing? (—Rashi[24])

These two sets of *berachot* parallel the two levels of our relationship to the Messianic ideal. On the one hand, there needs to be a confirmation that history has specific direction and significance: there will come a time of consummation, of *Kets*. There will come a time when dreams will be fulfilled, when compassion will triumph, when excellence will be rewarded and darkness dispelled.

On the other hand, we must accept the process, growing towards the *Kets*. We must treasure the chaotic passage, cherish the confusing journey. We must never misrepresent or misconstrue the time-to-come through the distorting lens of our own fragmentary and incomplete vision, as if it were a mere extrapolation of a parochial present and a personalized moment.

Life can only be understood backwards; but it must be lived forwards.
SÖREN KIERKEGAARD

So too with blessings. There are blessings that provide bearings in history and confirm its substance and its relevance. These are the blessings that drive us to find our unique place in the scheme of a vision of the whole which is the *Kets* – the realistic and credible apocalypse. They are the blessings at the source, given to the sons of Ya'akov.

But there are blessings of another type, blessings that drive us to jump into the process, to expand and multiply and risk all, to "Go for it!" These are the blessings that urge us *to increase like fish* with all the diverse potential of Yisrael's gene pool, to transcend the personal and be servants of history instead of masters. They are the blessings to travelers through time, to the generations that follow the origins, to the Ephraims and Menashes of history who are fully themselves while forever remaining a part of the roots of Yisrael:

> *Ephraim and Menashe shall be like Re'uven and Shimon to me.* (48:5)

Climactic conclusions certainly make all the difference to a good plot, but the principal joy of a book is not its climax but its unfolding. It is the journey that is important, the development and the lives of characters. The deeper structure of the journey is revealed in a well crafted conclusion. When we reach the end, as we must, we experience the enjoyment of closure – but we are saddened that it is over.

The days of *Mashiaḥ* are no different. Without them, the extravaganza of history is futile and irrelevant. But when those days do arrive at last, we will be profoundly saddened that the journey is done.

> *Remember your Creator*
> *In the days of your youthfulness,*
> *Before the bad days come,*
> *And those years arrive of which you will say,*
> *"I have no desire in these. . . ." (Kohelet 12:1)*
> – *The years of no desire* refer to the Messianic era. . . .
>
> SHABBAT, 151b

It is only the "Apocalypse analyst" who is driven to know the end before completing the story. His desire for "secret knowledge" exposes a lust for power and specious control, within which lurks the danger of manipulative messianism. The demand for "*Mashiaḥ* or Bust!" is the desire to have your messiah and eat him too. Think of the compromises of morality, of halacha, of military judgment, of political sanity, and of simple common sense that have been made in the name of a messiah. Think of how ruinous messianism has proven in all its forms and under all its many names and political variants – in our own times perhaps more ruinous than ever before.

> *Begin at the beginning...and go on until you come to the end: then stop.*
>
> LEWIS CARROL, ALICE'S ADVENTURES IN WONDERLAND

The reason that the *Kets* must remain hidden is clear: It may not become known before its time because it is *unknowable* before its time. The *Kets* is not a piece of information or a date – it is a vision that encompasses Creation's entirety. The withdrawal of the Shechina left Ya'akov as blind as his children, for the *Kets* cannot be "remembered."

But the vision of the *Kets* was embodied in the *berachot*. Ya'akov's projection into the future was shaped by the revelation of historical design, direction, and integration. The more fully Ya'akov's personal blessings are lived and linked together, incorporated by the nation as a whole, the closer the approximation of Messianic integration.

> *Each according to his own blessing he blessed them.* (49:28)
>
> Why the change from the singular to the plural? To teach you that each of them was also linked to the blessings of the others. . . .
>
> TANḤUMA, VAYḤI, 16

The *Kets* must provide vision and direction, but nothing more. The moment it becomes the goal instead of the result, the objective instead of the course, it is no longer the *Kets*. It becomes instead the tool of personal messianic fantasy. It is reduced to the justification of an illusory cause that is limiting and destructive, a mirage that serves only to delay the advent of the real thing:

> *Mashiaḥ* only comes when you are not looking for him.
>
> SANHEDRIN, 97a

Yisrael lives a fabulous saga, and each passage is an element of the story's dramatic composition – consummated in elegance, turned coherent and lucid through a final and climactic chapter. It is *Mashiaḥ* who pulls it all together, who must expose and integrate the links that join all the details and adventures of lives scattered throughout the vicissitudes of history and permutating civilizations. It is the success and achievement of *Mashiaḥ* that vindicates, at last, the incalculable particulars of every individual life – of every action, thought, fleeting awareness, discovery, emotion, and relationship – as members of a unified composition.

All's well that ends well.
SHAKESPEARE

Dedication and service to that saga is the task of Yisrael. The acceptance of the servitude to history restored the departed Shechina to Ya'akov, and brought about the first integration of Yisrael as a nation with a burning sense of historical presence:

> Such integration had never existed from the moment of Creation until the day that Ya'akov lay on his deathbed. Avraham stood on his right, Yitzḥak on his left, and then he told his children, "*Gather round* (49:2)," and at that moment there was wholeness. They all sang spontaneously, "*To You,*

God, is the grandeur and the power. . . ."
This is why it is said: 'Ya'akov *Avinu* never died'.[25]

ZOHAR, I:235a

As long as that vision lives in history, Ya'akov lives; yet, expose that vision and it is debased. So it was that they – and we all – were sworn into that servitude to history which became Yisrael's renown:

And Yosef bound the children of Yisrael by oath, saying: God will surely remember you and you must take my remains with you from here. (50:25)

And Yosef bound them by oath to implant in their children:
You are now entering into servitude in Egypt.
You must never defy this by attempting to leave until such time as two messengers arrive with the following exact words: *God has surely remembered you. . . .*

TARGUM YONATAN

And so it was that God Himself had the Travelers take this same oath in a later exile:

I made you swear, daughters of Jerusalem . . . not to awaken or arouse the love until its moment. (Shir haShirim 2:7)

He made us swear not to expose the *Kets* and not to force or press the *Kets* prematurely. . . .

KETUVOT, 111a[26]

We are a nation gifted in living a vision of history as vindication but not as goal. The power of our accomplishment lies in our willingness to live life fully within history, unspoiled by the End. For we know that the *Kets* exists for Creation itself[27] rather than for the personal benefit of those few who live to see it. The duality of knowing the vision while living in the present is expressed every single day in the same words uttered around the deathbed of Ya'akov:

When the *Shechina* withdrew [as Ya'akov was about to expose the *Kets*], Ya'akov said, "Perhaps among you there is someone unsuitable? . . ."
Said his children to him, "*Shema Yisrael . . . Listen, Yisrael! The Lord our God, the Lord is One!* Just as in your heart there is Unity, so too in ours."
At that moment, Ya'akov exclaimed, "Blessed be the Name of

His honored Majesty forever and ever," which we say now together with the *Shema* – but in a *whisper*.

PESAḤIM, 56a

Open proclamation of the *Shema* even in the darkest moments goes hand-in-hand with whisper of the End, together defining the quiet but relentless work of Yisrael through history.

How mysterious the future in Egypt must have seemed to them in those minutes, standing around Ya'akov's bed. How long the centuries must have stretched. We take for granted the fabulous drama of their future which is our past, but how extravagant it has been! Our own drama stretches out before us along with a sense of approaching closure and climax, which we silently await, sadly and joyously. We must live with that electrifying excitement, while at the same time remembering the finality of the closing words of the Book of Bereishit, the end of *Vayḥi*, the end of the beginning:

Yosef died…and was placed in a coffin in Egypt. (50:26)

Yosef died…and was sealed in a coffin, which was then lowered into the Nile of Egypt.

TARGUM YONATAN[28]

Click.

1 *The Economist*, December 22, 1990, p. 91.

2 *The New Republic*, volume 203, p. 16.

3 *The Nation*, volume 246, number 20, p. 702.

4 Bereishit Rabba, 98:2.

5 Ibid.

6 Cf. Ramban, Bereishit 49:10. Of further interest is Bereishit Rabba, 99:2, and *Tanḥuma*, 14:1.

7 Bereishit Rabba, 99:2; 99:6; *Tanḥuma*, 8,14.

8 Bereishit Rabba, 98:16,17,18; *Tanḥuma, Vayḥi* 11; Rashi, Bereishit 49:21, s.v. *Hanoten*, ד״ה הנותן.

9 Bereishit Rabba, 98:6,7; 99:3,8,11; Rashi 49:8,9,27.

10 Bereishit Rabba, 99:2; *Tanḥuma, Vayḥi*, 14; Rashi 49:27.

11 Targum Yonatan, 49:18.

12 Bereishit Rabba, 98:13,14; 99:11; Rashi 49:16-19.

13 Bereishit Rabba, 98:2,4,5; 99:5; Rashi 49:6.

14 Sanhedrin, 5a; Rashi 49:10.

15 Or "mysteries of the King," as per Bereishit Rabba, 98.

16 Introduction to Chapter *Ḥelek*.

17 S.v. *Ad*, ד״ה עד.

18 Bereishit Rabba, 99:4; 100:12; *Tanḥuma* 8,16; Devarim Rabba, 11:1; Rashi and Rashbam, 49:28. The confusion leads Ibn Ezra and *Ḥizkuni*, 49:1, to maintain that these words of Ya'akov are prophecies, not blessings.

19 Bereishit 49:4-7; Bereishit Rabba, 98:4,5; 99:6,8; *Tanḥuma*, 9,10; Rashi 48:8, s.v. *Vayomar*, ד״ה ויאמר.

20 Ibn Ezra and Radak, Bereishit 2:3.

21 A "pool" can also mean "a subterranean accumulation of liquid."

22 Ramban, Shemot 25:24; Metsudat David, II Kings, 4:2 Cf. Tosefta, Berachot, 6.

23 Bereishit 49:4-7; Bereishit Rabba, 99:6; Midrash Shoḥar Tov, 90; Cf. Rashi Devarim 33:7, s.v. *Ve'ezer*, ד״ה ועזר, and Ramban, Devarim 33:6.

24 S.v. *Vayomar*, ד״ה ויאמר; Cf. *Tanḥuma*, 6:1.

25 Ta'anit, 5b.

26 See Rashi, op. cit., s.v. *Shelo*, ד״ה שלא יגלו, and s.v. *Ve'shelo*, ד״ה ושלא ירחקו.

27 Bereishit Rabba, 2:4.

28 Cf. Sotah, 13a.

ACKNOWLEDGMENTS...

ברוך החונן לאדם דעת שהחיינו וקיימנו והגיענו לזמן הזה

To my long-suffering wife and children (especially BatNadiv, who proved invaluable for her careful editing) who tolerated their missing husband and father philosophically, and even sent me off for weeks at a time for uninterrupted thinking and writing.

To the many dedicated students, friends, and others (thanks especially to their forbearing families) who joined in the weekly all-night sessions during which these essays were mercilessly reviewed and criticized before their initial release. I wish I could accurately mention all of you by name, but those who lasted longest include Aharon Katz, Aharon Leibowitz, Avraham Goldhar, David Krongold, Meir Perry, Morris Gindi, Moshe Handel, Moshe Wilshinsky, Shlomo Seidman, Yisrael Petlak, and Yonatan Gershan.

Writing a book was an adventure.
To begin with it was a toy, an amusement.
Then it became a mistress, then a master, and then a tyrant.
WINSTON CHURCHILL

To the receptive and undaunted backers of the Foundation for Jewish Publications, unstinting in their intrepid support of ideas that found little other venue, and to my every category of editors and designers, dedicated beyond any possible call of duty. They include Barnea Selavan, Elly Schiff, David Willner, Yechezkel ("the Doc") Missle, Lillian Cohen, Sandee Hier, along with quite a few volunteers who made serious contributions.

To each and every subscriber to the outrageously priced fax-journal, *FrameWorks*, through which the FJP originally circulated and market-tested these essays: You helped prove the viability of this project, provided critical moral and financial support, and on many occasions contributed ideas and criticism.

To my friends over the long haul, the committed partners in this first volume, who have dedicated the following....

FrameWorks Bereishit
Helen and Joe Berman
in honor of their children,
grandchildren, and great grandchildren

Parashat Noaḥ
Gabriel Betesh

Parashat Lech-Lecha
Hélène & Ari Bousbib
in honor of Lilian & Moshe Bousbib

Parashat Vayera
Rachel and Jeff Sutton
in honor of Frieda and Joseph Sutton and
for the *refuah shelema* of their daughter Frieda

Parashat Ḥayei Sara
Moshe and Grizzy Miller
and family

Parashat Toledot
Tzvi and Anette Medresh
and family

Parashat Vayetze
Linda and Howard Sterling
and family

Parashat Vayishlaḥ
Mazal and Gabriel Menaged
and children

Parashat Vayeshev
Moises and Esther Jafif
and family

Parashat Miketz
Yisrael and Naomi Petlak

Parashat Vayigash
Freddie and Pauli Harari
and children

Parashat Vayḥi
Morris and Devora Smith
and children

Glossary

Adam: man as species; also the Primal Man.

Aggada: lit. 'the telling', or the 'binding together'. Passages in classical Torah literature treating non-legal issues, such as Jewish thought and theology, providing an integrated conceptual framework for Torah.

Aishet Ḥayil: lit. a 'woman of valor'.

Akeida: the sacrificial 'binding' of Yitzḥak by Avraham on Mount Moriah.

Amida: the silent prayer said three times daily; lit. the 'Standing'.

Av (father) pl. *Avot*: The Patriarchs, Avraham, Yitzḥak and Ya'akov. Also means 'archetype', 'paradigm'.

Avoda: lit: 'work', closest English equivalent is 'worship'. Often used as synonym for offerings or prayer.

B'nei Noaḥ: Sons of Noaḥ, gentiles.

Bamidbar: lit. 'In the Desert'. The *Book of Numbers*.

Bereishit: lit: 'In the Beginning'. The *Book of Genesis*.

Beit Mikdash: the Temple in Jerusalem.

Bechora: primogeniture, the birthright of the firstborn.

Beracha pl. *berachot*: blessings, benedictions.

Bina: wisdom, intuition.

Bitaḥon: 'trust' in God.

Brit basar: lit. 'Covenant of Flesh'. Circumcision.

Brit milah: circumcision

Da'at: knowing, connection.

Devarim: lit. 'Words'. The *Book of Deuteronomy*.

Din: loosely translated as 'Judgement' or 'Justice'. The archetypal hallmark of Yitzḥak, the *Av* reflecting the equivalent metaphysical Attribute.

Divrei haYamim: The *Book of Chronicles*.

Edom: lit. the Red. The land, kingdom and exile of Eisav; can also refer to Eisav himself.

Eisav: Esau, Ya'akov's twin brother, seen as Roman archetype and ancestor. Represents the exile of Rome.

Elohim: name of God denoting the Attribute of Justice, thus can also mean the 'court'.

Em (mother), pl. *Emahot*: The Matriarchs, Sara, Rivka, Rachel and Leah. Feminine parallel to *Av* as archetype.

Emunah: faithfulness.

Eretz Yisrael: the Land of Israel.

Galut: exile, the state of exile, or a historical period of exile, as in *Galut* Bavel, the Babylonian Exile. See *Golah*.

Gog and Magog: A confrontation at the "End of Days." Often confused with the Christian Armageddon described in Rev. 16.

Golah: the lands of the exile; the Diaspora.

Haftara: the "After Reading." A selection from the Prophets chosen to match the theme of the weekly portion or the holiday. Originally it was instituted as a substitute for the Torah reading as a reminder of its content during a historical period when Jews were forbidden to read from the Torah itself in public. Later it was retained as part of the service.

Haggada: The liturgical 'Recitation' said at the "Seder" on the first night of Passover, compiled mostly during the Tannatic\Mishnaic era, before circa 200 CE.

Halacha: Jewish law.

Ḥen: charisma, charm, favor.

Ḥesed: loosely translated as 'loving-kindness'. The archetypal hallmark of Avraham, the *Av* reflecting the equivalent metaphysical Attribute.

Iyov: Job; the *Book of Job*.

Kedusha: sanctity, implies consecration and specificity.

Kets: the end, apocalypse.

Kohelet: the *Book of Ecclesiastes*, traditionally ascribed to King Solomon.

Lulav: a palm frond, tied together with myrtle and willow, and shaken together with a citron on the holiday of Succot (Tabernacles).

Mashiaḥ: the Messiah, lit. the "Anointed One."

Me'arat haMachpela: lit. the doubled cave. The burial site of the *Avot* and *Emahot,* purchased by Avraham.

Middat haDin: God's "Attribute of Pure Justice," often personified.

Midrash (plural: *midrashim*): Classical rabbinic interpretation and exposition of biblical passages. From the root meaning 'seek out' or 'inquire', it is a term for interpretive study of the Torah, and the name of the collections in which the interpretations were recorded.

Milah: circumcision.

Mishkan: The Tabernacle in the desert and the first centuries in Israel, later superceded by the Temple in Jerusalem; lit. the 'Dwelling'.

Mishlei: the *Book of Proverbs,* traditionally ascribed to King Solomon.

Mishna: The primary text of the oral tradition. Collected and edited by R. Yehudah haNassi.

Mishne Torah: lit. review of the Torah. The name of Maimonides' masterpiece encompassing all Jewish Law; also a term for the *Book of Deuteronomy*.

Olam Habah: lit. the 'World to Come', afterlife.

Olam Hazeh: lit. 'This World', present existence.

Pesaḥ: the festival of Passover. Can also refer to the paschal offering.

Rambam: acronym for Rabbi Moshe ben Maimon (1135-1204); Maimonides.

Rashi: acronym for Rabbi Shelomo Yitzḥaki (1040-1105), foremost commentator on the Torah and Talmud.

Re'uven: Reuben. The oldest of Ya'akov's sons.

Rosh haShana: The Jewish New Years, which is also considered the *Yom haDin,* day of Judgment.

Rivka: Rebecca.

Rosh Yeshiva: Dean of the Academy.

Sanhedrin: generally referring to the Supreme Court, the ultimate legal authority of the Jewish People; also a name for lower courts empowered to deal with capital crimes.

Shemot: lit. 'names'. The *Book of Exodus.*

Seder: the procedure of the Passover night service conducted at home; lit. the 'Order'.

Sefer Torah: the Torah scroll, written by a trained scribe in a precise manner with perfect textual accuracy.

Shechina: the Divine Presence, the embodiment of the relationship between God and Man.

Shema: lit. 'Hear!' or 'Listen!'; referring to the verse *Hear O Israel the Lord Our God, the Lord is One.* (Deuteronomy 6:4), the opening verse of the paragraphs placed in the *mezuza* scroll on doorposts and in the *tefillin* worn on head and hand. It is a veritable catechism of Jewish faith, recited every morning and evening, at special personal and national moments, and on the deathbed.

Shemona Esrei: the quotidian *Amidah* ("Standing" prayer) recited thrice daily; lit. the 'Eighteen' referring to its eighteen benedictions originally formulated by the Men of the Great Assembly with Ezra the Scribe. After the destruction of the Second Temple it was reformulated by Rabban Gamliel and the Sanhedrin in Yavne to its present form, in which the 'Eighteen' contains *nineteen* blessings

Shir haShirim: *Song of Songs*. Traditionally ascribed to King Solomon.

Succah: an outdoor hut made for Succot (the holiday of Tabernacles).

Talmud: lit. 'The Learning'. Exposition of the Oral Law, based on the Mishna. Compiled between 200-500 CE separately in Palestine and Babylon, it is a vast compendium of law, philosophy, ethics, and lore.

Tanach: the entire Jewish Bible, a Hebrew acronym for *T*orah, *N*evi'im, *K*etuvim—the Five Books of Moses, the Prophets, and the Writings, respectively.

Tanḥuma: A collection of *midrashim* on the Pentateuch.

Targum: lit: Translation. Term for any of the Aramaic translations of Torah during the last centuries BCE, and early centuries CE.

Tehillim: from the root of "praise", the *Book of Psalms*.

Teshuva: lit. 'return', loosely translated as 'repentance'.

Tiferet: loosely translated as 'Beauty' it also implies Truth and Harmony; the archetypal hallmark of Ya'akov(Jacob) the *Av* reflecting the equivalent metaphysical Attribute.

Tikkun: lit. 'repair', the opportunities for and role of humanity in healing creation.

Tohu: Chaos.

Toledah: 'offspring', relates to birth and to consequence or implication.

Tzion: Zion, lit. marked, remarkable, signpost.

Tzizit: specially constructed fringes prescribed for certain garments; can refer informally to the garment itself.

Yavan: Greece.

Yefeh To'ar: beauty; lit. of beautiful appearance.

Yeḥezkel: Ezekiel.

Yehudah: Judah.

Yerushalayim: Jerusalem.

Yisrael: Israel, Jacob, or the Jewish People.

Yitzḥak: Isaac. The second of the three *Avot;* lit. "he will laugh".

Vayikra: lit. 'and He called', the *Book of Leviticus.*

Zaken: lit. 'aged', or as a noun, 'Elder', a title of respect.

Zohar: lit. the Radiance; traditionally attributed to R. Shimon bar Yoḥai, it is the most important text of Jewish mysticism.

Index of Sources

Tanach

Babylonian Talmud

Midrash

Zohar and related works

Targum

Commentators

Other Works

Rambam (Maimonides)

COMMENTARY ON MISHNA,

MISHNE TORAH,

Siddur

Haggada

Subject Index

this book may be ordered directly from the publisher

The Foundation for Jewish Publications
15 School Street
Boston, Massachusetts 02108
1-877-FJP-BOOK

in New England, call 617-227-7979
in Israel fax 972-2-628-9991

www.fjp.net